NEW ZEALAND
THE BEAUTIFUL
COOKBOOK

NEW ZEALAND THE BEAUTIFUL COOKBOOK

EDITED BY TUI FLOWER
RESEARCH EDITOR: ROBYN MARTIN

Editorial Co-ordinator: Merren Parker

Principal photographer: Judith Long

Art Director: Bruce Wallace

Designers; Helen Saunderson, Rosanne Hyndman, Astrid Mensink.

First published by Shortland Publications in 1984
Reprinted in 1988 twice,
Reprinted in 1990 by Weldon Publishing,
a division of Kevin Weldon & Associates Pty Ltd.
372 Eastern Valley Way, Willoughby NSW 2068.

© Kevin Weldon & Associates Pty Ltd
© design Kevin Weldon & Associates Pty Ltd

Typeset in New Zealand by Taranaki Newspapers Limited.

Printed by Griffin Press, Australia.

National Library of Australia Cataloguing-in-publication data

New Zealand The Beautiful Cookbook
Includes index.
ISBN 1 875410 22 8.
1. Cookery, New Zealand. I. Flower. Tui.
641.5993

CONTENTS

INTRODUCTION

Everyone is involved with food. It is a topic so universally important, that anyone will discuss it with you even if only to give their reasons for not liking it. Interests in it range from inquiring curiosity to gourmet enthusiasm.

For every New Zealander, it is more than just a talking point, as the quality of our land, waters, and climate provides for the production of a variety of top grade foodstuffs that are renowned world wide, thus making food the life-blood of our economy.

The Maori and the early settlers knew the richness of the lands and seas and the foods they provided. Succeeding generations have nurtured and husbanded this potential, until today we enjoy the produce of the sea, the fertile plains, the rolling hills, and the rugged high country — the fish, the grain, the dairy produce, and the tender lamb.

The technology of farming in its many areas has become an industry in itself, ensuring that New Zealand can export the best quality food in top condition to all parts of the world.

From the time of early settlement through to the present day, our culinary culture has gained from the many ethnic peoples who have come to our shores to seek fortune and a new life style. So we have Chinese, Indian, Polynesian, Yugoslav, Greek, Italian, German, and Dutch influences on what started as a largely British cuisine. Increasingly, our eating habit has changed from using just what the land provided, so that now, with the help of modern technology, our diet can be more varied throughout the year, and thus better suited to the variable climate we live in.

Apart from the need to have food to live, interest in cooking has become a craft skill for many, providing that satisfying hobby that is an enjoyment for all.

Cooking as a cultural heritage, a practical economy, a creative art, or an enthusiastic experiment, can all be part of the pleasure of the kitchen and the satisfaction of the cook.

Tui Flower

FISH STORIES

Our long and varied coastline provides a wondrous selection of fish. The oysters, crayfish, mussels, tuatua, pipi, and the now elusive toheroa were staple food of the Maori people. European settlers, too, have enjoyed this shellfish bounty, as well as the fish that come from more distant and deeper waters. A liking for the delicate flounder, the tasty snapper, tarakihi, and the colourful gurnard make these the most popular of fish. The recently acceptable orange roughy, coming from the deep, is challenging other white fish for top billing.

Where our West Coast rivers sweep to the sea, in Spring, it is whitebait time, and hundreds of thousands of these delicate whole fish find their way to the gourmets' tables.

Inland, clear babbling rivers are the home of the brown and rainbow trout which grow to a large size, making the New Zealand trout fisherman's sport the envy of all other river fishermen.

Traditional fish and chips are still most popular in New Zealand; however, our fish cooking has come a long way from that traditional British image, to the imaginative use of the sea harvest, be it squid or snapper.

Captions to preceding 6 pages.

Page 14/15: Preparing a fishing net on 90 Mile Beach, Northland (Photograph Peter Morath).
Page 16/17: Islands of the Hauraki Gulf viewed from the Coromandel Peninsula (Photograph Eric Taylor).
Page 18/19: Sea harvest. A formidable choice of fish when offered freshly caught. An exciting and colourful bounty from the seas which surround our island nation.
Page 20: A fishing boat moored at Lyttelton Harbour near Christchurch. (Photograph Peter Morath.)

Hoki

This almost sprat-shaped fish is, in fact, quite sizeable; it can weigh up to 1.5 kilograms.

It is abundant around the South Island, but also occurs around the North Island. It is a very large resource, being available most of the year.

The flesh is delicate, white, and moist. It flakes very easily when cooked, and for that reason, should not be overcooked or it will break into pieces.

Crumb-Top Hoki

300 grams hoki fillets

½ teaspoon grated lemon rind

2 tablespoons chopped parsley

½ cup fresh breadcrumbs

Freshly ground pepper

3 tablespoons melted butter

About 2 tablespoons melted butter for brushing

Lemon wedges

Parsley

Mix together lemon rind, parsley, breadcrumbs, pepper and the first measure of melted butter.

Cut hoki fillets into serving-size lengths. Place on grill rack. Brush one side of the fish with second measure of melted butter. Grill for 3 to 4 minutes on one side.

Turn over, brush the other side with melted butter, and sprinkle with breadcrumb mixture. Place under grill for 3 to 4 minutes or until the fish is cooked and breadcrumbs are golden.

Serve hot, garnished with lemon wedges and parsley.
Serves 3 to 4.

Whitebait

Whitebait — that distinctively New Zealand delicacy which measures 4.5 to 5.5 centimetres in length, is eaten whole.

It is not related to the European whitebait, and is caught during the spring in the tidal river estuaries, as the fish move upstream from the sea.

While this is mostly recreational fishing, there is commercial fishing on the West Coast of the South Island. Fishing for whitebait is controlled by regulation.

The juvenile smelt of an unrelated species, fished in the northern half of the North Island, is often sold as Waikato Whitebait.

Whitebait has a very delicate flavour, and for this reason, should be cooked with care. Cooking needs to be brief and simple.

Whitebait Omelet
(photograph right)

3 eggs

½ teaspoon salt

25 grams butter

1 cup whitebait

In a small bowl, beat eggs and salt with a fork. Heat butter in a medium frying pan. Pour in beaten eggs. Reduce heat slightly until the omelet is half set, lifting the edges.

While the top of the omelet is still liquid, spread the whitebait over it. Continue to cook until the egg is almost set. Season with salt.

Remove the pan from the heat, and leave omelet to stand for about 2 minutes.

Roll up the omelet, and place join downwards on a plate. Cut into 4 diagonal slices. Serve hot or cold.
Serves 4.

Whitebait Deauville
(photograph right)

¼ cup whitebait

1 tablespoon flour

¼ teaspoon salt

Pepper

25 grams butter

Lemon wedge

Drain the whitebait, and place in a bowl. Sprinkle with flour, salt and pepper.

Heat butter in a small frying pan. Add whitebait all at once, and cook, turning constantly, for about 1 minute.

Pile on to a warm plate, and serve with a lemon wedge.
Serves 1.

Whitebait Fritters

1 egg

1 tablespoon flour

¼ teaspoon salt

½ cup whitebait

25 grams butter

1 tablespoon oil

In a small bowl, whisk the egg until frothy. Fold in the flour and the salt. Add the whitebait, and stir to just combine.

Heat the butter and oil in a frying pan. Drop spoonfuls of whitebait batter into hot butter. When golden brown, turn to cook second side. Serve hot.
Serves 3.

Crayfish Salad

4 small crayfish tails

Salt and pepper

Lettuce

Avocado

Dressing:

2 spring onions

¾ cup mayonnaise

2 tablespoons dry white wine

1 tablespoon tomato sauce

¼ cup sour cream

Pinch cayenne pepper

Remove the flesh from the crayfish tails by slitting the underside of the tail with scissors, then with a little applied pressure, remove the flesh in large pieces. Trim off the soft undershell. Cut the flesh into bite-sized pieces, and season with salt and pepper. Refill the shells with the seasoned flesh.

Thinly slice the lettuce, and place a bed on each of 4 plates.

Put the filled crayfish tails on the beds of lettuce. Spoon the dressing down the centre of each crayfish tail. Decorate with peeled, stoned and thinly sliced avocado.

Dressing: Slice the spring onions thinly. Mix with the mayonnaise, wine, tomato sauce, sour cream and cayenne pepper.
Serves 4.

Sprats

Every youthful fisherman will at some time have caught a variety of little fish usually called sprats. Great pleasure is given such fishermen when Mum makes something from that catch. For her, the greatest involvement is the need to remove bones from such little fish. Do this by slitting the fish along the length of stomach, remove gut, and wash out. Open out flat on a wooden board, skin side up, and roll lightly with a rolling pin. Lift out backbone.

Soused Sprats
(photograph left)

10 sprats
1 onion
1¼ cups cider vinegar
½ cup white vinegar
¾ cup water
1 teaspoon peppercorns
1½ teaspoons mustard seed
2 bay leaves
2 cloves garlic
2 tablespoons sugar

Remove heads and tails from the sprats. Clean, and remove the bones.

Cut onion into rings.

In a saucepan, place cider vinegar, white vinegar, water, peppercorns, mustard seeds, bay leaves, onion rings, peeled and sliced garlic, and sugar. Heat to boiling. Reduce heat, and simmer for about 10 minutes. Cool.

With the skin side outwards, roll up the boned sprats tightly. Place in a glass, china or plastic container with a non-metallic lid. Pour the cooled liquid over the rolled sprats. Cover with lid. Place in refrigerator.

Allow 3 to 4 days for flavour to develop and fish to become white. **Serves 6 to 8.**

Mustard Crumbed Sprats
(photograph left)

10 to 12 small sprats
Oil

Topping:
50 grams butter
2 cups fresh white breadcrumbs
2 tablespoons prepared mustard
1 teaspoon Worcestershire sauce
½ teaspoon grated lemon rind
Salt and pepper

Remove heads and tails from the sprats. Clean and gut the sprats and remove the bones. Split in half along back.

Place sprats skin side up on a grill pan. Brush skins with oil. Grill for 4 to 5 minutes. Turn sprats skin downwards.

Spoon breadcrumb topping on top of sprats. Grill until topping is golden.

Topping: Melt butter, blend in breadcrumbs, mustard, Worcestershire sauce and lemon rind. Season with salt and pepper.
Serves 4 to 5.

Bluff Oysters

To the oyster lover, there is nothing to equal the Bluff oyster which, for so long, was the most readily available oyster in New Zealand.

Although it is available all around the shores of New Zealand, the only commercial areas are Foveaux Strait and Tasman Bay. The Bluff oyster is taken by dredge, and it is not cultivated.

The season for these oysters is March 1 to August 31.

The Rock Oyster, also a native species, is very like the Sydney rock oyster. It occurs naturally in bays and inlets in the northern North Island — the Bay of Islands, Kaipara Harbour, and parts of the Hauraki Gulf.

This oyster is being cultivated as well, but is being superseded by the faster growing and larger Pacific oyster, an accidental introduction to New Zealand waters. It flourishes around northern North Island from the Manukau to the Bay of Plenty.

Oyster Cocktail

¼ cup tomato sauce
2 tablespoons Worcestershire sauce
1 tablespoon lemon juice
Pinch chilli powder
1 tablespoon finely chopped parsley
1 tablespoon grated onion
2 tablespoons dry sherry
¼ teaspooon sugar
About 2 cups finely shredded lettuce
At least 2 dozen well-drained oysters
4 lemon wedges.

Measure tomato and Worcestershire sauces, lemon juice, chilli powder, parsley, onion, sherry and sugar into a screwtop jar. Shake it well, then put in the refrigerator to chill.

Near serving time, arrange shredded lettuce in stemmed glass dishes. On the lettuce, arrange 6 or more oysters. Chill briefly.

Just before serving, spoon 3 tablespoons of the sauce over each dish of oysters. Garnish with lemon wedges.
Serves 4.

Oyster Soup
(photograph below)

1 small fish head
4 cups water
1 bay leaf
1 sprig parsley
1 x 435 gram tin oyster soup
2 tablespoons cream
1 dozen Bluff oysters
Salt
Freshly ground pepper

Wash fish head. Place in saucepan with the water, bay leaf and parsley. Cover the saucepan, and cook for about 45 minutes.

Strain stock. Bring to the boil, and reduce in volume to about 2 cups. Mix in tinned oyster soup and fish stock, and heat gently until heated through.

Just before serving, add cream, oysters and oyster juice. Season to taste with salt and pepper. Heat gently for 2 to 3 minutes. Serve immediately.
Serves 4.

Oysters Kilpatrick
(photograph right)

1 rasher bacon
1 teaspoon butter
1 dozen Bluff oysters
Oyster shells
Salt
Freshly ground pepper
Worcestershire sauce
Parsley
Lemon wedges

Remove bacon rind, and chop finely. Heat butter in a small frying pan, and fry bacon for 3 to 4 minutes.

Arrange oysters on half oyster shells on a grill rack. Season lightly with salt and pepper. Sprinkle with Worcestershire sauce. Scatter bacon pieces over each oyster.

Place under grill for about 3 minutes, or until heated through. Serve on a plate garnished with parsley and lemon wedges.
Serves 1 to 2.

Note: If no shells are available, use small ovenproof dishes.

Seasoned Tomato Oysters
(photograph below)

2 tomatoes
¾ cup fresh breadcrumbs
2 tablespoons chopped parsley
1 teaspoon finely chopped chives
¼ teaspoon paprika
2 tablespoons melted butter
Freshly ground pepper
1 dozen Bluff oysters
¼ cup cream

Peel and deseed tomatoes. Chop very finely. Mix together tomatoes, breadcrumbs, parsley, chives, paprika, melted butter and pepper.

Take half breadcrumb mixture and make a layer in the bottom of 4 individual greased ovenproof dishes.

Drain oysters, reserving juice. Arrange 3 oysters on top of the breadcrumb layer in each dish. Sprinkle remaining breadcrumb mixture on top.

Mix together reserved oyster juice and the cream. Pour it over breadcrumb layer.

Bake at 180 degrees C for about 10 minutes, or until heated through.
Serves 4.

Baked Oysters Raymond

2 dozen oysters
3 tablespoons oil
3 tablespoons lemon juice
½ teaspoon salt
Shake pepper
½ teaspoon curry powder
1 teaspoon dry mustard
1 cup soft breadcrumbs
25 grams buttter
3 slices bacon

Drain the oysters well. Mix the oil, lemon juice, salt, pepper, curry powder and mustard, and leave the oysters in it to marinate for half an hour.

Heat the butter in a pan, and stir in the crumbs until they are lightly coloured.

Drain the oysters, and pat dry on a paper towel. Roll the oysters in the crumbs. Place them in a shallow baking dish. Bake at 220 degrees C for about 20 minutes or until they are puffed and crisp.

Cut the bacon into pieces, and grill until crisp. Serve with the oysters as an entree.
Serves 4 to 6.

Snapper

One of the most popular and best known fish in the country, snapper has a good flavour, and is suitable for most cooking methods.

Snapper Salad

The fish for this must be fresh.

500 grams skinned and boned snapper
1 onion
¾ cup lemon juice
6 radishes
2 stalks celery
2 to 3 spring onions
Salt
Freshly ground black pepper

Cut fish into two centimetre cubes. Peel and slice the onion. Place fish, onion and lemon juice in a china or glass bowl. Toss to coat evenly.

Cover with plastic film, and refrigerate for a minimum of 12 hours, or until fish is white.

Drain off liquid, and reserve. Wash radishes and cut into quarters. Slice celery. Wash and trim the spring onions.

Arrange fish, onions, radishes, celery and spring onions in a serving bowl. Pour over the reserved liquid. Season with salt and pepper.
Serves 4 to 5.

Snapper Country Style

4 snapper fillets
6 black peppercorns
1 bay leaf
¾ cup dry white wine
2 green peppers
4 small onions
2 tomatoes
Salt
1 clove garlic
Cooked rice
Paprika

Skin the snapper fillets. Place the fish in a dish with peppercorns and bay leaf, pour wine over them, and leave to marinate for a short time.

Remove the seeds from peppers, and slice. Peel and slice onions and tomatoes. Dust the sliced vegetables lightly with salt.

Take a large, heavy pan, and rub the base and side with the cut clove of garlic. Pour in enough oil to cover the bottom of the pan, and when this is hot, add the marinated fish and vegetables. Cook for 8 to 10 minutes, turning ingredients over carefully once during that time.

When cooked, serve on a hot plate with white rice. Dust with paprika.
Serves 4.

Snapper with Remoulade Sauce

2 large snapper fillets
1 cup water
1 cup white wine
1 teaspoon salt
4 peppercorns
2 cloves
1 sprig thyme
1 bay leaf
1 sprig parsley
1 onion
1 carrot

Sauce:

1 cup mayonnaise
1 tablespoon chopped parsley
½ teaspoon prepared french-type mustard
1 tablespoon chopped chives
Chopped watercress and tarragon leaves if available

Trim the fish and remove bones. In a shallow pan, mix the water, wine, salt, peppercorns, cloves, thyme, bay leaf, parsley, sliced onion and sliced carrot. Simmer, covered, for 30 minutes.

Place fish in the court-bouillon. Cover and simmer until the fish is cooked. Do not let the liquid boil.

Remove from the heat and allow to cool in the court-bouillon, then lift carefully on to a serving plate.

Sauce: Mix the mayonnaise with the mustard and the finely chopped green herbs. Use this to decorate the fish thickly. Serve cold.
Serves 4 to 6.

Cold Snapper Casserole

2 onions

1 clove garlic

¼ cup oil

1 teaspoon salt

1 tablespoon sugar

Shake pepper

1 cup tomato pulp

¼ cup white wine

4 to 6 pieces of snapper steaks or fillets

Chopped parsley

Peel and chop the onions and garlic. In a pan, heat the oil and fry the onion and garlic until tender, but not coloured. Sprinkle in the seasonings, add the tomato pulp, and simmer the sauce for 5 minutes. Add the wine, and cook for another 2 minutes.

The fish can be steaks or halved large fillets. They should be trimmed neatly and placed in an oiled oven-ware dish. Pour the tomato mixture over them.

Cover, and cook in a 180 degree C oven for about 30 minutes or until the fish is tender.

Chill thoroughly before serving. Sprinkle generously with parsley.
Serves 4 to 6.

Baked Whole Snapper

1 whole snapper

Filling:

½ cup rice

1 onion

50 grams butter

2 tomatoes

1 green pepper

2 tablespoons chopped parsley

3 to 4 leaves basil

1 egg

Wipe the inside and skin of the snapper with a damp cloth. Fill cavity with stuffing, and secure with skewers. The extra stuffing is placed around the fish. Place in a greased baking dish, and cover lightly with greased foil.

Bake at 180 degrees C for about 30 minutes, depending on size of fish.

Filling: Cook rice in lightly salted boiling water until barely tender. Drain.

Chop onion finely. Heat butter, and cook onion until tender but not brown.

Skin, and remove the seeds from tomatoes; chop flesh. Deseed and chop green pepper.

Mix cooked rice, onion, tomatoes, green pepper, parsley and chopped basil together in a bowl. Beat egg lightly, and add enough to bind the mixture. Season well with salt and pepper.
Serves 4.

Crispy Snapper

4 pieces skinned and boned snapper

Salt and pepper

3 to 4 tablespoons flour

1 egg

2 tablespoons oil

25 grams butter

Wipe the snapper with a damp cloth. Sprinkle with salt and pepper. Cover, and allow to stand for 5 minutes. Place flour on a large piece of paper. Lightly beat egg and pour on to a plate.

Heat oil and butter in frying pan until very hot, but not smoking.

Coat fish pieces first in flour then in beaten egg. Cook for about 5 minutes each side, according to the thickness of the fish.
Serves 4.

Mussels

The recent farming of mussels has brought a marked increase in the supply which is available fresh, on the half shell, cooked, marinated and smoked.

There are two main varieties — the blue mussel and the green mussel. The blue mussel averages 50 to 70 millimetres in size. The green averages about 100 millimetres, but can grow appreciably larger.

In both varieties, the creamy-white coloured mussels are the males, and the reddish-orange or apricot ones are the females.

While both varieties are being farmed, the green mussels are obtained from both farming and dredging. The blue mussel is cultivated to a lesser extent.

Mussel Turnovers

500 grams flaky pastry

3 cooked mussels

1 small onion

1 tablespoon chopped parsley

2 tablespoons breadcrumbs

Salt and pepper

Squeeze of lemon juice

1 egg yolk

1 tablespoon water

Roll out the pastry to 2 millimetre thickness, and cut into 5 centimetre rounds with a pastry cutter. Place the pastry on an oven tray, and chill in the refrigerator while preparing the filling.

Chop cooked mussels into small pieces, and mix with the finely chopped onion, parsley, crumbs, seasonings and lemon juice.

Place small amounts of the filling on one half of the pastry circles, dampen the edges, fold over the pastry, and press down well. Mark with a fork around the edges, and brush the top of the pastry lightly with egg yolk glaze.

Bake at 220 degrees C for about 15 minutes. Serve hot as a cocktail savoury.
Makes 36.

Turn mixture out on to a floured board. Divide evenly into 12 pieces. Using floured hands, roll each piece into a cylinder. Straighten croquettes, using floured knives or spatulas. Square ends with the knives.

Dip each croquette in beaten egg. Brush egg carefully all over it. Allow any excess egg to run off.

Place croquettes on to a sheet of paper which is covered in breadcrumbs. Roll, to evenly coat the surface. Again, square up the croquettes with knives or spatulas. If not being deep-fried immediately, refrigerate.

Fry at 195 degrees C for 5 to 7 minutes, or until golden and heated through. Drain on paper. Serve at once.
Makes 12.

Poisson Creme Grille

2 flounder

Butter

8 large scallops

8 small mushrooms

Salt and pepper

Cayenne pepper

1 cup milk

½ cup cream

Parmesan cheese

Skin the flounder, and cut four fillets from each fish.

Butter an oblong ovenware dish of size suitable for taking the length of the fish fillet across the dish. Place the fillets along the dish so the bottom is completely covered. Arrange the scallops, so there is one on each fillet of fish.

Wash the mushrooms, trim the stalks to a point, and place with the scallops. Season lightly with salt, pepper and a pinch of cayenne.

Mix the milk and cream together, and carefully pour over the dish to cover the fillets completely, leaving the mushrooms and scallops showing. Sprinkle the dish generously with parmesan cheese.

Place the dish under a hot grill for 5 minutes. Lower the heat, and continue cooking under the grill for 15 to 20 minutes.

Alternatively, cook in the top part of the oven at 230 degrees C for 15 to 20 minutes or until golden brown. Serve immediately.
Serves 8.

Tomato Baked Mussels

1 onion

1 clove garlic

1 tablespoon oil

1 x 420 gram tin tomatoes in juice

Pinch ground cloves

2 tablespoons chopped parsley

¼ teaspoon salt

Freshly ground pepper

400 grams cooked mussels

¼ cup fresh breadcrumbs

1 tablespoon grated parmesan cheese

Peel and finely chop onion. Crush garlic.

Heat oil in a saucepan. Add onion and crushed garlic, and cook until soft but not brown. Add tomatoes in juice, ground cloves, parsley, salt and pepper. Simmer until mixture thickens, stirring occasionally.

Remove from heat, and stir in mussels. Pour mixture into an ovenproof dish. Mix together the breadcrumbs and parmesan cheese. Sprinkle over mussel mixture.

Bake at 180 degrees C for 20 to 25 minutes, or until top is golden brown. Serve immediately.
Serves 4.

Smoked Fish Croquettes
(*photograph above*)

50 grams butter

¼ cup flour

1 cup milk

1 x 312 gram tin smoked fish

2 tablespoons finely chopped onion

2 tablespoons finely chopped parsley

1 tablespoon lemon juice

Salt and pepper

1 egg

Fine breadcrumbs

Oil for frying

Melt the butter in a saucepan. Stir in the flour, and cook for 1 to 2 minutes. Remove from the heat, and add the milk a little at a time, stirring to a smooth sauce after each addition.

Return to the heat and bring to the boil, stirring constantly. Simmer for 3 to 4 minutes.

Drain the smoked fish and remove any bones. Flake finely with a fork.

Add smoked fish, finely chopped onion, chopped parsley, lemon juice, salt and pepper, to the mixture. Mix well. Spread on to a shallow plate. Cover with plastic film, and refrigerate until cold and firm.

Eel

In this country, eel is becoming known as a quality smoked fish product.

Its fat content makes it a good fish to smoke.

The firm, white flesh of fresh eel is suitable for baking or stewing.

Smoked Eel Cream

100 grams smoked eel

2 hard-boiled eggs

1 tablespoon butter

1 tablespoon mayonnaise

1 tablespoon chopped fennel

1 teaspoon lemon juice

¼ teaspoon salt

Freshly ground black pepper

Chop the smoked eel and eggs finely. Soften the butter and add with the mayonnaise, fennel, lemon juice, salt and pepper. Beat the mixture until smooth and creamy.

Pile into a small dish and garnish with fennel. Serve with crisp bread or crackers.
Serves 6 to 8.

Smoked Eel Mousse

2½ teaspoons gelatin

2 tablespoons water

100 grams cucumber

250 grams smoked eel

¼ cup mayonnaise

¼ teaspoon salt

Freshly ground black pepper

2 teaspoons lemon juice

1 tablespoon chopped parsley

1 teaspoon chopped chives

½ cup cream

Black olives

Cucumber slices

Soak the gelatin in the water until it swells, then dissolve over hot water.

Peel the cucumber, and remove the seeds. Cook flesh in boiling, salted water for about 5 minutes. Drain well, and sieve, or puree in a food processor.

Flake the smoked eel, and add to the sieved cucumber. Add the dissolved gelatin, mayonnaise, salt, pepper, lemon juice, parsley and chives. Mix together thoroughly.

In a small bowl, whip the cream, and fold into smoked eel mixture.

Oil a 2 cup mould and pour in the mousse. Refrigerate for at least 4 hours or until firmly set. Unmould before serving, and garnish with black olives and cucumber slices.
Serves 8 to 10.

Squid

Two varieties of squid are available — the arrow squid and the broad squid. Both have white, dense, firm flesh with a faintly shellfish flavour about it. The broad squid is very similar to the European calamari.

Savoury Stuffed Squid
(photograph left)

2 broad squid

1 onion

4 tablespoons oil

1½ cups fresh white breadcrumbs

1 tablespoon lemon juice

2 tablespoons chopped parsley

4 tablespoons anchovy essence

Chopped parsley

Tomato slices

Wipe squid with a damp cloth.

Chop onion finely. Heat oil in frying pan, and cook onion until tender but not brown.

In a bowl, place the breadcrumbs, lemon juice, chopped parsley and anchovy essence. Add cooked onion, and mix well to combine. Season with salt and pepper.

Fill the cavity of the squid with the prepared stuffing. Secure opening with a wooden toothpick. Place squid on a plate. Cover with plastic film.

Microwave on full power for 3 minutes. Turn squid over, and microwave for a further 2 minutes or until squid is white. Remove wooden toothpicks. Garnish with chopped parsley and tomato slices. Cut into 2 pieces.
Serves 4.

Note: If not cooked in microwave, cover with foil, and bake at 160 degrees C for about 20 minutes or until tender.

Squid Rings with Tangy Mayonnaise
(photograph left)

2 to 3 broad squid

Salt and pepper

1 egg

Brown breadcrumbs

Oil for frying

Tangy Mayonnaise:

1 cup mayonnaise

2 teaspoons finely chopped spring onion

1 teaspoon finely chopped parsley

1 teaspoon finely chopped gherkin

1 teaspoon hot water

Wipe squid with a damp cloth. Cut in rings of about 0.5 centimetre in width. Sprinkle lightly with salt and pepper.

Beat egg lightly, and pour on to a plate. Have breadcrumbs on a sheet of paper. Dip squid rings first into egg, then into breadcrumbs. Chill for about 15 minutes.

Heat oil in deep fryer. Fry a few squid rings at a time until golden. Drain on absorbent paper. Serve hot with accompanying sauce.
Serves 5 to 6.

Tangy Mayonnaise: In a bowl, place mayonnaise, spring onion, parsley and gherkin. Thin to dipping consistency with hot water if necessary.

Squid Balls
(photograph left)

500 grams arrow or broad squid

2 tablespoons finely chopped onion

¼ teaspoon salt

Pinch white pepper

1 tablespoon cornflour

Breadcrumbs

Oil or fat for frying

Wipe over squid. Put through the mincer, or process finely in the food processor. Add the onion, salt, pepper and cornflour to the squid, and mix well.

Using two spoons, make into balls about 3 centimetres in diameter, and coat with breadcrumbs.

Deep fry in hot oil or fat until golden brown. Drain on absorbent paper. Serve hot with chilli sauce.
Makes 18.

Fish and Chips

Fish and chips, the favourite of so many people, is a meal not usually cooked at home, yet there are areas of the country where there are no handy fish shops, and there are those who like to produce a home-cooked meal.

Baking Powder Batter

1 egg

½ cup milk

¼ cup water

1 cup flour

¼ teaspoon salt

1 tablespoon melted butter

½ teaspoon baking powder

Separate the egg, and beat the egg yolk with the milk and water.

Sift the flour and salt into a bowl. Make a well in the centre. Pour in the liquid, and beat until smooth. Add melted butter and stiffly beaten egg white.

Leave to stand for at least 30 minutes.

Just before use, gently stir baking powder into batter.

Beer Battered Fish

(photograph below)

Flat beer can be used in this recipe.

Beer Batter:

1 cup flour

¼ teaspoon salt

1 egg

1 tablespoon oil

½ to ¾ cup beer

Fish:

600 grams white fish fillets

Seasoned flour

Oil for frying

Beer Batter: Sift flour and salt together.

Separate egg. Beat yolk, oil and beer into flour to form a smooth batter. Beat egg white until stiff, and fold into batter when ready to use.

Fish: Cut fish into serving-sized pieces. Dust lightly with seasoned flour. Shake off surplus. Dip fish in the batter so that it is completely coated. Lift out, allowing fish to drain on the side of the bowl.

Fry in deep oil, preheated to 185 degrees C, until golden and crisp. Lift out with a perforated spoon on to absorbent paper to drain off the oil. **Serves 4 to 6.**

Seafood Platter

Lettuce leaves

6 small whole tomatoes or 6 wedges of tomato

About 300 grams smoked snapper

100 grams smoked roe

1½ dozen oysters

12 fingers buttered wholemeal bread

1 lemon

½ cup thick mayonnaise

Salt and pepper

Pinch cayenne pepper

Parsley sprigs

Wash the lettuce, and allow to drain thoroughly. Wash the tomatoes. If whole, cut almost right through into quarters. If large, cut into segments.

Skin the snapper, and cut the flesh into large pieces. Cut the roe into thick slices.

Poach the oysters briefly in their own liquor, until they just become cloudy. Leave to drain.

On small plates, arrange individual salads, beginning with a few lettuce leaves on the base, then tomato, a slice of roe, and 1 or 2 pieces of smoked snapper.

Prepare the buttered bread, and cut into fingers.

Cut 6 neat wedges from the lemon, reserving the remaining lemon to use as juice. Add this juice to the mayonnaise, together with salt, pepper and cayenne to get preferred sharpness.

Place 3 oysters on each platter, in a central position, but not on any of the fish. Garnish with a small mound of mayonnaise, 2 buttered bread fingers, and a sprig of parsley. Serve at once.
Serves 6.

Smoked Roe Dip

Smoked roe

Sour cream

Lemon juice

Chopped chives

Mix the smoked roe and sour cream together in about equal amounts, and season with a dash of lemon juice and a scattering of chopped chives.

Chill until ready to serve as a dip with crackers or crisps.

Baked Fish Roll

1 cup cooked flaked fish

2 cups mashed potatoes

2 tablespoons lemon juice

1 hard-boiled egg

1 beaten egg

Salt and pepper to taste

¾ cup dried breadcrumbs

2 tablespoons melted butter

Lemon slices for garnish

Make sure the fish is free of bones, and blend it with the potato, lemon juice, chopped hard-boiled egg and beaten egg. Season with salt and pepper. Shape into a roll about 18 centimetres long.

Leave to chill to make for easier handling, then roll in breadcrumbs.

Place in a lightly buttered dish, brush with the melted butter, and bake at 180 degrees C for about 30 minutes. Serve hot or cold. Garnish with slices of lemon and, if wished, accompany with a sauce.
Serves 6.

Crumb Topped Hapuku Steaks

4 hapuku steaks

Salt and pepper

Butter

1 cup breadcrumbs

½ teaspoon finely grated lemon rind

1 tablespoon chopped parsley

1 tablespoon chopped onion greens or chives

2 tablespoons melted butter

Sprinkle the fish with salt and pepper, and place in a buttered ovenware dish, large enough to take fish in a single layer.

Mix the lemon rind, parsley, chives, salt and pepper into the crumbs, and bind with the melted butter. Divide this mixture over the steaks, using it to coat the top of each one.

Place in the oven at 200 degrees C, and cook for 15 minutes or until fish is cooked through and the topping is golden.
Serves 4.

Smoked Fish with Egg Parsley Sauce

750 grams smoked snapper

1½ cups milk

3 tablespoons butter

3 tablespoons flour

2 hard-boiled eggs

3 tablespoons finely chopped parsley

Salt and pepper

Remove skin and bones from the smoked fish. Place fish in a shallow frying pan, and pour the milk over. Cover the pan, and bring the milk to the boil. Lower heat, and simmer slowly for 20 minutes.

Remove the fish from the liquid, and keep hot. Strain the cooking liquid.

Melt the butter in a saucepan. Add the flour, stirring to form a smooth paste. Cook for 1 to 2 minutes. Remove from the heat, and add the milk the fish was poached in, a little at a time. Stir well after each addition to form a smooth sauce.

Return to the heat and bring to the boil. Simmer for 3 minutes. Add the chopped hard-boiled eggs and chopped parsley. Season with salt and pepper.

Place fish on a serving plate, spoon the sauce over the top.
Serves 4 to 5.

Gurnard Creole

4 to 5 gurnard fillets

50 grams butter

1 medium onion

2 stalks celery

1 green peppeer

2 sprigs parsley

¾ cup tomato paste

1 lemon

1 x 420 gram tin tomatoes in juice

1½ teaspoons salt

¼ teaspoon pepper

1 teaspoon basil

Pinch cayenne pepper

2 tomatoes

Place the fillets in a greased baking dish.

Melt the butter in a large frying pan. Chop the onion, celery, half of the green pepper and the parsley. Cook in the butter for 4 to 5 minutes. Stir in the lemon juice, the tomato paste, tomatoes in juice, and seasonings. Heat thoroughly, and pour the sauce over the fillets.

Bake at 190 degrees C for 20 to 30 minutes or until the fish flakes easily with a fork. Garnish with tomato wedges and green pepper rings.
Serves 4.

Bream Bay Pate

375 grams smoked snapper

75 grams grated processed cheese

1 clove garlic

½ cup cream

100 grams butter

1 to 2 tablespoons lemon juice

Salt

Pinch cayenne pepper

Lemon slices

Remove the snapper flesh from the skin and bones, and mince or process it finely. Put the cheese, crushed garlic, cream and softened butter into a bowl, and beat with an electric mixer. Alternatively use a food processor. Beat in the lemon juice, salt to taste and the cayenne pepper.

Put into individual ramekin dishes or a 1½ cup terrine, and chill.

Garnish with lemon slices. Serve with crackers or fingers of toast.
Makes 1½ cups.

Gulf Fish Stew

Fish for stews needs to be firm, and it is best to include a variety. Any shellfish can be used to garnish the dish.

1 kilogram mixed fish
8 small onions
2 tablespoons butter
1 clove garlic
1 bay leaf
1 sprig thyme
1 sprig parsley
1 celery top
200 grams mushrooms
1 teaspoon salt
1/4 teaspooon pepper
1 cup white wine
1 cup water
2 tablespoons butter
1 tablespoon flour

Trim fish and cut into pieces about 5 centimetres square.

Peel onions and leave whole. Peel and crush garlic. Cook onions in butter, without letting them colour.

Tie bay leaf, thyme and parsley together. Wash mushrooms well.

Place these ingredients with the onions in a large saucepan. Add salt, pepper, wine and water. A little more wine and water may be needed to bring liquid to cover the fish. Simmer gently for 20 minutes.

Lift the fish out with a draining spoon and place on a serving dish. Keep warm.

Cream butter and flour well, and stir small pieces into the liquid until it boils and thickens. Correct the seasonings.

Lift out onions and mushrooms, and arrange them around the fish. Strain the sauce, and pour around the fish. Serve the stew with toasted bread.

Serves 4 to 6.

Dark meat inside brightly coloured paua shells.

Seafood Turnovers

2 scallops
1 fillet white fish, 50 to 75 grams
50 to 75 grams, prawns or shrimps
1 shallot
1/4 cup white wine
2 tablespoons water
1 tablespoon butter
1 tablespoon flour
1/4 teaspoon salt
Pinch paprika
2 tablespoons top milk
1 tablespoon chopped parsley
500 grams puff pastry
Egg yolk

Prepare the fish as necessary. If tinned prawns or shrimps are being used, drain.

Chop the shallot, and place with the scallops, white fish, white wine and water in a saucepan. Poach gently until the fish is just cooked.

If prawns or shrimps are not tinned, poach them in the cooking liquor also. Drain off the cooking stock, and reserve it.

Break up the white fish, chop the shellfish into small pieces, and mix together.

In a small saucepan, heat the butter and stir in the flour. When this is frothy, gradually add the cooking liquor, and cook, stirring all the time, until the sauce thickens. Season well with salt and paprika. Blend in the top milk and parsley.

Mix this sauce with the seafood, and leave to go cold.

Roll out the pastry, and from it, cut rounds about 7 centimetres in diameter. On one half of each of these, put a spoonful of the seafood mixture. Dampen the edges, fold over the remaining pastry, and decorate the edge. Brush lightly with egg yolk. Bake at 230 degrees C for 8 to 10 minutes.

Serve warm as an hors d'oeuvre.

Makes 60.

Paua

This is a shellfish restricted to New Zealand waters, although it is a member of the abalone family. It is best known for its irridescent shell, which is roughly oval. The shellfish is found clinging firmly to rocks with its large muscular foot.

Flesh of the paua is dark, the outer layer being the darkest. This is also the tough portion, requiring beating to break up the fibres and make it suitable for eating.

The flesh has a high iodine content and is suitable for cooking quickly. Lengthy cooking tends to toughen it. The tough outer portions are best minced, and can then be made into fritters or soup.

Freshly gathered paua that can have the outer layer beaten as soon as possible, tend to be less tough than those stored for a length of time.

Paua in Chilli Sauce

400 grams fresh paua
200 grams pork fillet
1 clove garlic
1 teaspoon chopped fresh ginger
2 tablespoons oil
1 cup fish stock
1 tablespoon cornflour
1 tablespoon water
1 teaspoon chilli sauce
Salt and pepper

Beat the dark edges of the paua to tenderise. Cut the paua and pork into thin strips. Crush the garlic, and finely chop ginger.

Heat the oil in a frying pan with the garlic and ginger. Add pork slices, and stir-fry until lightly cooked. Remove from pan.

Stir-fry the paua slices for only 5 to 10 seconds, stirring quickly. Remove from pan. Add fish stock to pan. Mix cornflour with water; stir until thickened. Add chilli sauce. Season with salt and pepper.

Return cooked pork and paua to frying pan to quickly heat through. Serve over rice or noodles.

Serves 4.

Paua Fritters
(photograph above)

4 paua

2 egg whites

3 tablespoons flour

Salt and pepper

2 tablespoons oil

25 grams butter

Mince the paua, or chop very finely.

Beat the egg whites until they hold soft peaks. Sift flour, and fold into egg whites. Lightly mix in minced paua. Season with salt and pepper.

Heat oil and butter in frying pan. Place tablespoonfuls of the mixture in hot oil and butter. Cook until golden on both sides. Drain on absorbent paper. Serve hot.
Makes about 8.

Lemon Fish

Lemon fish, commonly on the market, is another name for Rig which is a small variety of shark. It is a firm textured, white fleshed, boneless fish which does not flake readily.

Hauraki Soup

3 cups water

1 cup dry white wine

2 carrots

1 onion

2 stalks celery

10 black peppercorns

Bouquet garni

500 grams lemon fish

2 egg yolks

4 tablespoons cream

Salt and pepper

Chopped parsley

Lemon slices

Place the water and wine in a large saucepan. Peel and slice the carrots and onion. Chop the celery. Lightly crush the peppercorns with the flat blade of a knife.

Add carrots, onion, celery, peppercorns and bouquet garni to the liquid. Bring to the boil, and simmer for 30 minutes. Remove from the heat.

Place fish in a second saucepan. Strain the liquid over the fish. Bring to the boil, then reduce the heat so the liquid is just simmering. Poach for 7 to 10 minutes until fish is cooked. Remove fish from liquid, and cut into bite-sized pieces.

Beat egg yolks and cream together. Add 2 tablespoons of the hot liquid to the egg-cream mixture, and whisk to combine. Pour this back into the saucepan, whisking at the same time.

Return fish to the saucepan. Season with salt and pepper to taste. Heat, without allowing to boil, before serving. Serve sprinkled with chopped parsley and a lemon slice.
Serves 4 to 5.

Scallops in White Wine Sauce

Potato Border:

500 grams potatoes

25 grams butter

4 to 6 tablespoons milk

Melted butter

4 scallop shells

Filling:

250 grams scallops

½ cup water

1 tablespoon lemon juice

1 small onion

50 grams butter

2 tablespoons flour

¼ cup water

¼ cup dry white wine

½ teaspoon salt

¼ teaspoon pepper

1 egg yolk

1 tablespoon cream

Potato border: Peel and wash the potatoes. Cook in boiling salted water until tender. Drain well.

Place a lid on the saucepan, and return to low heat, to dry out the potatoes. Move saucepan about a little. Potatoes will go quite white around the edges. Mash well, or pass through a food mill. Add butter and milk to mix.

Put mixture into a piping bag, fitted with a 1 centimetre star-shaped nozzle. Pipe the potatoes around the edge of each scallop shell. Brush lightly with melted butter.

Filling: Poach scallops in first measure of water and the lemon juice for about 5 minutes. Drain, and reserve the liquid. Peel and finely chop the onion.

Melt half the butter in a saucepan, add onions, cover with a lid, and cook gently for about 3 minutes. Remove from heat and add to the scallops. Set aside.

In another saucepan, heat the remaining butter. Stir in the flour, and cook until frothy. Remove from heat.

Combine the poaching liquor with second measure of water and the wine. Add salt and pepper. Return saucepan to heat. Gradually add the liquid, and cook, stirring continuously, until the sauce thickens. Remove from heat. Beat the egg yolk and cream together. Stir into the hot sauce. Add scallops and onion mixture to sauce. Stir until thoroughly combined.

Divide the scallop mixture equally among the 4 scallop shells.

Place under griller until pale golden. Serve immediately.
Serves 4.

Fish en Papillotes

200 grams mushrooms

2 tablespoons butter

1 shallot

1 tablespoon chopped parsley

½ teaspoon salt

3 tablespoons butter

3 tablespoons flour

Salt and pepper

1 cup milk

6 sheets white paper, 20 by 25 centimetres

Butter

6 fillets of fish, preferably flounder

Lemon juice

Prepare the sauce by washing and finely chopping the mushrooms. Cook these in the first measure of butter, add the finely chopped shallot and parsley, and continue cooking until all the liquid is used up. Season with salt.

In a small saucepan, melt the second measure of butter and stir in the flour. When this froths, gradually add the milk, and cook with constant stirring until the sauce thickens. Season with salt and pepper, and blend with the mushroom mixture.

Prepare the papillotes by folding the paper in half and cutting it into a rough shield or heart shape. Butter the paper well.

Trim fillets free of skin and bone. Wipe them, then sprinkle with salt and pepper, and squeeze a little lemon juice on them.

Spread a spoonful of mixture on one half of a buttered papillote, and place a prepared fillet of fish on it. Spread more mushroom sauce over the fish, and fold the paper over. Fold the edges of the paper to form a tight hem which will not let steam or juices escape.

Place the papillotes on a dry baking tray or dish, and bake at 180 degrees C for 20 to 30 minutes, depending on the thickness of the fish. The paper will be lightly browned.

Lift the papillotes on to hot plates and serve as they are. The fish is eaten from the paper. If you wish, the paper can be cut just inside the folded edges with the point of a sharp knife or kitchen scissors, so facilitating opening by the diner.
Serves 6.

Fish Mousse

Mousse:

1 x 1 kilogram tarakihi

3 egg whites

1½ cups cream

3 teaspoons salt

Pinch cayenne pepper

Sauce:

2 cups water

¼ cup dry white wine

1 onion

1 carrot

1 bay leaf

3 peppercorns

1 teaspoon salt

50 grams butter

¼ cup flour

1 cup strained fish stock

½ cup top milk or cream

2 teaspoons tomato paste

Crayfish meat or prawns

2 or 3 hard-boiled eggs

Mousse: Skin the fish fillets, and remove the bones. Save the trimmings for making the fish stock.

Mince the fish. Place in a bowl standing in a large bowl of ice.

With a wire whisk, beat in the unbeaten egg whites a little at a time, until a smooth paste-like mixture is formed. Gradually beat into this, the cream, salt and cayenne pepper.

Turn the mixture into a well-buttered mould of about 6-cup capacity. Cover this with a piece of buttered paper, fitting closely and neatly to the mixture.

Stand the mould in a dish of hot water, and put in a 160 degree C oven. Cook in this way for about 45 minutes, or until the mousse has set.

Sauce: Take the skin and bones of the fish, and put with the water and wine, sliced onion, sliced carrot, bay leaf, peppercorns and salt, and simmer for about an hour; then strain and reserve the stock.

Melt the butter in a saucepan, and stir in the flour. When this has frothed, gradually add the measured amount of fish stock, and cook, stirring, until the sauce thickens. Cook over very low heat with regular stirring for a further 5 minutes.

Blend in the cream and tomato paste, and correct the seasonings as necessary. Set aside and keep warm until ready to use.

Have the crayfish meat removed from the shell and cut into large pieces. Reserve the legs for garnish.

If prawns are being used, have them shelled and ready for serving.

Slice the hard-boiled eggs.

When ready to serve, unmould the mousse into the centre of a platter. Arrange the crayfish or prawns around the mould, using the hard-boiled egg and legs decoratively with it. Carefully spoon the pale pink sauce over the mousse.
Serves 8.

Curried Fish Salad

2 cups flaked cooked fish
2 cups cooked rice
1 onion
1 clove garlic
1 slice root ginger
2 tablespoons oil
1 tablespoon curry powder
½ teaspoon grated lemon rind
1 cup coconut cream
1 green pepper
Salt to taste

The fish can be mixed varieties or of one sort, cooked and chilled.

The rice should be cooked until tender, and chilled.

When ready to mix the salad, chop the onion, garlic and root ginger finely. Heat the oil in a frying pan. Fry onion, garlic and ginger in the oil until just tender, but not coloured.

Stir in the curry powder, lemon rind and coconut cream. Lower the heat and simmer for about 5 minutes.

Remove the seeds from the green pepper, and dice the flesh. Mix the fish, rice, and pepper flesh, and season lightly with salt.

When the sauce has cooked, allow to go cold, then stir through the fish-rice mixture. Chill until ready to serve.
Serves 4 to 6.

Poached Gurnard au Gratin

1 onion
1 carrot
2 cups water
1 bay leaf
6 black peppercorns
½ teaspoon salt
4 or 8 gurnard fillets, depending on size
50 grams butter
2 tablespoons flour
¼ cup dry white wine
½ cup milk
1 cup grated tasty cheese
Salt and pepper to taste
Pinch ground nutmeg
2 tablespoons breadcrumbs

Slice onion and carrot. Place the water, onion, carrot, bay leaf, salt and black peppercorns in a large saucepan. Bring to the boil, then lower the fish fillets into the hot liquid. Gently poach, without allowing to boil, for 7 to 8 minutes or until the fish is cooked.

Remove fish from liquid, and drain well. Reserve ¼ cup of cooking liquid. Remove any skin and bones from the fish.

Heat butter in a small saucepan. Stir in the flour. Cook for two minutes, stirring constantly. Remove from the heat. Gradually add the wine, and cook, stirring all the time, for a further 2 to 3 minutes. Gradually add the reserved cooking liquid and the milk, stirring well after each addition. Bring to the boil, stirring all the time, then simmer for 3 to 4 minutes.

Remove from the heat. Stir in ¾ cup of the grated cheese. Season to taste with salt, pepper and nutmeg.

Arrange the cooked fish on the bottom of a lightly buttered shallow ovenproof dish. Cover with the sauce. Mix the remaining cheese with the breadcrumbs. Sprinkle evenly over the sauce.

Place under a grill or in the top of the oven until the sauce is lightly browned and bubbling.
Serves 4.

A fishing boat brings in its catch at dawn.

FIRST CATCH YOUR...

To the sporting New Zealander, catching your food is a bonus on the excitement of the chase. Fishermen, river and sea, hunters of birds or deer or wild pig, all enjoy the beauty of the land, the challenge of the sport, and the rewarding pleasure of eating their catch.

From the simplest cooking of a trout on the riverbank, to the complicated procedures of marinating and cooking a piece of venison, or the hanging and roasting of feathered game, there is something for all hunters and those who cook for them.

The marlin that is smoked for the deep sea fisherman competes with the roast of wild pork from the pig shooter. The braised pheasant from the shooting season vies with the rabbit stew from the farmer's gun.

New Zealand has an abundance of fish, fowl, and flesh to be caught, cooked, and enjoyed.

Captions to preceding 4 pages.

Page 38/39: Mirror-like reflections of mountains and sky in Lake Tekapo, South Island. (photograph Eric Taylor).

Page 40/41: Trout. Success and achievement. The undeniable joy of a trout fisherman and the pleasure of sampling the catch in the quiet surroundings of the stream.

Facing page: The proud stance of a Wapiti deer. (photograph Michael De Hamel — Photobank).

Venison

Like any other meat, it can be cooked in a variety of ways.

By nature, venison is light on fat, and benefits from being marinated.

Most people like the thought of roast meat, and roast venison is delicious after being marinated, and when roasted covered with strips of bacon.

It is now possible to have farmed venison, as well as that taken in the wild.

Venison Steaks and Mushrooms in Foil
(photograph right)

1 onion
¼ cup red wine
2 tablespoons brandy
2 tablespoons oil
Salt
Freshly ground pepper
4 venison steaks
2 rashers bacon
100 grams mushrooms
4 juniper berries
25 grams butter
4 teaspoons butter

Sauce:

1 onion
1 carrot
1 tablespoon oil
2 tablespoons flour
1 cup beef stock
1 tablespoon tomato paste
Bouquet garni
¼ cup red wine vinegar
3 black peppercorns
¼ cup red wine

Peel and finely chop the onion. Mix together with red wine, brandy, oil, salt and pepper. Marinate steaks for about 4 hours, or overnight, if possible.

Remove the rind, and chop the bacon finely. Wash and chop mushrooms finely. Crush juniper berries. Mix together bacon, mushrooms, and juniper berries. Set aside.

Drain steaks from marinade, reserving the liquid.

Heat the first measure of butter in a heavy-based frying pan. Brown the steaks on one side only. Remove from the pan, and spread the browned side with a thick layer of mushroom mixture.

Wrap each steak in foil. Dot each with 1 teaspoon of butter.

Place in an ovenproof dish. Bake at 200 degrees C for 30 minutes, until tender. Serve with sauce.
Serves 4.

Sauce: Peel and finely chop the onion and carrot. Heat oil in a saucepan, and brown onion and carrot. Stir in the flour. Gradually add the beef stock and tomato paste. Add bouquet garni.

Simmer gently for 30 minutes, stirring occasionally. Strain, and set aside.

Heat the red wine vinegar in a saucepan. Add the reserved marinade and crushed peppercorns.

Reduce mixture to half by boiling briskly. Strain, and add to beef stock mixture. Simmer for a further 20 minutes. Add the red wine, and reheat before serving.

Venison Ragout

500 grams stewing venison
3 cups water
Salt
1 teaspoon paprika
2 cloves
1 bay leaf
3 to 4 peppercorns
1 onion

Sauce:

50 grams butter
2 tablespoons flour
Salt
1 tablespoon lemon juice
2 tablespoons wine
¼ teaspoon sugar
1 pickled gherkin

Cut the meat into cubes about 3 centimetres square.

Bring the water to the boil. Add the meat, salt, paprika, cloves, bay leaf, peppercorns and quartered onion. Cover, and bring to the boil. Lower the heat, and simmer for 1 to 1½ hours, or until tender.

Lift out the meat and reserve the stock.

Sauce: Melt the butter in a saucepan. Add the flour, and cook for 1 to 2 minutes, stirring well. Add 2½ cups of the strained stock. Season with salt, lemon juice, wine and sugar. Add the meat, and leave it to simmer 10 minutes.

Dice the gherkin and add to the ragout.
Serves 4 to 5.

Braised Topside of Venison
(photograph right)

1 cup red wine vinegar
1 cup water
5 whole allspice berries
8 peppercorns
1 teaspoon brown sugar
1 onion
1 bay leaf
1 carrot
1 stalk celery
1 sprig thyme
750 grams to 1 kilogram topside venison
8 juniper berries
6 black peppercorns
½ teaspoon chopped thyme
1 onion
3 rashers bacon
25 grams butter
½ cup red wine
12 prunes
1 peeled and diced apple
¼ cup walnut halves

In large saucepan, place vinegar, water, whole allspice, peppercorns, brown sugar, sliced onion, bay leaf, sliced carrot and celery and sprig of thyme. Bring slowly to the boil, and simmer for 30 minutes. Remove from the heat and allow to cool.

Place the venison piece in a non-metallic bowl, and pour over it the cool marinade. Cover, and place in refrigerator for a minimum of 24 hours.

Drain, reserving half a cup of marinade. Dry the meat with a paper towel. Tie the meat with string.

Crush the juniper berries, black peppercorns and thyme together. Rub the surface of meat with the crushed mixture.

Slice onion finely. Remove rind, and chop the bacon.

In a heavy-based casserole, heat the butter. Cook bacon and onions together until golden. Remove from casserole.

Lightly brown meat in the residual butter. Return onions and bacon to casserole. Pour in reserved marinade and the wine, prunes, diced apple and walnuts.

Cover tightly, and simmer for 1½ to 2 hours, until meat is tender. Serve sliced with sauce spooned over.

Serves 5 to 6.

Venison Pepper Steaks

| 100 grams mushrooms |
| 3 tablespoons black peppercorns |
| 2 tablespoons juniper berries |
| 4 venison steaks |
| 2 tablespoons butter |
| ¼ cup brandy |
| ½ cup sour cream |

Wash and slice the mushrooms finely. Crush the peppercorns and juniper berries with the flat blade of a large knife. Press on to both sides of the steaks.

Heat butter in a large heavy-based frying pan until very hot. Cook the steaks quickly on both sides. Remove steaks from pan, and keep warm.

Add the mushrooms to the pan. Cook 2 to 3 minutes. Add the brandy, then sour cream. Stir well. Pour over the steaks.

Serves 4.

Roast Venison

| 800 to 900 grams venison roast |
| Pork crackling to fit around venison |
| **Red wine marinade:** |
| 1 clove garlic |
| ¼ cup oil |
| ½ cup red wine |
| ½ teaspoon dry mustard |
| 2 bay leaves |
| Freshly ground pepper |

Crush the garlic. Combine with oil, red wine, mustard, bay leaves and pepper. Marinate venison in this for at least 24 hours, turning occasionally. Drain well.

Wrap pork crackling around the venison. Tie securely with string.

Weigh the prepared joint to calculate cooking time, allowing 45 minutes per 500 grams. Roast at 190 degrees C for the first hour, then reduce temperature to 180 degrees C for the remaining cooking time. Remove crackling to serve.

Note: If wished, a sauce can be made to serve with the roast using some of the marinade.

Grilled Venison Steaks

| 1 onion |
| 5 tamarillos |
| 2 cloves garlic |
| 2 teaspoons Worcestershire sauce |
| ½ teaspoon prepared mild mustard |
| 2 tablespoons brown sugar |
| ¼ cup tomato puree |
| ¼ teaspoon chilli powder |
| 6 venison steaks |

Peel and chop the onion and tamarillos. Mix together onion, tamarillos, crushed garlic, Worcestershire sauce, mustard, brown sugar, tomato puree and chilli powder.

Place venison steaks in a shallow dish. Pour over marinade. Cover, and leave for 24 hours, basting occasionally.

Place steaks on a grill rack, reserving the marinade. Grill for about 4 to 5 minutes on each side, until tender.

Meanwhile, heat the reserved marinade in a saucepan. Bring to the boil, and cook until tamarillos are tender. Press through a sieve, and return to saucepan. Heat through, and serve hot with grilled steaks.

Serves 6.

Venison Stew with Potato Dumplings

(photograph page 45)

1 kilogram thick flank venison

25 grams butter

2 tablespoons flour

2 cups beef or venison stock

1 cup water

Salt

1 onion

6 peppercorns

1 bay leaf

2 tablespoons lemon juice

½ cup red wine

Potato Dumplings:

1 kilogram potatoes

1 onion

5 slices white bread

¼ cup water

Salt and pepper

1 tablespoon chopped parsley

2 eggs

About ¼ cup flour

Wipe the meat, then pat dry and cut into 3 centimetre pieces. In a heavy casserole, heat the butter and brown the meat, a few pieces at a time. Remove meat from pan. Add flour, and cook until frothy. Pour in the stock, water and salt.

Cook, stirring, until sauce thickens. Add the chopped onion, peppercorns, bay leaf and lemon juice. Simmer for 5 minutes.

Return meat to saucepan. Cover, and simmer for about 1½ hours until tender. Add wine, then simmer uncovered for about 10 minutes until well reduced.

Serve with Potato Dumplings.

Serves 4 to 5.

Potato Dumplings: Wash, peel and grate the potatoes. Squeeze to remove liquid. Peel and grate the onion. Soak bread in measured water, and squeeze firmly.

Mix bread, salt, pepper, grated onions and parsley. Add well-drained grated potatoes. Beat eggs, and add.

Form mixture into balls of about 2 centimetres in diameter. Roll balls in flour. Place balls in a large saucepan of simmering water.

Cover tightly, and cook for about 15 minutes. Drain well.

Note: Depending on the type of potatoes, a small amount of flour may need to be added to bind the mixture to a consistency that will keep its shape during cooking. Cook one dumpling first to see if it holds.

Venison Soup

About 1.25 kilograms venison neck chops or pieces

1 onion

2 carrots

2 stalks celery

5 black peppercorns

1 bay leaf

2½ litres water

1 onion

1 clove garlic

50 grams butter

¼ cup flour

¼ cup port wine

Salt

Freshly ground pepper

Chopped parsley

Wipe the venison, and place in a large saucepan.

Peel the first onion and the carrots. Cut into 3 or 4 pieces. Cut celery in half. Arrange prepared vegetables, black peppercorns and bay leaf around meat. Pour water over. Bring to the boil, cover, and simmer for 3 hours.

Strain off liquid. Remove meat from the bones, and set aside.

Return stock to the saucepan; boil rapidly until reduced to about 6 cups. Remove from heat.

Chop the second onion, and crush the garlic. Heat butter, and gently fry onion and garlic until soft, but not brown. Stir in flour, cook until frothy. Gradually add reduced stock, stirring continuously, until boiling.

Reduce heat to simmering, add port, and season with salt and pepper. Simmer gently for 15 minutes.

Add reserved meat and heat through gently. Serve hot, garnished with chopped parsley.

Serves 6 to 8.

Individual Venison Pies

500 grams venison

Pinch ground mace

Pinch allspice

½ teaspoon salt

Freshly ground black pepper

2 tablespoons flour

¼ cup red wine

¼ cup malt vinegar

½ cup beef stock

1 onion

2 teaspoons tart red jelly

1 tablespoon finely chopped parsley

300 grams flaky pastry

Glaze:

1 tablespoon water

1 egg yolk

Cut the venison into 2 centimetre cubes. Combine the mace, allspice, salt, pepper and flour. Coat the meat in this.

Place coated meat in a saucepan. Pour over it the wine, vinegar and beef stock. Chop onion finely and add it. Cover, and simmer 1½ hours, or until tender.

Leave until cool. Stir in the jelly and parsley.

Roll out pastry to line and cover four 9 centimetre individual pie dishes. Fill with venison mixture, and cover with pastry. Make 2 or 3 slashes in the tops. Brush glaze over the tops of the pies.

Bake at 220 degrees C for 20 to 25 minutes.

Glaze: Mix water and egg yolk together with a fork.

Makes 4 pies.

Roast Wild Pork
with Pink Apple Sauce
(photograph above)

Pork:

Joint wild pork

1 cup brown sugar

2 teaspoons dry mustard

1 teaspoon salt

Apple Sauce:

1 small onion

4 cooking apples

2 teaspoons butter

¼ cup water

3 tablespoons stiff red currant jelly

Weigh the pork to determine cooking time, allowing 25 minutes per 500 grams, and 30 minutes extra.

Mix the brown sugar, mustard and salt together in a bowl. Rub the sugar mixture over the top fatty surface of the pork. Place the meat in a roasting dish, and roast at 180 degrees C, basting often with the drippings that come from the meat. Cook for required time, then rest for 10-15 minutes before carving.

Pink Apple Sauce: Peel and dice the onion finely. Peel, core, and slice the apples. Place onion, apples, butter and water in a saucepan. Cover, and simmer until apples are tender — about 15 minutes. Puree to make a sauce. Just before serving, stir in the red currant jelly, so a flecked appearance is achieved.
Serves 6.

Wild Pork Urewera
Style

1 boned joint of wild pork

3 cups fresh breadcrumbs

1 onion

1 cooking apple

1 tablespoon butter

1 egg

1 tablespoon chopped parsley

1 teaspoon thyme

Salt and pepper

1 tablespoon flour

1 tablespoon brown sugar

Weigh the meat. Score the skin of the meat and flatten it, cutting if necessary.

Place the breadcrumbs in a bowl. Finely chop the onion. Peel, core and finely chop the apple. Melt the butter.

Add the onion, apple, melted butter, egg, parsley, thyme, salt and pepper to the breadcrumbs, and mix well. Add a little water to combine, if necessary

Spread the stuffing on the cut side of the meat. Roll the pork up, and tie at regular intervals. Rub the outside of the meat with salt and pepper, and sprinkle the flour and brown sugar over.

Place in a roasting dish, and bake at 180 degrees C, allowing 35 minutes per 500 grams plus 30 minutes extra. Remove the string before serving.

The number of servings will depend on the size of the joint.

Wild Pork

The texture and flavour of wild pork is influenced by the food the animal consumes in the bush. Certain roots, for instance, cause the flesh to become dry and the flavour medicinal.

Rabbit

Rabbit with Prunes

10 to 12 prunes

1 rabbit

2 rashers bacon

2 large onions

2 tablespoons butter

About 1½ cups water

Salt

Pepper

Thyme

1 bay leaf

2 tablespoons flour

1 tablespoon vinegar

1 tablespoon water

Soak the prunes in water until plump. Cut the rabbit into portions. Cut the bacon into pieces. Peel and chop the onions.

Heat the butter in a large frying pan, and gently fry the bacon and onion until lightly coloured, then remove. Fry the rabbit pieces until golden brown, and return the bacon and onion to the pan. Add enough water to almost cover meat. Season with salt and pepper, and add thyme and bay leaf. Bring to the boil. Cover, then reduce heat to simmer until the rabbit is almost tender — about 10 to 15 minutes. Add the drained prunes, and cook 10 to 15 minutes longer.

Mix the flour, vinegar and water together, and stir into the pan, boiling to allow to thicken.
Serves 5 to 6.

Rabbit Braised in Beer

2 rashers fatty bacon

1 rabbit

2 tablespoons flour

Salt

Pepper

8 tiny onions

1 cup beer

1 tablespoon mild mustard

1 teaspoon brown sugar

Cut the bacon into pieces, and place in a roasting pan. Place in a 200 degrees C oven, and cook until fat starts to draw from the bacon pieces.

Dust the rabbit in seasoned flour, and place in bacon fat, turning to coat well.

Peel onions, and leave whole. Place in the pan with the rabbit, and return to the oven for about 15 minutes. Turn once or twice during this time.

Mix beer, mustard and brown sugar, and pour into the pan. Lower oven heat to 180 degrees C, and cook the rabbit, basting frequently, until tender — about 30 minutes.
Serves 4.

Note: If wished, a gravy can be made from the pan drippings.

Rabbit Terrine

350 grams rabbit

100 grams pork fat

Pinch turmeric

¼ teaspoon mace

¾ teaspoon salt

¼ teaspoon pepper

½ teaspoon fresh thyme

150 grams chicken livers

150 grams sausagemeat

1 tablespoon tomato sauce

Salt

Pepper

4 to 6 thin rashers bacon

Cut the rabbit meat from the bones. Using a mincer or food processer, mince the rabbit meat and pork fat to get a smooth grind. Season with turmeric, mace, salt, pepper and thyme, and set aside.

Mince the chicken livers and add the sausagemeat, salt, pepper and tomato sauce.

Line a deep 2½ cup terrine or ovenware dish with the rindless bacon rashers, reserving some for covering the top.

Spread one layer of the sausagemeat mixture on the bottom, then a layer of rabbit, pressing down firmly. Repeat.

Cover the top with the remaining rashers of bacon. Cover with a lid or foil. Stand in a roasting dish half-filled with water.

Bake at 180 degrees C for 1 to 1¼ hours.

Remove from the oven, and place a weight on top of the foil to press down the terrine. When completely cold and set, turn out and accompany with thin slices of toast or savoury biscuits.
Serves 10 to 12.

Jugged Hare

1 hare

50 grams butter

4 rashers bacon

2 tablespoons flour

1 cup beef stock

1 cup red wine

1 sprig parsley

1 bay leaf

1 sprig thyme

1 clove garlic

1 onion

1 teaspoon grated lemon rind

6 cloves

Clean and joint the hare. Brown in the melted butter in a large flame-proof casserole or a heavy-based saucepan.

Remove the rind from the bacon and cut into small pieces. Add to the hare and fry lightly. Stir in the flour, and cook gently for 2 to 3 minutes. Add the stock, wine, herbs, crushed garlic and grated lemon rind to the dish. Stud the onion with the cloves, and add this.

Cover, and cook at 180 degrees C for 1½ hours.

Alternatively, simmer on top of the stove for 1½ hours.

Remove the clove-studded onion before serving. Serve with red currant jelly.
Serves 4 to 6.

Pheasant

Pheasant Terrine
(photograph below)

1 x 815 gram pheasant

2 tablespoons sherry

2 tablespoons brandy

600 grams belly pork

2 to 3 shallots

1 clove garlic

1 teaspoon salt

1 egg

1 cup fresh white breadcrumbs

Freshly ground black pepper

4 tablespoons finely chopped parsley

2 tablespoons finely chopped thyme

Skin and carefully remove breast meat from the pheasant carcass. Cut into strips 1 centimetre thick. Marinate in sherry and brandy for at least 2 hours.

Remove remaining meat from the pheasant carcass; reserve carcass and trimmings for soup.

Cut away pork rind thinly; slice about one third of pork. With the blade of a knife, stretch and flatten these thin pork slices. Use to line a 4 to 5 cup loaf tin or terrine. Reserve 2 or 3 slices for top of terrine.

In a food processor or mincer, finely mince the pheasant pieces, and the remaining two-thirds of pork.

Finely chop shallots. Mash garlic in salt.

Combine minced pork and pheasant, shallots, mashed garlic and salt, egg and breadcrumbs. Mix well, and season with pepper.

Drain pheasant strips; pour the marinade into minced mixture. Combine finely chopped fresh parsley and thyme. Roll breast strips in herbs.

Divide minced mixture into 3; spread one third over the base of terrine. Layer half of the breast strips; spread with the second portion of minced mixture; then layer with remaining breast strips and minced mixture. Cover terrine with pork slices.

Cover with foil or a lid. Stand in a roasting pan of hot water, and cook at 180 degrees C for about 1 hour.

Remove from the oven, and cover with 2 or 3 layers of greaseproof paper. Press with weights as the terrine cools.

Unmould, and scrape fat from the surface. Serve chilled.
Serves 6 to 8.

Roast Pheasant and Game Chips
(photograph below)

1 pheasant

3 to 4 tablespoons melted butter

Salt

Freshly ground black pepper

Game Chips:

250 grams small potatoes

Oil for deep frying

Wipe the pheasant inside and out with a clean, damp cloth. Weigh pheasant to calculate cooking time. Allow 15 to 20 minutes per 500 grams plus 15 to 20 minutes. Brush pheasant with melted butter, and season with salt and pepper.

Roast at 220 degrees C for first 30 minutes; reduce oven temperature to 180 degrees C for remaining cooking time. Baste frequently. Serve with game chips and cranberry sauce.

Game Chips: Peel potatoes. Cut into paper-thin rounds. This is especially easy with a slicer or food processor.

Soak the slices in cold water for about an hour, drain well, and dry thoroughly.

Deep fry a few at a time in hot oil until lightly coloured. Drain well on absorbent paper, and keep hot until remaining chips are cooked.
Serves 2.

Matahura Quail
(photograph below)

2 tablespoons raisins

½ cup hot water

4 quail

Salt

Pepper

¼ cup melted butter

1 cup chicken stock

Soak the raisins in the hot water for a few minutes until they swell.

Wipe the prepared quail with a damp cloth. Do not wash. Salt and pepper inside and out. Stuff with the raisins. Brush the quail generously with melted butter.

Place quail in a roasting dish with a lid. Bake uncovered at 220 degrees C for about 15 minutes or until brown.

Reduce temperature to 180 degrees C, add chicken stock, and baste the birds well with the stock and any remaining melted butter. Put the lid on, or cover tightly with foil, and bake a further 20 to 25 minutes, or until tender.

Allow 2 quail per person, unless the quail are very large.
Serves 2.

The prize of the sportsman and the skill of the cook makes pleasure for the family.

Country Fried Pheasant
(photograph below)

1 pheasant

¼ cup flour

½ teaspoon salt

¼ teaspoon black pepper

¼ teaspoon paprika

25 grams butter

½ cup water

½ cup milk

1 onion

Cut the pheasant into convenient serving pieces. Put the flour, salt, pepper and paprika into a paper or plastic bag. Add pieces of pheasant, a few at a time, and shake about to thoroughly coat them with the seasoned flour.

Heat the butter in an electric frypan or a pan with a close fitting lid. Add pheasant pieces, and brown them well on all sides. Reduce heat, and add water and milk.

Slice the onion in rings, and place the slices on top of the pieces of pheasant. Adjust heat until just simmering. Simmer 1 to 1½ hours, or until tender, adding more water and milk if necessary. Remove pheasant to a serving dish, stir the sauce well, and pour it over the top of the dish.
Serves 4.

Stuffed Roast Pheasant
(photograph below)

Stuffing:

1 onion

50 grams butter

1 apple

1 cup fresh breadcrumbs

¼ teaspoon sage

¼ teaspoon thyme

¼ teaspoon black pepper

½ teaspoon salt

The Pheasant:

1 pheasant

2 rashers bacon

Hot water

Gravy:

3 tablespoons flour

¼ cup cold water

Salt

Pepper

¼ cup Madeira or orange juice

Stuffing: Chop the onion finely. In a saucepan, heat the butter and cook the onion until transparent. Remove from pan, heat and grate the apple. Add the apple, breadcrumbs, herbs and seasonings, mix well.

The Pheasant: With a damp cloth, wipe the bird inside and out. Fill the cavity with stuffing. Close opening securely, and truss the bird. Place rashers of bacon over the breast. Wrap pheasant in foil, and place in a roasting dish. Add hot water to a depth of about 5 centimetres. Cover the dish with a lid or foil.

Bake at 160 degrees C for 2 to 3 hours or until tender, depending on the age of the bird.

Remove the lid, unwrap the pheasant, and drain off 1½ cups of the juices, and return the bird to the oven to brown.

While the bird is browning, make the gravy.

Gravy: Mix flour and cold water to a smooth cream. Stir into hot pan juices, and stir until boiling. Add salt and pepper to taste, and Madeira or orange juice just before serving.
Serves 3 to 4.

Port and Orange
Pheasant Casserole
(photograph page 49)

1 x 815 gram pheasant
25 grams butter
1 onion
½ cup port wine
1 cup chicken stock
1 teaspoon finely grated orange rind
½ cup orange juice
1 tablespoon cornflour
3 tablespoons water
Salt
Freshly ground black pepper
Orange slices
Parsley sprigs

Wipe the pheasant inside and out with a clean, damp cloth. Heat the butter, and brown pheasant all over. Drain, and transfer to an ovenproof casserole.

Finely chop the onion; fry gently in residue butter, until soft but not brown. Add port, chicken stock, orange rind and juice to the frying pan. Bring to the boil, and pour over pheasant.

Cover, and cook at 160 degrees C for 2 to 2½ hours, until pheasant is tender. Drain off cooking liquid.

Mix cornflour in water; combine with half the cooking liquid. Return to the pan with remaining liquid.

Bring to the boil, and simmer gently for 2 to 3 minutes as sauce thickens. Season with salt and pepper.

Serve the sauce spooned over the pheasant. Garnish with quarter slices of orange and parsley sprigs.
Serves 3 to 4.

Pheasant Parcels
(photograph page 49)

1 pheasant
1 to 2 tablespoons melted butter
Salt
Freshly ground black pepper
Filling per Pheasant Parcel:
25 grams butter
1 rasher bacon
2 tablespoons dry white wine

Wipe the pheasant inside and out with a clean, damp cloth. Brush with melted butter and season with salt and pepper.

Roast at 200 degrees C for 20 minutes. Remove from the oven, cut pheasant in half or, if large, into quarters.

Cut greaseproof paper into 50 by 30 centimetre sheets. Allow 2 sheets of greaseproof per portion of pheasant. Heat butter, and brush liberally over one side of greaseproof paper.

Remove rind from bacon. Wrap each pheasant portion in bacon. Place on buttered paper, and spoon over wine. Divide the roasting juices between parcels. Seal edges all round by twisting over firmly so that none of the juices can escape. Place the parcels on a roasting dish.

Cook at 180 degrees C for 30 to 40 minutes, until tender. Serve parcels individually so each person opens one.
Serves 2 to 4.

Casserole of Swan

Breasts and legs of a swan
Milk
3 rashers bacon
25 grams butter
1 clove garlic
1 onion
1 teaspoon salt
1 tablespoon brown sugar
½ cup dry sherry
1½ to 2 cups water
100 grams button mushrooms
2 tablespoons chopped parsley

Remove the skin from the swan. Place the meat in a dish, and pour over the milk. Leave overnight, turning occasionally.

Remove the meat from the milk, and dry with a paper towel.

Cut the rind from the bacon rashers. Fry the bacon in a hot pan, then place in an ovenproof casserole.

Add the butter to the bacon fat. Crush the garlic and chop the onion. Fry the garlic and onion until cooked, but not coloured. Place in the casserole dish.

Brown the swan meat, and place on top of the onion. Sprinkle the salt and brown sugar over the meat.

Pour the sherry and water into the pan drippings, and bring to the boil. Pour over the meat.

Cover the casserole, and bake at 160 degrees C for 1¼ to 1½ hours. Add the mushrooms and cook, uncovered, for a further 15 minutes, or until the meat is tender. Sprinkle with chopped parsley before serving.
Serves 4 to 6.

Mutton Birds

These sea birds,
the young of the sooty shearwater,
live in burrows,
and are rich in a greasy fat
which is found in the crop
and as a thick coating
over the body of the bird.
The fat gives the bird
a strong flavour,
but if it is removed
during the cooking process,
the taste is more acceptable.
The cooked flavour of these birds
has a fishy note to it.

1 mutton bird
Water
Lemon wedges

Wash the mutton bird in warm water, and place in a saucepan. Cover with water, and bring to the boil.

Drain, and repeat the boiling process.

Place the bird in a heated frying pan or under a hot grill. Cook slowly until the fat is crisp and brown, turning once.

Serve with lemon wedges.
Serves 2.

Breasts of Wild Duck
(photograph left)

2 wild ducks	
2 rashers bacon	
1 apple	
1 onion	
½ cup water	

Sauce:

3 cups chicken stock	
¼ teaspoon salt	
1 tablespoon chopped onion	
1 bay leaf	
3 peppercorns	
1 clove	
2 sprigs parsley	
1 sprig thyme	
2 tablespoons flour	
Pinch cayenne pepper	
¼ cup orange juice	
1 teaspoon grated orange rind	

Wipe the wild ducks with a damp cloth. Place a rasher of bacon over the breast of each duck. Peel the apple and onion. Put the apple inside one duck, and the onion in the other.

Set the birds in a shallow roasting dish, and add the water. Bake at 250 degrees C for 20 to 25 minutes, or until tender.

Remove from the oven, and carefully remove the breasts, and set aside.

Sauce: Put the duck carcasses and legs in a saucepan. Add the chicken stock, salt, chopped onion, bay leaf, peppercorns, clove, parsley and thyme. Bring to the boil and simmer gently for 1 hour. Strain. Measure out 1½ cups of the stock.

Add the flour to the drippings in the roasting pan, and stir until smooth. Gradually stir in the strained duck stock and cayenne pepper. Continue stirring until it boils and thickens. Add the orange juice and rind and the duck breasts, and heat 2 to 3 minutes, or until the duck is heated through.

Serve with boiled rice.
Serves 4.

Note: If the duck has been frozen, allow it to thaw completey before cooking.

Pukeko Soup
(photograph above)

Stock:

1 pukeko	
1 carrot	
1 onion	
1 stick celery	
1 bay leaf	
1 sprig thyme	
1 sprig parsley	
6 peppercorns	
2 cloves	
1 teaspoon salt	
Cold water	

Soup:

2 cups diced vegetables	
¼ cup chopped breast meat	
4 cups stock	
Salt	
Pepper	

Stock: Joint the prepared pukeko. Chop the carrot, onion and celery. Place pukeko, vegetables, bay leaf, thyme, parsley, peppercorns, cloves and salt, in a saucepan, and cover with cold water. Bring slowly to the boil, and simmer gently about 3 hours.

Strain off liquid and use this to make the soup. It should measure about 4 cups.

Soup: Remove some of breast from the pukeko and chop it finely across the grain. In a saucepan, place diced vegetables, chopped meat, and the stock. Simmer for 25 to 30 minutes. Season to taste. Serve hot, garnished with parsley.
Serves 5 to 6.

Wild Duck in a Clay Pot
(photograph above)

2 wild ducks	
2 tablespoons oil	
1 sprig thyme	
6 juniper berries	
Salt	
Pepper	
1 onion	
1 carrot	
1 stick celery	
4 rashers bacon	

Soak the clay pot in cold water for 15 minutes, or as directed for its use.

With a clean, damp cloth, wipe the ducks inside and out. Chop the thyme finely. Mix together with the oil, and rub over the ducks. Put 3 juniper berries inside each duck, and season with salt and pepper.

Chop the onion, carrot and celery, and place in the clay pot. Arrange the ducks on the vegetables and place the rashers of bacon over the breasts. Put the lid on the clay pot, and place in a cold oven and turn on to 230 degrees C.

Bake about 1½ hours, or until tender.
Serves 4 to 5.

Smoked Marlin Salad

*The delight
of the deep sea fisherman
is to enjoy his sporting catch
delicately smoked.*

1 lettuce

2 to 3 tomatoes

1 small cucumber

1 small green pepper

2 spring onions

300 grams smoked marlin or
smoked trout

Salad dressing

Wash and dry the lettuce, and tear into small pieces. Cut tomatoes into wedges. Score cucumber skin, and slice it. Cut green pepper into rings. Wash and trim the spring onions.

Remove bones, and break the smoked marlin into chunky pieces about 3 centimetres square.

Arrange vegetables and smoked fish in a serving bowl. Chill until ready to serve. Serve salad dressing separately.
Serves 4 to 5.

Soused Salmon

1 salmon about 1.25 kilogram

4 cups water

6 peppercorns

1 teaspoon salt

1 sprig parsley

1 sprig thyme

1 bay leaf

1 stalk celery

1 onion

1 carrot

1 cup vinegar

Lemon slices

Parsley

Cut the salmon into steaks, and place in a large casserole or baking dish. Cover with the water, and add the peppercorns and salt.

Tie the parsley, thyme, bay leaf and celery together. Slice the onion and carrot and place in the dish along with the tied herbs and celery. Pour over the vinegar.

Cover with a lid or aluminium foil and cook at 150 degrees C for 1½ hours.

Allow to cool in the refrigerator, and when cold, lift the fish on to a plate, and garnish with lemon slices and parsley. The cooking liquid will form a gel, if given sufficient cooking and cooling time.
Serves 6.

Trout Kedgeree

About 500 grams trout as fillets or steaks.

½ cup white wine

Water

1 teaspoon salt

6 peppercorns

1 bay leaf

1 strip lemon peel

½ cup raw rice

Boiling salted water

25 grams butter

1½ tablespoons flour

50 grams butter

Salt and pepper to taste

2 hard-boiled eggs

Parsley for garnish

Place the prepared pieces of trout in a shallow pan, and add the wine with about an equal volume of water, enough to just cover the fish. Add the salt, peppercorns, bay leaf and lemon rind, and cover with a lid. Poach gently for about 15 minutes, or until the fish is cooked.

While the fish is cooking, put the rice in boiling salted water, and cook until tender. Drain well.

Take the fish from the poaching liquid, and leave to go cold, then flake. Strain the liquid and retain it.

In a saucepan, heat the first measure of butter, and stir in the flour. When this bubbles, gradually stir in 1 cup of the reserved fish stock, and cook with constant stirring, until the sauce thickens. Check seasonings.

Heat the second measure of butter in a large pan, and lightly cook the rice, fish and the coarsely chopped whites of the eggs. Stir until heated through, but do not let it colour.

Pile into a serving dish, and pour the hot wine sauce over the mixture. Garnish with the sieved egg yolks and a sprig of parsley.
Serves 4 to 6.

Black and White Trout

*The simplest and most delicious
way with trout.*

1 trout

Salt

6 to 8 double page sheets of
newspaper

Fresh water

Clean the trout, leaving the head, tail and fins intact. Sprinkle the fish with salt.

Wrap the trout in one sheet of newspaper, and wet thoroughly with fresh water. Repeat this wetting and wrapping process until all the newspaper is used.

Place the wet parcel in a fire among glowing embers, and cook for about 30 minutes. Take the trout parcel out of the embers and remove the charred paper.
Serves 4 to 6.

Tongariro Trout

1 trout

Salt and pepper

1 onion

Pinch sage

Pinch thyme

2 to 3 rashers bacon

Clean the trout, and sprinkle the cavity with salt and pepper. Peel and slice the onion, and place in the cavity of the trout, along with the sage and thyme.

Remove the bacon rind and arrange the rashers along the trout. Wrap the trout in greased foil and place in an ovenproof dish.

Bake at 180 degrees C for 45 to 60 minutes, for a trout of about 1 kilogram. To serve, remove the foil from the fish, and place on a serving plate.

The number of servings will depend on the size of the trout.

MEAT...

The fact that the whole world doesn't eat meat at least once a day is not always an easy idea for many New Zealanders to accept. Throughout our history, there has been an abundance of meat, mainly sheep meat. It was not uncommon in the recent past, for rural people to eat sheep meat two, or even three times a day.

Our knowledge of food and nutrition, and the advantages of freezing and refrigeration have modified this habit. Nevertheless, meat is still the base of the main daily meal of most New Zealanders.

The fine quality sheep meats, from delicate spring lamb, through the tasty and tender cuts of hogget, to the mature mutton, all have a place in our cooking. Beef, too, is of high quality to enjoy in all styles of cooking.

The raising of pork is increasing, with special pigs being developed for the more exacting cuts now required.

The white meat of poultry has gained popularity in the interests of lower fat intake, as well as for its appeal for flavour and versatility.

We are meat eaters with top quality products to enjoy.

Captions to preceding 4 pages.

Page 54/55: Beef cattle at Paradise, Central Otago. (photograph Peter Morath).

Page 56/57: Meat is the foundation of most main meals in New Zealand. Here we choose a dish to make from the wide selection of cuts and varieties available to us.

Facing page: Local farmers gather at the Blenheim saleyards. (photograph Alisdair Drew).

Lamb, Hogget and Mutton

Lamb is a selected male or female carcass, under the age of 12 months.

Hogget is a sheep of either sex, over 12 months old. It is called a 2-tooth because it has 2 permanent incisors.

Mutton is a selected older sheep, graded according to the quality. It has more than 2 permanent incisors.

Braised Orange Lamb

4 shoulder chops

1 clove garlic

1 small onion

1 cup beef stock

Salt and pepper

1 small sprig fresh rosemary

1 sweet orange

2 teaspoons cornflour

1 tablespoon cold water

Trim the chops, and brown on both sides in a hot, heavy-based frying pan. Lift the chops out of the pan, and in the fat that remains, cook the crushed garlic and finely chopped onion. Pour in the stock. Season with salt and pepper, and add the sprig of rosemary, bringing the liquid to the boil.

Place the chops back in the pan, and put a thick slice of peeled orange on each chop. Cover the pan with a close-fitting lid, and simmer for about 40 minutes.

Lift chops with orange on to a serving plate, and into the pan gravy, mix the cornflour blended with water. Bring to the boil, and boil for 1 minute. Serve with chops.
Serves 4.

Lamb Pilaf

2 cups cooked lamb

¾ cup rice

2½ cups chicken stock

¼ teaspoon ground cinnamon

Pinch ground cloves

¼ teaspoon pepper

1 teaspoon salt

¼ cup currants

50 grams butter

¼ cup cashew nuts

Have the cooked meat cut into small dice and free of all fat or gristle.

Put the rice in a saucepan, together with the chicken stock, spices, salt and currants. Bring to the boil, cover, and simmer gently for about 15 minutes, or until the liquid has been absorbed by the rice.

While this is cooking, heat half the butter in a pan, and lightly fry the diced meat.

When the rice is ready, add the remaining butter to it and stir through.

Add the cashew nuts to the meat, and heat through. Place the meat in a pile in the centre of a ring of rice.
Serves 3.

Blue Lamb Chops

8 rib chops

Oil

Salt

Black pepper

100 grams blue vein cheese

2 tablespoons cream

Trim any excess fat from the chops. Brush chops with oil, and sprinkle both sides with salt and pepper.

Heat the griller. Put about 1 centimetre of water in the grilling pan, and place the rack in position. Arrange chops on rack, and grill for 5 to 6 minutes on each side.

Meanwhile, mix the cheese and cream to a smooth paste.

Remove chops from griller, and spread cheese mixture on one side of each chop. Replace under griller, and heat until cheese is bubbling and lightly browned.
Serves 4.

Braised Shanks

1 tablespoon fat or oil

4 hogget shanks

4 stalks celery

4 small onions

1 teaspoon salt

Pepper

¼ cup water

In a large heavy saucepan or flame proof casserole, heat the fat until very hot. In it, brown the shanks all over. Lower the heat, cover with a close-fitting lid, and braise for about 30 minutes.

Have the celery cut into pieces about 15 centimetres long, and the onions peeled, but whole. Add these to the dish; season, and add the water. Cover, and continue cooking for a further 40 to 50 minutes, or until the meat and vegetables are tender.

Serve the meat on a platter, and surround it with the vegetables.

If wished, the remaining liquid can be lightly thickened with flour, or it can be served as it is.
Serves 4.

Kerikeri Roast Lamb

1.75 to 2 kilogram leg of lamb

Salt

¼ cup orange juice

¼ cup honey

4 tablespoons flour

Salt

Pepper

2 cups vegetable water

Lightly score the skin of the meat, and rub with salt. Place in a roasting pan and roast at 160 degrees C for about 2½ hours.

Mix the orange juice and honey together, and brush this over the meat. Do this about every 20 minutes during roasting.

When the lamb is cooked, remove to a hot serving dish.

Pour off all but 4 tablespoons of the pan drippings. Stir in the flour, adding salt and pepper to taste. Cook until bubbling. Gradually add the vegetable water, stirring until it boils and thickens. Serve sauce separately.
Serves 6 to 8.

Fox Glacier above green South Island farmland.

Lamb Patties with Apricots

2 onions

50 grams mushrooms

500 grams lean minced lamb

½ cup fresh white breadcrumbs

1 tablespoon Worcestershire sauce

1 egg

Pinch cayenne pepper

1 teaspoon salt

½ cup dried apricots

Cold water

1 tablespoon oil or dripping

1 tablespoon flour

½ cup dry white wine

2 tablespoons cream

Pinch salt

Pepper

Watercress

Finely chop the onions and mushrooms. Place in a large bowl with the minced lamb, breadcrumbs, Worcestershire sauce, egg, cayenne pepper and salt, and mix well.

With wet hands, shape into 6 patties, about 8 centimetres across.

Cover the apricots with cold water, and bring slowly to the boil. Lift out, and place the apricot halves on the lamb patties. Leave 2 to 3 hours.

Heat the oil or dripping in the frying pan. Lift the apricots off the patties. Fry the patties for about 6 to 7 minutes on each side. Remove to a warm plate, and keep hot.

Pour off any excess fat. Cook the apricots about 1 minute on each side, until lightly golden. Remove, and keep hot.

Mix the flour and wine until smooth. Pour into the frying pan, and stir until bubbling. Add cream and salt and pepper to taste.

Reheat, but do not boil. Spoon sauce over patties and apricots. Garnish with watercress. Serve hot. **Serves 4.**

Apple Lamb

750 grams hogget steaks or leg chops

2 onions

3 to 4 potatoes

1 tablespoon flour

1 cup stock or water

Salt and pepper

½ cup white wine

2 to 3 apples

2 tablespoons grated cheese

Brown the meat on both sides in a heavy-based pan, then lift out.

In the fat that remains, adding a little oil if necessary, fry the sliced onions and sliced potatoes.

Place half of this in a deep casserole and arrange the meat on top. Put the remaining vegetables over the meat.

Into the fat in the pan, stir the flour, then gradually add the stock and bring to the boil. Season well and add wine, then pour over the casserole.

Peel and core the apples, cut into slices, and cover the vegetables with this. Sprinkle with grated cheese. Cover with a lid and place in a 180 degree C oven for about 1 hour.

When the vegetables and apples are tender, remove the lid, and brown the top of the casserole. **Serves 4.**

Marinated Leg of Lamb

1 x 2 kilogram leg of lamb

2 cups red wine

½ cup wine vinegar

¼ cup cooking oil

12 bay leaves

¼ teaspoon salt

¼ teaspoon pepper

Place the leg of lamb in a non-metallic bowl.

Combine wine, vinegar, oil, bay leaves, salt and pepper. Pour the marinade over the meat. Turn and baste 3 to 4 times a day for 3 days.

Alternatively, the meat may be placed in a large plastic bag with the marinade, and stood in a bowl.

At the end of three days, drain the meat on a rack for 30 minutes. Just before roasting, dry thoroughly with paper towels. Place on a rack in the roasting dish.

Place in a 220 degree C oven for 15 to 20 minutes, basting every five minutes. Turn the oven down to 180 degrees C, and roast without basting for a further 2 to 2½ hours.

Serves 6 to 8

Baked Smoked Mutton
(photograph left)

This meat is first corned,
which tenderises it,
then it is smoked
to produce its unique flavour.

1 smoked leg of mutton

4 cups water

Soak the smoked mutton in water for 3 to 4 hours, or preferably overnight. Drain and weigh mutton to calculate cooking time, allowing 25 minutes per 500 grams. Place in a large roasting dish and pour in water. Cover with foil.

Bake at 180 degrees C for calculated time, or until tender when meat is pricked with a fork. Remove and allow to cool.

Serve cold, with Cranberry and Apple Relish.

Cranberry and Apple Relish
(photograph left)

2 green apples

2 tablespoons cider vinegar

1 teaspoon finely grated orange rind

¼ cup orange juice

½ teaspoon mixed spice

¼ cup brown sugar

1 x 227 gram tin whole berry cranberry sauce

Peel, core, and slice apples. Place apple slices in saucepan; add cider vinegar, orange rind and juice, and mixed spice. Cover, and simmer gently for about 20 minutes, or until apples are tender, but not breaking up. Add sugar, heat until dissolved, then boil rapidly for 2 to 3 minutes.

Add contents of tin of cranberry sauce. Heat through gently. Stir to combine thoroughly. Allow to cool.
Makes 2 cups.

Keeps for about 1 week in refrigerator.

The smoking of mutton produces a mutton ham, a pleasing alternative to the more usual ham from pig meat.

Crown Roast of Lamb
(photograph above)

The rib loin of the sheep
is often referred to as the 'rack'.
It is the part of the loin
that has the long rib bones on it.
The meat is very sweet,
providing particularly good eating,
and it is sufficiently tender
for quick cooking techniques
such as grilling, frying or roasting.

2 matching pieces rib loin lamb comprising 6 to 7 cutlets each

2 tablespoons melted butter

Have the butcher trim and chine the meat. If necessary, trim as much fat as possible from the base end of each loin. Cut and scrape the top 4 to 5 centimetres of meat and fat from the top of the bones so that they are completely clean. If it has not been done by the butcher, cut the lower half of the cutlets between each bone.

Sew the two pieces of meat together, bone side out, with a trimming needle and fine string. Weigh the Crown to calculate cooking time, allowing 30 minutes per 500 grams.

Fill the centre cavity of the Crown with tamarillo or other stuffing.

Cover the tips of the bones with foil. Brush with melted butter.

Roast at 180 degrees C for calculated time, or until meat is tender.
Serves 6 to 8

Tamarillo Stuffing
(photograph above)

½ leek

1 tablespoon butter

2 tamarillos

½ apple

1¼ cups fresh white breadcrumbs

2 tablespoons freshly chopped parsley

1 teaspoon brown sugar

Freshly ground black pepper

1 egg

Finely slice leek. Fry gently in butter until soft, but not brown. Skin the tamarillos, and chop roughly. Finely chop the apple.

Combine tamarillos, apple, breadcrumbs, parsley, brown sugar, pepper, egg and cooked leek. Use to fill the cavity of the Crown Roast.
Makes 2 cups.

Note: This stuffing can also be used for a Guard of Honour.

Braised Forequarter

(photograph right)

Boned forequarter lamb or hogget about 1.5 kilograms

Salt

Freshly ground black pepper

3 small sprigs rosemary

4 sprigs parsley

2 bay leaves

2 cloves garlic

2 tablespoons oil

25 grams butter

6 small onions

3 sticks celery

1 green pepper

6 tomatoes

1 tablespoon tomato puree

2½ cups lamb or chicken stock

½ cup dry white wine

Salt

Freshly ground black pepper

Place the boned forequarter out, skin side down. Season well with salt and pepper. Place rosemary, parsley and bay leaves on meat. Peel garlic, and cut cloves in half. Place well apart on the meat. Roll the meat up, and tie securely with string.

Heat oil and butter in a large frying pan, and brown the meat on all sides. Remove, and put aside.

Peel onions and leave whole. Chop celery into four centimetre pieces. Chop green pepper roughly. Lightly fry onions, celery and green pepper in remaining oil and butter. Skin and seed tomatoes, and roughly chop.

Put fried vegetables in the bottom of a large ovenproof dish. Place the browned, rolled forequarter on top.

Combine tomatoes, tomato puree, stock and wine. Season with salt and pepper. Pour over the meat and vegetables so that the vegetables are just covered. Cover with a lid.

Cook at 180 degrees C for 1¾ to 2 hours, until the meat is tender.
Serves 8.

Roast Forequarter with Cranberry Stuffing

(photograph right)

1 small onion

1 tablespoon butter

½ teaspoon finely grated orange rind

1 x 227 gram tin whole berry cranberry sauce

1 tablespoon chopped parsley

1 cup fresh white breadcrumbs

1 egg yolk

Salt

Freshly ground black pepper

1.5 kilograms boned forequarter lamb or hogget

1 tablespoon melted butter

Finely chop onion. Fry gently in butter until soft, but not brown.

Mix together the cooked onion, orange rind, whole cranberry sauce, parsley, breadcrumbs and egg yolk. Season with salt and pepper.

Place boned forequarter out, skin side down, and season with salt and pepper. Place stuffing on the meat. Roll up, and tie securely with string. Brush with melted butter.

Roast at 200 degrees C for 20 minutes. Reduce temperature to 180 degrees C for about 1 hour and 20 minutes. Baste regularly during cooking. Remove string before serving.
Serves 8.

German Roast Lamb

(photograph left)

1 leg of lamb, 1.5 to 2 kilograms

2 to 3 cloves garlic

3 tablespoons oil

2 tablespoons fresh mixed herbs including parsley, rosemary and thyme

2 tablespoons prepared hot mustard

Salt

Freshly ground black pepper

1 tablespoon dried breadcrumbs

½ cup dry vermouth

½ cup water

½ cup sour cream

½ cup cream

½ cup water

Cut through the skin of the meat in a criss-cross pattern. Peel and cut garlic into slivers, then insert a sliver where each cut crosses.

Roast at 190 degrees C for 45 minutes.

Combine the oil with the chopped herbs, mustard, salt, pepper and breadcrumbs.

Pour off fat from meat. Spread breadcrumb mixture over the meat.

Mix vermouth, first measure of water, sour cream and fresh cream together.

Reduce oven temperature to 180 degrees C. Pour second measure of water into roasting pan. Pour a little of the cream liquid over meat and return to oven.

About every 10 minutes, pour a little more of the cream liquid over the meat, until it is all used up. Continue cooking for about another 45 minutes, basting meat regularly. Strain the pan juices through a sieve to serve as gravy.
Serves 8 to 10.

Guard of Honour

(photograph page 63)

2 matching pieces rib loin lamb comprising 6 to 7 cutlets each

2 tablespoons oil

2 tablespoons lemon juice

2 tablespoons thin honey

As with the crown roast, ask the butcher to prepare it. Cut and scrape the top 6 to 7 centimetres of meat and fat from the top of the bones, so they are completely clean.

The two pieces of meat are then joined, skin outside, so the bones meet and criss-cross on top. Tie together neatly with string. Cover the tips of the bones with foil to prevent browning.

Weigh the Guard to calculate the cooking time, allowing 30 minutes per 500 grams.

In a small saucepan, gently heat oil, lemon juice and honey. Mix well. Brush Guard with lemon-honey mixture.

Roast at 180 degrees C for the calculated time, or until meat is tender. Baste the meat freqently during cooking.
Serves 6 to 8.

Veal

In New Zealand, the majority of veal available is from calves up to 12 months of age.

A small amount of white veal, that is to say, meat from animals fed solely on milk or milk products, and not over 18 weeks of age, is available. This is the European style of veal.

Scaloppine Navona

6 slices veal

3 tablespoons flour

½ teaspoon salt

Shake pepper

3 tomatoes

2 tablespoons butter

1 tablespoon oil

1 tablespoon sweet sherry

2 tablespoons white wine

¼ teaspoon salt

Pepper

6 small thin slices ham

6 small thin slices Mozzarella

Trim the meat and beat it out thinly. Season the flour with salt and pepper, then dust it over the meat.

Skin the tomatoes, and chop them roughly, then simmer in a very little water until they are pulp-like.

While the tomatoes are cooking, heat the butter and oil in a large frying pan, and in it fry the veal on both sides until it is lightly brown. This will take about 5 minutes on each side. Lift out the meat, and place it in an ovenproof dish.

Pour sherry and wine into the frying pan, and season with salt and pepper. Spoon this sauce over the meat.

Place a slice of ham on each piece of meat, and on top of it arrange the slices of cheese. Spread the pulped tomatoes on top of the cheese.

When ready to serve, place under a grill for a few minutes until the cheese melts.
Serves 6.

Blue Vein Stuffed Veal

100 grams blue vein cheese

½ cup drained crushed pineapple

½ teaspoon chopped thyme

Salt and pepper

6 slices schnitzel veal

Toothpicks

1 egg

1 cup fine fresh breadcrumbs

Oil for frying

Chopped parsley

Crumble the cheese into a bowl. Add pineapple and thyme, and season with salt and pepper to taste. Mix well.

Divide the mixture into 6. Put 1 portion of the mixture on each slice of veal. Roll each one up and secure with a toothpick.

Beat the egg lightly in a basin, and have the crumbs on a piece of paper. Dip the veal rolls first in egg, then in crumbs. Chill for half an hour.

Fry in deep, hot oil for about 5 minutes. Drain well. Serve garnished with a sprinkling of parsley.
Serves 6.

Paupiettes de Veau

1 onion

1 tablespoon butter

100 grams minced veal

100 grams minced ham

1 egg yolk

Salt and pepper

¼ teaspoon thyme

1 teaspoon chopped parsley

4 slices veal schnitzel

Salt and pepper

1 tablespoon seasoned flour

25 grams butter

¾ cup chicken stock

¼ cup white wine

Bouquet garni

Peel and finely chop the onion. Melt the first measure of butter in a saucepan, and cook the onion gently until soft but not coloured. Combine this with the veal, ham, egg yolk and seasonings in a bowl.

Place the pieces of schnitzel out flat, and season with salt and pepper. Put a quarter of the stuffing in the centre of each slice of schnitzel and fold up like a parcel, so that the stuffing is completely enclosed. Tie these paupiettes securely with string, then toss in seasoned flour.

Heat the second measure of butter in a frying pan, and cook the paupiettes about 5 minutes until brown all over. Place them in a 5 cup ovenware dish with the stock, wine and bouquet garni. Cover and cook at 160 degrees C for 1½ hours.

Remove the string and bouquet garni. Serve hot.
Serves 4.

Veal with Asparagus

4 to 6 slices veal steak, cut thick

50 grams butter

4 spring onions

2 tablespoons flour

Salt and pepper

1¾ cups chicken stock

18 to 24 asparagus spears, fresh, frozen or tinned

½ cup sour cream

Lemon juice

Chopped parsley

Trim the veal so that the steaks are uniform in size.

Melt the butter, and cook the chopped spring onions in it, without letting them colour. Lift out the onions, and brown the veal. Remove this from the pan, and sprinkle the flour, salt and pepper into the butter, stirring well. Add the chicken stock, and cook, stirring, until the sauce thickens. Return the meat and onions to this mixture. Cover and simmer gently for about 20 minutes, or until the meat is tender.

If using fresh or frozen asparagus, trim off the tips to about 5 centimetres in length, and reserve. Cook remaining stalks in lightly salted water until tender, then put through a food mill or food processor, to give an asparagus puree. Cook the tips in lightly salted water until just tender. Drain and keep warm.

If using tinned asparagus, the tips can be cut off in the same way, and heated through when needed in a little of the juice. The remaining part of the stalk is turned into a puree without further cooking.

When the meat is tender, add about ½ cup of pureed asparagus to the sauce and stir in the sour cream. Add a squeeze or two of lemon juice.

Return the sauce to the heat, but do not boil once the sour cream has been added.

Serve the meat on a platter, with a little of the sauce poured over. Garnish with cooked asparagus tips, and sprinkle with parsley.
Serves 4 to 6.

Sesame Chicken

1 chicken about 1.25 kilograms

50 grams butter

1 tablespoon lemon juice

1 to 1½ cups fine white breadcrumbs

2 tablespoons chopped parsley

1 teaspoon salt

¼ teaspoon pepper

1½ tablespoons sesame seeds

Cut the chicken into serving-sized portions.

Melt the butter and blend with the lemon juice.

On a plate, mix the crumbs, parsley, salt, pepper and sesame seeds. Dip the chicken first in the melted butter mixture, then roll in the crumb mixture. Place the chicken in a lightly greased ovenware dish, spooning any remaining butter mixture over the chicken.

Bake at 180 degrees C for about 45 minutes or until the chicken is cooked through.
Serves 4.

Chicken Vol-au-Vent

800 grams puff pastry

1 egg yolk

Filling:

2 rashers bacon

100 grams mushrooms

25 grams butter

1 cup cooked chopped chicken

50 grams butter

¼ cup flour

1½ cups milk

Salt and pepper

Roll out the pastry to a circle 20 centimetres in diameter. Using a 10 centimetre pot lid, mark a circle within the big one, but do not cut right through. Chill the pastry on a baking tray for 15 minutes. Brush with beaten egg yolk.

Bake at 230 degrees C for 10 minutes. Lower the heat to 190 degrees C, and continue to bake for about 20 minutes.

When cool, carefully remove the marked out circle.

Filling: Chop the bacon and slice the mushrooms. Fry the bacon and mushrooms in the first measure of butter. Combine bacon, mushrooms and chicken.

Melt second measure of butter and stir in the flour. Cook until frothy. Add the milk and cook until thick, stirring all the time. Season to taste. Fold the mushrooms, bacon and chicken into the sauce. Use to fill the centre of the pastry case, and top with the cut out pastry lid.
Serves 6.

Chicken Galantine

(photograph page 8)

This recipe is challenging, and has many exacting steps, but it is highly recommended as a cold-cut winner.

1.5 kilogram chicken
1 pork fillet
1 teaspoon salt
4 peppercorns
8 cups water
250 grams fresh pork fat, in the piece
2 spring onions
1 teaspoon salt
4 peppercorns
1 bay leaf
1 sprig thyme
1 sprig parsley
¼ cup sweet sherry
Salt and pepper
2 eggs
125 grams lean ham
375 grams cooked calf's tongue, in the piece
A piece of wet cotton cloth

Cut the chicken all the way down its back. Using the point of a sharp knife, work as much flesh as possible away from the bones. Lift out the carcass.

Remove the leg meat and the breast meat from the skin, taking care not to damage the skin. Reserve the leg meat.

Slice each chicken breast lengthways into 6 strips.

Cut off one third of the pork fillet, and reserve, with the leg meat, for mincing. Cut 6 strips from the remaining pork fillet.

Put the chicken bones and giblets into a saucepan with the first measures of salt and peppercorns, and the water, and simmer gently for 2 to 3 hours. Strain the stock and reserve for later use.

Cut the pork fat into 12 neat strips, similar in size to those of the chicken and pork. Reserve remaining fat for mincing with the leg meat.

Put all the strips of chicken, pork and pork fat in a bowl.

Finely chop the spring onions, and add these, together with the second measures of salt and peppercorns, the herbs and sherry to the bowl. Cover, and leave the meat to marinate in the refrigerator for several hours, preferably overnight.

Put the reserved chicken meat, pork fillet and fat through a mincer or food processor. Season with salt and pepper, and add the lightly beaten eggs. Mix well and set aside.

Cut the ham and the tongue into 6 strips each.

Drain the marinating meat, and blend the marinade into the minced mixture.

Now, assemble the Galantine. To do this, place the piece of cloth on a board, and place the chicken skin on this, outside down. Draw the leg and wing skin through to the inside. Divide the minced mixture into 4, and the mixed meat strips into 3 groups. Spread one quarter of the mince over the skin, and on this, arrange one third of the meat strips in alternating rows, to form a colour pattern with the various meats. Repeat the layers of minced meat and strips, ending with a layer of minced meat.

Using the cloth, roll the meat up to form a sausage, firmly held by the skin. Sew the join up with needle and thread, securing the ends. Similarly, sew up the holes where the leg and wing skins are tucked in. Roll the cloth firmly around the chicken skin, and tie the ends.

Put the reserved chicken stock in a large saucepan, and bring to the boil. Place the Galantine in it, and simmer gently for 1¾ to 2 hours.

Lift the Galantine from the stock, place on a level surface, and allow to cool until it can be handled.

Remove the wet cloth, and roll a dry cloth around the Galantine, firmly tying the ends. Chill thoroughly, then untie. Serve cut into crosswise slices, which will show a decorative pattern of coloured meats.
Serves 8.

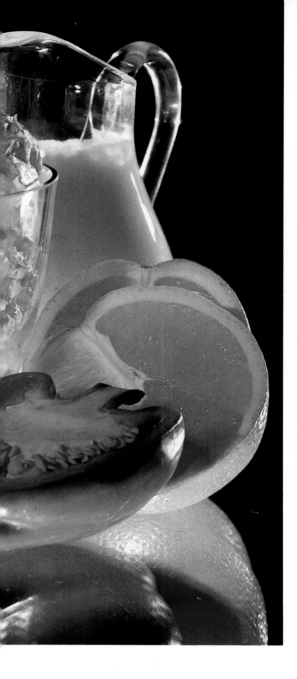

Put the chicken into a bowl and add the toasted almonds.

Soak the ground almonds in the orange juice for 15 minutes. Mix the soaked almonds and juice into the chicken.

Peel the orange thickly, and carefully remove the segments. Cut a slice off the top of the pepper and remove all seeds. Cut the pepper in half, then into thin slices.

Add orange segments and pepper slices to the chicken, then set aside to chill.

Dressing: Melt the butter. Beat the eggs, and gradually beat in the butter and sour cream.

Bring vinegar to the boil and beat into the egg mixture, a little at a time. Add the seasonings.

Pour the mixture into the top of a double boiler, and cook over steadily boiling water until the mixture thickens. On no account must the mixture be allowed to boil. Chill before using.

Just before serving, fold the dressing into the chicken mixture. Arrange some lettuce leaves on the base of a serving bowl and pile the salad on top.

Serves 4.

Orange and Almond Chicken Salad
(photograph above)

4 cups cooked diced chicken
½ cup whole toasted almonds
2 tablespoons ground almonds
¼ cup orange juice
1 orange
1 small green pepper
Lettuce leaves
Dressing:
50 grams butter
2 eggs
¾ cup sour cream
3 tablespoons white vinegar
½ teaspoon salt
Pinch pepper

Creamy Chicken Casserole
(photograph page 57)

1 x 1.5 kilogram chicken
Water
1 teaspoon salt
6 peppercorns
1 bay leaf
1 onion
1 sprig parsley
2 onions
2 carrots
3 stalks celery
75 grams butter
2 tablespoons flour
½ cup top milk
Paprika

Have the chicken cut into serving-sized portions. Place it in a large saucepan, and generously cover with water. Add the salt, peppercorns, bay leaf, whole onion and parsley. Bring to the boil, and simmer gently for about an hour, or until the chicken meat is tender. Lift out the meat, and strain the stock.

Peel the second measure of onions, and cut into rings. Dice the carrots and the celery.

In a small saucepan, heat half the butter, and in it lightly cook the onion until it is transparent, but not coloured. Add the carrots and celery, and continue cooking, without letting the vegetables colour. Add 1½ cups of the strained chicken stock. Cover, and simmer gently until the vegetables are tender.

Cream the remaining butter and flour together to form a soft paste, and when the vegetables are tender, crumble this into the saucepan, stirring briskly, so that a smooth sauce is formed. Continue cooking until the sauce boils and thickens.

Remove from the heat, add the top milk, and stir well. Place the chicken in a casserole, and pour the vegetable sauce over it.

Place in a 180 degree C oven, and cook for about 20 minutes, or until thoroughly heated through. Before serving, sprinkle generously with paprika.

Serves 4 to 6.

Cold Crumbed Ham
(photograph left)

Whole uncooked ham

2 to 3 cups dry white breadcrumbs

Weigh, then soak the uncooked ham overnight. Drain.

Place in a large roasting dish. Pour in sufficient cold water to come halfway up the sides of the dish. Cover with foil, and bake the ham at 160 degrees C, allowing about 40 minutes per kilogram.

Remove rind; this peels off readily when sufficiently cooked. Allow to cool.

Toast breadcrumbs carefully, turning frequently. Sieve toasted crumbs, and press into the fat on the ham. Decorate knuckle with paper frill. Serve with Cumberland Sauce.

Allow 100 to 150 grams per serving.

Glazed Bacon
(photograph left)

1 shoulder boiling bacon, about 2.5 kilograms

1 onion

1 carrot

1 bay leaf

4 black peppercorns

Cloves

Glaze:

¼ cup brown sugar

1 teaspoon dry mustard

1 tablespoon rum

Weigh the uncooked bacon, then soak it overnight.

Place in a large pan, rind side up. Cover with fresh cold water. Peel and quarter the onion and carrot; add to the pan with bay leaf and peppercorns. Bring slowly to the boil and simmer gently until the meat is tender. Allow about 35 minutes per kilogram.

Remove from cooking liquid, peel off rind, and place on rack in a baking dish. Score fat to a depth of about 3 millimetres in a diamond pattern. Stud each diamond with a clove.

Mix together brown sugar, dry mustard and rum. Spread over bacon.

Bake at 160 degrees C for about 30 to 40 minutes. Baste frequently with glaze.
Serve hot.

Cumberland Sauce
(photograph left)

1 orange

1 lemon

¼ cup fresh orange juice

2 tablespoons lemon juice

½ cup redcurrant jelly

¼ cup port wine

Thinly pare rind from orange and lemon. Chop finely into strips. Place in a small saucepan, and cover with cold water. Bring to the boil, reduce heat, and simmer for about ten minutes until tender. Drain well.

Combine the orange juice, lemon juice, redcurrant jelly and port. Heat gently until jelly has melted. Add cooked rind. Serve hot or cold with ham.
Makes about 1¼ cups.

Crumbed Pork Schnitzel

4 pork schnitzels

Flour

Salt

Freshly ground black pepper

1 egg

Fine white breadcrumbs

25 grams butter

1 tablespoon oil

4 gherkins

2 hard-boiled eggs

The pork schnitzels should be trimmed of any ragged ends, and lightly beaten. Dip each schnitzel into seasoned flour, and dust off any excess.

Beat the egg, and dip the meat into it. Drain off excess.

Coat with crumbs. Pat off excess.

Heat oil and butter in a heavy-based fry pan. Fry the schnitzels in the butter, turning once. Allow 3 to 4 minutes per side. Garnish with gherkin fans and slices of hard-boiled eggs.
Serves 4.

Gherkin Fans: Slice each gherkin lengthways 4 or 5 times, without cutting right through at one end.

Spread out slices like a fan, holding them at uncut end.

Oriental Chops

4 pork loin chops

Salt and pepper

Sauce:

2 centimetres fresh root ginger

1 spring onion

¼ cup boiling water

¼ cup soy sauce

2 tablespoons sherry

1 tablespoon honey

1 tablespoon cornflour

¼ cup cold water

Season chops with salt and pepper.

Heat grill, and cook chops for about 10 minutes each side, until cooked through to the centre.

Sauce: Slice ginger and spring onion finely, and place in saucepan. Pour boiling water on to ginger and onion. Add soy sauce, sherry and honey. Allow to stand 15 minutes.

Heat to boiling.

Mix cornflour with cold water then add to soy sauce mixture. Allow to thicken. Spoon over chops.
Serves 4.

Dalmatian Pork Chops

1 onion

25 grams butter

2 cooking apples

¼ cup currants

4 pork loin chops

2 tablespoons seasoned flour

2 tablespoons oil or lard

Chop onion finely. Heat butter, and cook onion until soft, but not brown. Peel, core and slice apples.

Add sliced apple to onion and allow to simmer for 2 minutes, stirring constantly. Add the currants.

Remove bones from chops. Coat with seasoned flour. Heat oil or lard in a frying pan and fry chops until golden.

Make a pocket in each chop by slicing lengthways through the eye of the meat and fat, almost reaching the skin. Fill stuffing into pocket. Place chops close together, cut side uppermost, in an ovenproof dish.

Cook in a 190 degrees C oven for about 30 minutes, or until meat is tender.
Serves 4.

Steamed Pork Pudding

2 cups flour

½ teaspoon baking powder

¼ teaspoon salt

¾ cup grated suet

About ½ cup water

2 apples

2 onions

500 grams pork

Salt and pepper

½ teaspoon dried sage, or 4 to 5 fresh sage leaves

¼ cup water

Sift the flour, baking powder and salt into a basin. Cut in the suet. Mix to a firm dough with the water. Roll out on a floured board.

Line a 5 cup pudding basin with three-quarters of the pastry, leaving the remaining quarter for the lid. Roll this into a circle to fit the top of the basin. Peel and slice the apples and onions.

Cut the meat into 1½ centimetre cubes. Season with salt and pepper.

Make layers of onion and apple, and meat in the basin. Sprinkle the top layer with the dried or finely chopped fresh sage, then add the water.

Cover with pastry lid, pressing join firmly. Cover with greased, grease-proof paper and foil.

Boil in a saucepan of water for about 3 hours.
Serves 6.

Pork with Creamy Prune Sauce

(photograph page 56)

12 prunes

1 cup dry white wine

4 pork loin chops

2 tablespoons seasoned flour

1 tablespooon oil

25 grams butter

¾ cup cream

Salt and pepper

Remove the stones from the prunes. Soak the prunes in the wine for at least 5 hours, or overnight. Simmer gently for about 30 minutes.

Coat chops in seasoned flour. Heat oil and butter. Fry chops until cooked through and golden on both sides — about 20 minutes. Reduce heat, cover, and cook for a further 15 minutes.

Place chops on a serving dish, and keep warm.

Strain the cooking liquid from the prunes into the pan. Scrape sides, and allow to boil hard until the volume reduces by half. Arrange prunes around chops. Add cream to the sauce. Heat until nearly boiling. Spoon over chops.
Serves 4.

Pork and Kumara Rolls

Stuffing:

50 grams mushrooms

1 tablespoon butter

3 spring onions

1 cup mashed, cooked kumara

Salt and pepper

Rolls:

4 Pork schnitzels

25 grams butter

2 tablespoons flour

¾ cup chicken stock

¼ cup orange juice

2 tablespoons sherry

¼ cup cream

Stuffing: Slice mushrooms finely. Heat butter, and fry mushrooms for about 2 minutes.

Chop spring onions finely. In a bowl, combine mushrooms, spring onions and cooked kumara. Season with salt and pepper.

Rolls: Beat pork schnitzels lightly. Divide filling evenly among the 4 schnitzels, spreading it over the meat. Roll up firmly. Tie with string, or secure with toothpicks.

Heat second measure of butter in a frying pan. Fry rolls quickly until golden brown and cooked. Remove string. Place rolls on a serving dish, and keep hot.

Add flour to pan drippings, stirring well. Cook until frothy. Gradually add stock, stirring well after each addition. Add orange juice, sherry and cream. Heat through gently without boiling.

Pour sauce over pork rolls.
Serves 4.

Yugoslav Meat Rolls

500 grams lean topside beef

1 teaspoon salt

¼ teaspoon pepper

1 onion

1 green pepper

2 tablespoons oil

1 tablespoon vinegar

Place the meat in the bowl of a food processor, and process until it becomes almost paste-like. Add the seasonings.

Shape into small sausage-like pieces, and thread on skewers.

Cook under a hot grill. Turn frequently until the meat is browned all over.
Serves 4.

Stuffed Braised Pork Fillets

2 pork fillets

10 to 12 prunes

1 small apple

1 tablespoon butter

¾ teaspoon salt

Shake pepper

½ cup water

Trim the fat from the pork fillets, and carefully cut right down the middle, without cutting to the bottom of the fillet.

If the prunes are soft, they can be stoned and used raw. If they are dry, soak them for several hours in water, or cook until soft, then remove the stones.

Peel the apple, and cut into 1 centimetre slices. Arrange the apple and prunes alternately along the opening made in the fillet. Draw the edges together and tie up securely with string, or hold firmly with skewers.

In a pan that has a lid, heat the butter, and lightly brown the fillets on all sides. Season with salt and pepper, and add the water. Cover and cook slowly for about 30 minutes, or until the meat is tender. If the lid is not close-fitting, more water may be needed. There should be a small amount of slightly thick sauce left. This can be served in a separate dish or spooned over the meat.
Serves 4 to 6.

Spiced Topside

1 kilogram round cut beef topside

1 teaspoon salt

¼ teaspoon pepper

1 tablespoon dry mustard

½ teaspoon fresh thyme or
¼ teaspoon dried thyme

1 sage leaf or a pinch of dried sage

1 cup water

1 tablespoon beef stock powder

½ cup tarragon vinegar (See page 187)

50 grams butter

2 tablespoons flour

¼ cup tomato puree

1 tablespoon wine

Parsley for garnish

Place the piece of beef topside in a large casserole with a close-fitting lid.

Mix together the salt, pepper, mustard, thyme, sage, water, stock powder and vinegar. Pour this over the meat, cover, and leave in a cool place for 3 days, turning daily.

On the fourth day, drain off the marinade and set aside.

Melt the butter in a large, heavy frying pan. Brown the meat on all sides, then remove it from the pan. Add the flour to the juices in the frying pan. Stir until well combined, then gradually stir in the marinade. Cook until the sauce thickens, stirring constantly.

Place the browned meat in a large casserole. Pour the sauce over. Cover, and cook in a 180 degree C oven for 1 to 2 hours or until the meat is tender.

Remove meat from the oven and cut into thick slices across the grain. Stir the tomato puree and wine into the sauce. Adjust the seasonings if necessary. Spoon some of the sauce over the meat. Garnish with chopped parsley.

Serve the remaining sauce separately.

Serves 6 to 8.

Shepherd's Pie

300 grams roast hogget or beef

1 clove garlic

1 stick celery

2 onions

3 tomatoes

25 grams butter

3 tablespoons red wine

1 tablespoon tomato puree

1 tablespoon chopped parsley

¼ teaspoon thyme

Salt and pepper

500 grams mashed potato

2 tablespoons breadcrumbs

Chop the meat. Peel and crush the garlic. Chop the celery. Peel and finely chop the onions and tomatoes.

Melt the butter in a frying pan. Add the garlic, celery and onions. Cook gently about 5 minutes until soft, but not coloured. Add the tomatoes and meat. Cook for five minutes. Add wine, tomato puree and seasonings.

Spread half of the potato on the bottom of a 6 cup greased ovenproof dish. Cover with the meat mixture. Spread remaining potato on top. Sprinkle with breadcrumbs.

Bake at 200 degrees C for 20 to 30 minutes, until heated through and golden brown on top. Serve hot.

Serves 4.

Russian Meat Patties

500 grams beef

½ cup breadcrumbs

¼ cup milk

75 grams butter

1 small onion

1 egg

Salt and pepper

½ cup flour

1 cup sour cream

½ cup stock

75 grams mushrooms

Mince the beef, and soak the breadcrumbs in the milk.

Heat 25 grams of the butter in a small pan, and in it fry the chopped onion.

Squeeze out the breadcrumbs, and add these and the cooked onion to the meat. Mix in the egg and seasonings, and beat thoroughly to get a smooth paste.

Roll small amounts of meat into oval shapes and flatten into cakes. Dust these with flour.

Heat the remaining butter in a pan, and fry the cakes quickly on one side until brown, then turn. When all are cooked, stir in the sour cream, stock and sliced mushrooms. Cover, and simmer gently for about 15 minutes, or until the mushrooms are cooked.

Serves 4.

Working with cattle on Molesworth Station, Tarndale.

Stir Fry Steak
(photograph right)

500 grams skirt steak

Freshly ground black pepper

1 leek

1 cucumber

1 green pepper

2 or 3 tomatoes

3 tablespoons oil

Salt

Remove any fat from the meat. Cut lengthways into 3 pieces, then slice finely across the grain of the meat. Sprinkle with the pepper.

Cut leek in half lengthways. Wash carefully, and slice diagonally into 1 centimetre strips.

Peel and cut cucumber into 5 by 1 centimetre strips. Discard seeds.

Cut green pepper into 2 centimetre squares, and tomato into quarters.

Heat oil until very hot in frying pan or wok. Quickly brown meat on both sides, turning constantly. Add leek and cucumber, then cook a further 2 minutes. Stir in pepper and tomatoes, and allow to heat through, turning constantly. Season with salt and pepper.
Serves 4.

Split Skirt
(photograph right)

3 medium kumara

25 grams butter

1 onion

2 slices bacon

3 to 4 tablespoons cream

1 teaspoon sugar

2 tablespoons chopped parsley

½ teaspooon salt

Freshly ground black pepper

500 grams skirt steak

2 tablespoons oil

Scrub kumara, and bake or boil in their skins until tender. Cool. Peel and mash flesh.

Heat butter. Chop the onion and bacon. Cook, without colouring, in the butter. Combine with mashed kumara, cream, sugar and chopped parsley. Season well with salt and pepper.

Cut a pocket in the side of the piece of skirt steak, or lift skin. Put stuffing into the pocket, or between meat and skin, and sew up with string, or secure with skewers. Rub surface of meat with oil.

Place, covered with foil or paper, in oven at 180 degrees C for 1¼ to 1½ hours.

Remove the string or skewers. Slice across the grain of the meat. Serve hot or cold.
Serves 4.

Czech Skirt
(photograph right)

500 grams skirt steak

2 tablespoons oil

3 onions

1 tablespoon flour

1 tablespoon paprika

1¾ cups stock

¼ cup sour cream or natural yoghurt

Salt

Freshly ground black pepper

1 tablespoon chopped fresh parsley

Cut steak across grain to 2 centimetre wide strips. Heat oil in a heavy pan, and fry steak until well browned. Remove from pan.

Cut onions into quarters, and cook in the pan until brown. Remove from pan. Stir in flour and paprika, and cook for three minutes, stirring constantly.

Remove from the heat; add stock. Bring to boil. Return onions and steak to the pan. Cover, and allow to simmer for 50 to 60 minutes, or until steak is tender.

Place steak and onions on a serving dish, and keep warm.

Boil the sauce hard to reduce its volume if necessary. Season with salt and pepper.

Just before serving, stir in the sour cream or natural yoghurt. Spoon it over the meat. Sprinkle with parsley. Serve with boiled flat noodles.
Serves 4.

Corned Silverside
(photograph Page 57)

Many people still associate corned meat with the old strong-flavoured meats of years ago, when the corning was for preserving.
Corning is now for flavouring.

1 kilogram piece corned silverside

Water

1 carrot

1 onion

1 tablespoon brown sugar

1 tablespoon vinegar

1 bay leaf

6 black peppercorns

Put the corned silverside in a deep saucepan. Cover it with fresh, cold water. Bring to the boil slowly, skimming any scum if necessary.

Peel carrot and onion, and cut in half. Add the carrot, onion, sugar, vinegar, bay leaf and peppercorns to the boiling water. Reduce heat, and simmer gently, allowing 1 hour per kilogram of meat.

Test the meat by piercing with a skewer for tenderness.

To serve hot: Remove from pan, and serve immediately with a hot sauce to accompany it.

If vegetables are wanted to serve with the meat, they can be boiled along with it. Carrots, parsnips, swede, onions, leeks and celery are suitable.

To serve cold: Allow meat to cool in the cooking liquor until it is a reasonable heat, then remove, and refrigerate. Place a crumpled piece of foil or a piece of waxpaper loosely on top to prevent the surface drying out.

Serve with fresh relish or home-made chutneys or pickles.

Note: If wished, while the meat is still warm, it can be put in a bowl or loaf tin, covered, and lightly pressed with a weight. Once cold, pressed meat slices very easily.

Cheesy Mince Crumble

75 grams blue vein cheese
1½ cups flour
½ teaspoon salt
Pinch pepper
50 grams butter
1 onion
1 carrot
1 stalk celery
2 tablespoons oil
500 grams beef mince
1 tablespoon flour
¾ cup water
1 teaspoon salt
¼ teaspoon pepper

Cut off 50 grams of blue vein cheese, and crumble coarsely.

Sift the flour and the first measure of salt and pepper into a bowl. Cut in butter until the mixture resembles breadcrumbs. Stir in the crumbled cheese.

Peel and chop the onion and carrot, and slice the celery into 1 centimetre lengths. Heat the oil and fry the vegetables until lightly browned. Add the mince and fry briskly until the redness has gone. Sprinkle flour over surface of the meat, then stir in water. Bring to the boil, stirring all the time.

Add the second measure of salt and pepper.

Turn half the mixture into a 5 cup ovenware dish. Crumble the remaining cheese over the meat, and spoon the remaining meat on top. Sprinkle cheese crumble mixture evenly over the surface of meat.

Bake at 200 degrees C for 40 to 45 minutes, until the crumble is crisp and brown.
Serves 4 to 6.

Beef en Croute

750 grams fillet steak
¼ teaspoon dry mustard
Salt and pepper
25 grams butter
200 grams mushrooms
1 tablespoon chopped parsley
500 grams puff pastry
1 egg

Season the surface of the beef with the mustard and salt and pepper. Heat the butter in a frying pan, and brown the beef to seal in the meat juices. Remove the beef to a plate, and allow to cool.

Wash the mushrooms and slice them thinly, then cook gently in the remaining butter in the pan. Stir in parsley, then allow mixture to cool.

Roll out the pastry to a 60 by 20 centimetre rectangle, and trim the edges. Cut in two across the shortest side, having one piece two-thirds larger than the other.

Scatter the mushroom mixture on the larger piece. Place the beef on top. Carefully press up the pastry around the beef. Brush the outside edges of the pastry with beaten egg.

Place the smaller piece of pastry over the top, and press the edges of the pastry together well. Brush all over with egg.

Roll out trimmings of pastry, and cut into leaves. Brush them with beaten egg, then arrange on top of the pastry case.

Bake in a 220 degree C oven for 40 to 50 minutes, until the pastry is well browned, and the meat tender when it is pierced with a fork. It may be necessary to lower oven temperature during final stages of cooking. Serve hot or cold.
Serves 6 to 8.

Savoury Apple Triangles
(photograph page 56)

500 grams short pastry
4 chipolata sausages
1 large cooking apple
1 onion
1 tablespoon oil
½ teaspoon mixed herbs
Salt and pepper
8 hard-boiled eggs
Oil for deep frying

Roll out pastry and cut into 15 centimetre squares. Cut the chipolatas into pieces, and grate the apple.

To make the filling, chop the onion and heat the oil, then gently cook the onion, chipolatas, grated apple, herbs, salt and pepper in the oil for 10 to 15 minutes. Allow to cool.

Place a hard-boiled egg and a little of the filling in a triangle on each pastry square. Dampen the edges of the pastry, and seal together firmly.

Deep fry at 190 degrees C for about 3 minutes. Serve hot or cold.
Makes 8.

Roast Brisket on the Bone

(photograph right)

1.5 kilograms fresh brisket

Salt and pepper

6 onions

6 carrots

Place meat in a roasting dish without any additional fat or oil. Cover loosely with foil. Roast at 160 degrees C for about 2 hours.

Peel onions, leaving the base end of the onion intact, so that it stays together during cooking.

Peel carrots, and cut into 5 centimetre lengths.

Remove the foil, season well, and place vegetables around the meat, basting with pan juices. Cook for a further two hours, or until meat is tender.

Place meat on a serving plate. Surround with onions and carrots.

Pour excess fat from roasting dish and make gravy from the juices in the pan.

Serves 6 to 8.

Spiced Brisket

(photograph right)

About 2 kilograms fresh brisket

3 tablespoons brown sugar

3 tablespoons salt

1 teaspoon crushed allspice

1 teaspoon powdered cloves

1 teaspoon powdered mace

½ teaspoon crushed peppercorns

½ teaspoon chopped fresh thyme

2 teaspoons crushed juniper berries

Remove bone from brisket, or ask your butcher to do this for you. Trim off any large pieces of fat.

Combine brown sugar, salt, allspice, cloves, mace, peppercorns, thyme and juniper berries in a basin. Mix well. Spread one-third of the spice mixture over both sides of the meat. Roll up and place in a plastic oven bag and stand on a plate in the refrigerator.

Next day, unroll meat and rub a further third of the spice mixture over the meat. Re-roll.

Repeat process on the third day.

On the fourth day, tie the meat in a roll at 3 centimetre intervals with string. Place in oven bag in the oven, and cook at 160 degrees C for 4 hours, or until tender.

Cool and refrigerate. Slice thinly to serve.

Serves 12 to 16.

Steak and Kidney Pudding

(photograph page 56)

Filling:

500 grams blade steak

2 sheep kidneys

Seasoned flour

1 large onion

½ teaspoon salt

¼ teaspoon pepper

¾ cup beefstock

Suet Dough:

1 cup flour

1 teaspoon baking powder

Pinch salt

½ cup suet

1 tablespoon lemon juice

¼ cup water

Filling: Cut the meat into 2 centimetre cubes. Core, skin and coarsely chop the kidneys. Roll steak and kidney in seasoned flour. Chop onion. Add salt and pepper to beefstock. Set filling ingredients aside. Grease a 4 cup pudding basin.

Half-fill a large saucepan which has a close-fitting lid with water, and put a trivet or similar in the base. Heat to boiling point.

Suet Dough: Prepare the dough by sifting flour, baking powder, and salt into a bowl. Add the suet, and mix well. Make a well in the dry ingredients. Add the lemon juice and enough water to make a light, but firm dough.

Turn out on to a floured board. Break off about one quarter of the dough. Set aside.

Roll out the remaining dough. Cut out a small circle to fit the bottom of the greased pudding basin. Roll out a strip, wide and long enough to line the sides of the basin. Place the small round of pastry in basin. Fit the strip on to it. Press all the edges together

firmly. There must be no gaps.

Roll out the remaining dough to a round to fit the top of the basin.

Place the steak, kidney and onion in the dough-lined basin. Add beefstock.

Fit dough lid on, pressing well to join dough. Cover with greaseproof paper which has a 2 centimetre pleat to allow for expansion of the pudding. Cover with another piece of brown paper. Tie securely with string.

Alternatively, cover with greased foil.

When water is boiling, place the pudding in the saucepan. The water should come three-quarters of the way up the basin. Cover the saucepan with a close-fitting lid. Boil for 3½ hours, adding more boiling water to the saucepan from time to time.

Serves 6.

Sausage and Apple Loaf

1 cup soft breadcrumbs

½ cup unsweetened stewed apple

500 grams sausagemeat

1 small onion

1 egg

1 teaspoon prepared mustard

Salt and pepper

1 apple

1 tablespoon brown sugar

1 tablespoon vinegar

1 teaspoon prepared mustard

In a bowl, mix together the crumbs, apple, sausagemeat and finely chopped onion until well blended.

Beat the egg lightly, and blend in the first measure of mustard and the salt and pepper. Stir this into the meat mixture until completely even. Press it into an 18 centimetre loaf tin.

Peel the raw apple and cut the flesh into segments. Press these into the top of the meat mixture in a pattern.

Blend the brown sugar, vinegar and the second measure of mustard together and pour over the top of the apple.

Bake at 180 degrees C for about an hour. Allow to cool a little in the tin before removing.

Serves 3 to 4.

...AND TWO VEG

The traditional Kiwi dinner has lightly been described as meat and two veg. Popular as meat is, we are also vegetable eaters. Dinner is not dinner for most, if there is no potato as well as at least one more accompanying vegetable.

The pride of many a gardener is to say, "and all of these vegetables are out of my garden." Our kind growing conditions allow for a wide selection of summer vegetables to be produced on our 'quarter acre'. Winter, too, means cabbage, caulis, leeks, and silverbeet are in fresh supply from home gardens.

While vegetables are usually served as an accompaniment to meat, increasingly, they are taking an important place as dishes in their own right.

Captions to preceding 4 pages.

Page 78/79: A field of maize near Hastings in Hawkes's Bay province. (photograph Bob Wells — Photobank).

Page 80/81: Kumara. Come March and it is time to harvest kumara. The tops are cut off, the digger turns the roots to the top of the soil, then the kumara are harvested.

Facing page: Market gardens line the hills at Bombay, south of Auckland. (photograph Laurie Thurston — Photobank).

Page 86/87: A barn of pumpkins for winter storage ensures soup in the pot.

Page 88: Harvesting rows of onions near Hastings. (Photograph Bob Wells — Photobank).

Dressings

French Dressing or Vinaigrette

(photograph left)
French dressing,
or vinaigrette as it is called,
is a particularly simple mixture
of good quality oil and vinegar.
This adage holds the secret for
successful vinaigrette:
Be a spendthrift with the oil;
Be a miser with the vinegar;
Be a counsellor with the salt;
And have a madman to shake them.

3 tablespoons good quality cooking oil, preferably olive oil

1 tablespoon white wine vinegar

Salt

Freshly ground black pepper

Shake all the ingredients together in a screw-topped jar until well combined and creamy.
    Use at once.
Makes about ¼ cup.

Blue Vein Dressing

1 x basic recipe French dressing

2 to 3 tablespoons blue vein cheese

Make French dressing according to directions.
    Crumble the blue vein cheese and add to the French dressing, shaking well before serving.
Makes about ¼ cup.

Garlic and Herb Dressing

(photograph left)

1 clove garlic

1 tablespoon mixed fresh herbs such as parsley, oregano, sage, thyme

1 x basic recipe French dressing.

Peel the garlic, but do not crush. Finely chop the herbs.
    Make up the French dressing according to directions given. Add garlic and chopped herbs. Mix well and leave to stand for several hours.
    Shake and serve at once.
Makes about ¼ cup.

Lemon Egg French Dressing

1 egg

3 tablespoons olive oil

4 teaspoons lemon juice

Salt and pepper

Hard boil the egg. Shell and cool under cold water. Mash the egg with a fork. Shake the oil, and salt and pepper together. Add the mashed egg to the dressing, mixing to a creamy consistency. Serve at once.
Makes about ¼ cup.

Asparagus

New Zealand asparagus is a green asparagus, giving it a distinctive flavour and tender quality, that provides us with the first real taste of spring.

Asparagus with Lemon Sauce

1 small onion

50 grams butter

1 bay leaf

Salt and pepper

3 tablespoons flour

2 cups chicken stock

Freshly ground nutmeg

2 egg yolks

1 tablespoon lemon juice

Hot cooked asparagus

Toast

Chop the onion finely, and fry it in the hot butter. Add the bay leaf, salt and pepper, and stir in the flour. When this froths, gradually add the chicken stock, stirring and cooking, until the sauce comes to the boil. Lower the heat, and simmer for 5 minutes. Discard the bay leaf. Add nutmeg.
    Beat the egg yolks lightly, and stir in the lemon juice, and blend into the hot sauce. Do not reboil the sauce.
    Place the drained, hot asparagus on toast, and pour the sauce over.
Makes 2 cups sauce.

Asparagus Salad

500 grams fresh asparagus

3 hard-boiled eggs

1 x 50 gram tin anchovy fillets

Lettuce

8 black olives

¼ cup salad oil

2 tablespoons white vinegar

½ teaspoon dry mustard

1 teaspoon sugar

Freshly ground black pepper

1 teaspoon chopped parsley

Cook the asparagus until just tender, then drain thoroughly and allow to cool.
    Quarter the hard-boiled eggs. Wash the fillets of anchovy, and pat dry.
    Have the lettuce washed and thoroughly dried. Arrange lettuce on a platter or in a bowl, and on it place spears of asparagus, 3 or 4 together. Arrange the hard-boiled eggs and olives in a pattern with the asparagus. On each group of asparagus spears, make a criss-cross with anchovy fillets, retaining 1 fillet for mashing in the dressing.
    Prepare the dressing by mashing the retained fillet and blending it with oil, vinegar, mustard, sugar, pepper and finely chopped parsley.
    Spoon this lightly over the salad.
Serves 4.

Asparagus Vinaigrette

Cold cooked asparagus

3 tablespoons olive oil

2 tablespoons wine vinegar

Salt and pepper

Chopped parsley

Place the drained cooked asparagus in a shallow dish.
    Shake the remaining ingredients together thoroughly, and pour over the asparagus.
    Leave for about 1 hour before serving. This can be served from the dish as an hors d'oeuvre, or arranged on lettuce leaves as side salads.
Serves 4.

Kumara

The New Zealand kumara is a purple-skinned and cream-fleshed sweet potato. The flavour is less sweet than many others, which makes it suitable for both savoury and sweet combinations.

Kumara Cakes

500 grams kumara

1 small onion

25 grams butter

2 eggs

Salt and pepper

1 cup soft breadcrumbs

Flour

Butter for frying

Boil the kumara until tender. Drain, and mash thoroughly.

Chop the onion finely, and fry in the butter until tender, but not coloured. Add this, the lightly beaten eggs, the seasonings and the breadcrumbs to the mashed kumara, and mix thoroughly.

Shape into small flat rounds. Dust the kumara cakes lightly with flour as necessary during the shaping.

Heat some butter in a frying pan, and fry the cakes until golden brown on one side, then turn and fry the second side.
Makes 16 to 20.

Sherried Kumara

900 grams to 1 kilogram kumara

1 tablespoon butter

¼ cup dry sherry

Salt and pepper

1 tablespoon brown sugar

Cook the kumara in boiling salted water until tender. Drain, allow to cool, and peel off the skins. Mash until the kumara are smooth and creamy. Add the butter and sherry. Season with salt and pepper.

Spread into a shallow baking dish. Sprinkle with brown sugar. Place under a grill until the top is lightly browned and the sugar is bubbly.
Serves 6 to 8.

Kumara with Orange

500 grams kumara

1 orange

3 tablespoons brown sugar

25 grams butter

1 teaspoon cornflour

¼ cup orange juice

Wash kumara, but do not peel. Cook in boiling salted water until tender — about 30 minutes. Allow to cool, then peel off skins. Cut into 1 centimetre cubes.

Remove skin and pith from the orange. Cut flesh into thick slices, then into cubes. Mix kumara and orange pieces together.

Place in a buttered 3 cup baking dish. Sprinkle the sugar evenly over the top. Dot with butter.

Mix cornflour to a smooth paste with 1 tablespoon of the orange juice. Add remaining orange juice. Pour over kumara.

Cover, and bake at 180 degrees C for 45 minutes.
Serves 5.

Orange Kumara

2 to 3 large kumara

1 orange

25 grams butter

3 tablespoons brown sugar

1 teaspoon cornflour

¼ teaspoon salt

¼ cup orange juice

¼ cup peanuts

Cook the kumara and cut into 3 millimetre thick slices. Peel the orange and cut into thick slices.

Butter thoroughly an ovenware casserole, and place the kumara and orange in it in an overlapping fashion.

Mix the soft butter with the sugar, cornflour and salt, then blend in the orange juice. Pour this over the casserole, and sprinkle with the nuts. Place in the oven at 180 degrees C and bake for about 45 minutes.

Serve with pork, ham or chicken.
Serves 4 to 6.

Dargaville Casserole

750 grams kumara

½ cup tinned or bottled apricots

½ teaspoon salt

1 tablespoon butter

½ cup cream

1 egg

Cook the kumara, and mash well.

Drain and mash the apricots. Add the salt, butter and cream to the mashed kumara, then stir in the apricots. Beat the egg and fold into kumara mixture.

Turn into a well-buttered 3 cup casserole.

Bake at 180 degrees C for 20 minutes. Serve with pork.
Serves 4 to 6.

Sauteed Kumara

4 kumara

2 spring onions

3 tablespoons butter

Salt and pepper

Wash kumara, but do not peel. Cook in boiling salted water for 20 minutes, or until almost tender. Cool, then peel off skins. Cut into about 3 centimetre cubes.

Chop spring onions. Heat butter in frying pan. Add spring onions and fry for 1 minute. Add kumara, and sprinkle with salt and pepper.

Continue to fry, shaking the pan to prevent sticking, until golden brown on all sides.
Serves 4.

Picking squash, North Auckland.

Kumara Puffs

1 cup cooked mashed kumara

¼ cup mashed banana

1 egg

1 tablespoon melted butter

2 to 3 tablespoons milk

Salt and pepper

Place mashed kumara and banana in a mixing bowl. Mix well together.

Separate the egg. Mix yolk, melted butter, milk, salt and pepper with the kumara and banana.

Using a clean dry beater, beat egg white until stiff. Fold into the kumara mixture. Place tablespoonful lots on a cold greased tray.

Bake at 250 degrees C for about 12 minutes, or until puffed and golden. **Makes about 10.**

Onion and Apple Pie

500 grams onions

2 to 3 apples

2 tablespoons butter

½ teaspoon celery seeds

2 eggs

½ cup sour cream

Salt and pepper

200 grams flaky pastry

Peel and slice the onions and apples.

Melt the butter in a frying pan. Add the onions and celery seeds. Fry gently until onions are transparent.

Place layers of onion and apple alternately in a 3 cup pie dish.

Beat eggs. Stir in the sour cream, salt and pepper. Pour over the apple and onion.

Roll out the pastry to ½ centimetre thick. Cut out a lid to fit the pie dish. Place lid over cooled apples and onions.

Bake at 200 degrees C for 30 minutes, then lower the temperature to 180 degrees C and bake for a further 20 to 25 minutes.
Serves 4 to 5

Drying shallots at Henderson.

Pumpkin Soup
(photograph Page 86)

500 grams peeled deseeded pumpkin

2 cups water

½ teaspoon salt

1 large onion

25 grams butter

Sour cream

Pinch nutmeg

Cook pumpkin in the boiling salted water until tender.

Peel and finely chop the onion. Melt the butter in a saucepan, and fry the onion for 5 minutes.

When the pumpkin is cooked, place in a blender or food processor, along with the cooking liquid and the onion, and process to a puree. Cook for a further 30 minutes.

Before serving, swirl with sour cream and sprinkle with a little nutmeg. Thin with milk if wished.
Serves 4.

Stuffed Marrow

2 centimetre thick rings of marrow

For each ring allow:

1 tablespoon raw rice

1 tablespoon finely chopped onion

¼ teaspoon salt

Shake pepper

For dish of 4 to 6 rings allow:

2 cups tomato pulp

¼ teaspoon fresh thyme

1 cup soft breadcrumbs

½ cup grated cheese

Wash the marrow and cut into rings. Leave the skin on, but remove seeds, keeping the rings intact.

Thoroughly grease a large baking dish, and set the marrow rings in it. Into the centre of each ring, put the rice and onion, and season well with salt and pepper. Mix the thyme into the tomato pulp, and pour over the marrow. Blend the breadcrumbs and grated cheese, and sprinkle liberally over the whole dish.

Bake at 180 degrees C for 30 to 45 minutes, or until marrow is tender and rice is cooked. Allow 1 ring of marrow for each serving.
Serves 4 to 6.

Souffle Mushrooms
Cup-shaped, not flat, mushrooms should be used for this recipe.

6 large mushrooms 10 centimetres in diameter

1 small onion

50 grams butter

2 tablespoons flour

½ cup chicken stock

Salt and pepper

2 eggs

Butter

Parmesan cheese

Wash the mushrooms carefully and cut out the stalk. Peel the onion and chop it and the mushroom stalks finely.

Melt the butter in a pan and fry the onion and mushroom stalks until soft. Stir in the flour, and when frothy, add the chicken stock, stirring well, until boiling. Season to taste. Cool slightly.

Separate the eggs, and beat the yolks into the cool sauce.

Beat the egg whites until stiff, and fold into the sauce.

Brush the mushroom caps with melted butter, and pile in the souffle mixture. Sprinkle with parmesan. Place the mushrooms on a greased baking sheet.

Bake at 200 degrees C for about 15 minutes, or until puffed and golden.
Serves 6.

Ginger Glazed Carrots
This is an excellent vegetable to serve with a steak.

500 grams carrots

2 tablespoons butter

2 tablespoons brown sugar

¼ teaspoon ground ginger

Scrape carrots and cut into uniform rings or pieces. Cook in boiling salted water until just tender, then drain thoroughly. Into the saucepan containing the carrots, put the butter, sugar and ground ginger, and heat quickly, tossing the saucepan to keep the contents moving until the carrots have taken on a glaze. Pay attention to the heat under the saucepan. It should be high, but not high enough to scorch.
Serves 4 to 6.

Egg and Potato Casserole

500 grams cooked potatoes

50 grams butter

6 hard-boiled eggs

1 tablespoon chopped, fresh, mixed herbs

Salt and pepper

Dry mustard

25 grams butter

2 tablespoons flour

1 cup milk

Salt and pepper

½ cup grated cheese

Slice the potatoes into 3 millimetre thick slices, and fry in the first measure of butter in a pan, until they are golden and crisp. Arrange these in the bottom and sides of an ovenware dish.

Shell the eggs and cut into large dice. Mix these with the chopped herbs and seasonings. Put the egg mixture into the potato-lined dish.

In a small saucepan, heat the second measure of butter and stir in the flour. When this is frothy, gradually add the milk, and cook with constant stirring, until the sauce thickens. Take from the heat, add the cheese, and pour over the egg and potato mixture.

Place in 230 degree C oven, and heat through for 10 to 15 minutes, or until the top is lightly browned. Serves 4.

Beered Potatoes

4 medium potatoes

25 grams butter

¾ teaspoon salt

2 cups beer

1 tablespoon chopped parsley

Peel the potatoes and cut into pieces about 2 centimetres wide and 4 centimetres long.

Melt the butter in a large frying pan. Add the potatoes and cook until lightly browned. Add the salt and beer to the pan, and cook, covered, for a further 10 minutes. Remove the lid, and cook, uncovered, for 5 minutes.

Remove the potatoes from the pan, and place in a serving dish. Sprinkle with chopped parsley. Serves 4.

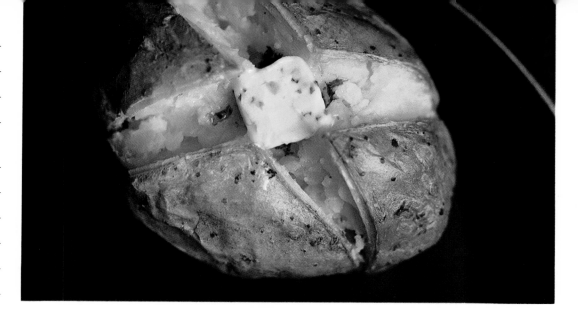

Potato Croquettes

500 grams potatoes

1 teaspoon salt

Pepper

1 tablespoon butter

1 teaspoon chopped parsley

2 tablespoons butter

2 tablespoons flour

½ cup milk

1 egg

1 cup toasted breadcrumbs

Oil for frying

Peel the potatoes, and boil gently until soft. Drain well, then mash until free from lumps. Beat in salt, pepper, first measure of butter, and parsley.

Melt second measure of butter, stir in flour, and cook until frothy. Remove from the heat and gradually add the milk, beating well. Cook until the mixture boils, stirring all the time.

Combine the potato and sauce mixtures until evenly blended. Turn the mixture on to a plate and allow to cool completely.

Divide into 8 even-sized pieces. On a lightly floured board, shape each piece into a cylinder.

Beat the egg lightly in a shallow plate. Have the breadcrumbs on a piece of greaseproof paper.

Dip each portion of potato first in the egg, then in breadcrumbs, making sure they are well coated.

Heat the oil to 190 degrees C. Carefully lower the croquettes into the oil, and fry until golden brown all over. Remove from the oil, and drain well before serving. Serves 4.

Baked Potatoes
(photograph above)

Wash potatoes thoroughly, then mark just through the skin in the form of a cross.

Bake in a 200 degree C oven for about 1 hour. When cooked, fold a cloth around the base of the potato, then press the base with the fingers, to spread the cross slightly.

To serve, garnish the cross with a knob of butter or, as we have done, with flavoured butter — or a sprinkling of paprika, a sprig of parsley, a strip of gherkin, slice of tomato, a spoonful of sour cream. Flavoured butters include butter mixed with chopped herbs, mashed anchovy, blue vein cheese, or crushed garlic.

Brussels Sprouts with Almonds

500 grams brussels sprouts

50 grams butter

2 tablespoons sliced blanched almonds

Salt and pepper

Trim the brussels sprouts free of untidy outside leaves, and cut a small cross in stem end. Wash thoroughly. Cook in lightly salted boiling water until they are just tender. The time will vary according to the size of the sprouts, but should be about 10 minutes. Drain.

Melt the butter, and in it lightly colour the almonds.

Pour this over the hot drained sprouts in a serving dish, and season lightly with salt and pepper. Serves 3 to 4.

Orange Beetroot

2 tablespoons butter

2 teaspoons cornflour

¼ teaspoon salt

2 tablespoons brown sugar

1 tablespoon cider vinegar

1 teaspoon grated orange rind

½ cup orange juice

½ cup water

750 grams cooked beetroot

Melt the butter in a saucepan, and stir in the cornflour, salt and sugar. Then stir in the vinegar, rind, juice and water, and cook until the sauce thickens.

Slice or dice the beetroot, and add to the sauce, cooking gently for about 10 minutes to completely heat the vegetable through.

Serve with pork, chicken or other meats.
Serves 6.

Broccoli Soup

1 onion

1 stalk celery

750 grams broccoli

25 grams butter

1 tablespoon flour

3 cups chicken stock

Salt and pepper

Whipped cream

Paprika

Chop the onion and celery. Remove the flower heads from the broccoli, and reserve to use as a separate vegetable. Chop the broccoli stalks.

In a saucepan, heat the butter, and fry the vegetables lightly. Stir in the flour, then gradually blend in the liquid. Cover, and simmer for about 20 minutes, or until vegetables are tender.

Pass through a sieve or put in blender or a food processor. Season to taste, and thin if wished with hot water.

Reheat soup and serve garnished with whipped cream and paprika.
Serves 6.

Creamy Leek Pie
(photograph right)

375 to 500 grams short pastry

1 to 2 leeks

50 grams butter

2 rashers bacon

3 egg yolks

¾ cup cream

Salt and pepper

Roll out the pastry, and cut from it a circle to cover the top of a 20 centimetre pie tin. Re-roll the pastry as necessary and line the pie tin with this.

Slice the white of leeks very thinly. Wash thoroughly, and measure two cups. In a pan, heat the butter, and in it cook the leeks very gently until they start to become tender, but do not colour.

Remove the rind from the bacon, and chop the flesh into small pieces. Mix bacon with leeks.

Allow to go cold, then put into the pastry-lined tin.

Beat the egg yolks and cream together and season well with salt and pepper. Pour this over the leeks. Place the pastry lid on top, and press it firmly to the edge of the bottom pastry.

Bake at 200 degrees C for about 20 minutes, then lower the heat to 180 degrees C, and continue to cook for a further 15 minutes, or until the custard mixture has set.
Serves 6 to 8.

Creamed Swede

2 swedes

1 tablespoon flour

Salt and pepper

¼ teaspoon curry powder

½ cup milk

Peel the swedes and cut into dice. Boil in lightly salted water until just tender, then drain.

Mix the flour, seasonings and milk together to form a smooth paste. Tip into the saucepan containing the drained swedes. Cook over gentle heat until the mixture thickens.
Serves 6

Cheese Chokos

2 large chokos

½ cup grated cheese

¼ teaspoon curry powder

Pinch thyme

Salt and pepper

Peel the chokos. Remove the seeds, and cut the flesh into 1½ centimetre cubes. Drop into boiling salted water, and cook until tender — about 10 minutes. Drain well, and hold chokos in the hot saucepan.

Mix together the grated cheese, curry powder, salt, pepper and thyme. Sprinkle the cheese mixture over the chokos in the saucepan, and cover with a lid.

Stand for a few minutes until the cheese has melted. Do not reheat or the cheese will go stringy.
Serves 4.

Cauliflower Polonaise
*This is a classical way
to serve this vegetable,
and is suitable for home meals
or entertaining.
The egg and breadcrumb mixture
can be prepared well in advance,
and the dish put together
just as it goes to the table.*

1 cauliflower

1 hard-boiled egg

3 tablespoons chopped parsley

2 tablespoons butter

¾ cup soft white breadcrumbs

1 tablespoon lemon juice.

Cook the cauliflower in boiling salted water until just tender. Drain thoroughly and break into large sections.

Put the hard-boiled egg through a sieve, and chop the parsley finely. Blend these two together.

Melt the butter in a small pan, and in it cook the breadcrumbs until golden brown.

Arrange the cauliflower in an ovenware dish and sprinkle the egg and parsley mixture over it. Sprinkle with lemon juice, and scatter the buttered crumbs over. Reheat if necessary.
Serves 4 to 6, depending on size of cauliflower.

Cauliflower Cheese
(photograph right)

1 cauliflower

3 tablespoons butter

3 tablespoons flour

Salt and pepper

½ teaspoon dry mustard

1½ cups milk

1½ cups grated gruyere cheese

2 rashers bacon

Remove any tough-looking stalk from the cauliflower, and make a deep cut in the stalk end with a knife. Wash cauliflower in salted water, then plunge into boiling salted water and boil steadily for about 20 minutes until tender.

Meanwhile prepare the sauce. Melt butter in a saucepan. Stir in flour, salt, pepper to taste, and mustard. When the mixture bubbles, remove from the heat and gradually stir in milk. Return to the heat and bring to the boil, stirring all the time. Fold in cheese, and stir well until the cheese has melted.

In a hot pan, fry the finely chopped bacon until crisp, then add it to the sauce.

Drain the cauliflower, and place in a warm serving dish. Pour the sauce over, and serve immediately.
Serves 4 to 6.

Salads

Mushroom Salad

500 grams firm mushrooms

¼ cup olive oil

2 small onions

2 tablespoons vinegar

2 to 3 tablespoons chopped parsley

Salt and pepper

Wash the mushrooms and trim the stalks. Drain well.

Heat the oil in a frying pan and cook the finely chopped onion and mushroom stalks for 5 minutes. Then add the sliced mushrooms and cook for 2 to 3 minutes only.

Tip into a bowl, and pour over the vinegar. Sprinkle in the parsley and seasonings. Cool and chill before serving.
Serves 6 to 8.

Cottage Cheese and Cucumber Salad

1 cup cottage cheese

1 tablespoon lemon juice

½ teaspoon salt

Shake pepper

1 tablespoon chopped mint

1 tablespoon chopped chives

1 large cucumber

Lettuce leaves

Paprika

In a bowl, mix together the cottage cheese, salt, pepper, lemon juice, chives and mint. Chill for about half an hour.

Meanwhile, peel the cucumber and cut into slices about 5 centimetres long and 1 centimetre wide. Mix the cucumber and cheese mixture, and chill again.

When ready to serve, arrange in lettuce leaves or a bowl lined with lettuce leaves, and sprinkle with paprika.
Serves 4.

Courgette Salad

12 courgettes

4 tablespoons oil

½ teaspoon salt

½ teaspoon sugar

½ teaspoon mustard

¼ teaspoon Worcestershire sauce

2 tablespoons vinegar or lemon juice

1 teaspoon finely chopped mint

1 teaspoon finely chopped parsley

Wash courgettes and remove the stalk ends. Cut into 2 centimetre slices, and cook in lightly salted boiling water for about 15 minutes until tender. Drain, and allow to cool completely.

Put the oil, salt, sugar, mustard and sauce in a bowl, and beat vigorously until smooth. Gradually beat in the vinegar.

Place the courgettes in a bowl, and mix the dressing through them. Pile the courgettes into a serving bowl, and garnish with the parsley and mint mixed together.
Serves 3 to 4.

Snow White Salad

500 grams New Zealand yams

1 red apple

1 tablespoon lemon juice

1 stick celery

Dressing:

2 mint leaves

½ cup sour cream

Trim the yams. Steam or boil them until just tender — about 5 minutes. Drain and allow to cool. When cool, slice into 2 centimetre rings.

Cut the apple into quarters, core, then dice. Pour lemon juice over to prevent discolouration.

Slice the celery. Combine with yams and apple.

Pour dressing on salad, and toss. Serve chilled.

Dressing: Finely chop mint leaves. Combine with sour cream.

Serves 4 to 5.

Director's Salad

500 grams green beans

1 small onion

1 rasher bacon

2 tablespoons olive oil

1 tablespoon wine vinegar

Freshly ground pepper

¼ teaspoon salt

1 tablespoon chopped parsley

2 tablespoons sliced blanched almonds

Lettuce leaves

Wash, trim and slice the beans. Keep the slices fairly coarse to retain the bean flavour. Cook in boiling salted water until fork-tender, then drain well and chill.

Meantime, chop the bacon and onion finely, and fry in a hot pan until tender, but not coloured.

Toss the beans with the bacon mixture.

Blend the oil, vinegar, salt and pepper, and pour over the beans, tossing them lightly, until all are coated with the dressing. Carefully mix in the sliced almonds and chopped parsley.

Serve in lettuce leaves.

Serves 6.

Celery Salad

Dressing:

½ cup mayonnaise

1 tablespoon capers

4 gherkins

1 tablespoon chopped chives

2 teaspoons prepared mustard

Pinch cayenne pepper

Salad:

4 to 6 stalks celery

Dressing: Chop the capers, gherkins and chives very finely. Mix these, the mustard and cayenne pepper into the mayonnaise thoroughly.

Salad: Wash, trim and remove any tough fibres from the celery. Chop into pieces about 1 centimetre in length. Toss the celery in the dressing, and chill.

Serves 6.

Brussels Slaw

250 to 375 grams brussels sprouts

2 spring onions

3 stalks celery

1 cup mandarin segments

3 tablespoons salad oil

2 tablespoons mandarin or orange juice

1 teaspoon sugar

1 tablespoon lemon juice

Salt and pepper

Wash the sprouts thoroughly, discarding the damaged outer leaves. Finely shred the sprouts and spring onions, and slice the celery. Mix these vegetables together lightly, and carefully stir the drained mandarin segments through them.

Mix the oil, orange and lemon juices, sugar and seasonings together, by shaking thoroughly. Pour this over the salad and toss lightly.

Serves 6.

Tomato and Nut Salad

6 large tomatoes

Salt

1 cup drained crushed pineapple

½ cup chopped roasted peanuts

½ cup diced celery

Salt and pepper

1 tablespoon oil

1 tablespoon white vinegar

Lettuce leaves

Cut a slice off the flower end of each tomato, and scoop out the seeds, leaving a thick, flesh cup. Sprinkle lightly with salt, and turn upside down on a plate to drain.

Take the scooped-out pulp and separate it from any seeds. Chop this pulp and mix it with the well-drained pineapple, nuts, celery, salt and pepper, oil and vinegar.

Chill both the tomato cups and the filling.

When ready to serve, pile the filling into the tomato cups, and place each one in a lettuce leaf.

Serves 6.

Pea Salad

1 kilogram frozen peas

1 small jar white cocktail onions

¼ cup salad oil

2 tablespoons lemon juice

Salt

Freshly ground black pepper

Mint sprigs

Lemon slices

Cook the peas in boiling salted water until barely tender, then drain thoroughly. Drain the cocktail onions. Mix these with the cold peas.

Shake together the oil and lemon juice, and season generously with salt and pepper. Stir this through the vegetables.

Pile into a dish, and garnish with mint sprigs and lemon slices.

Serves 6.

OUR PLACE IN THE PACIFIC

As part of the Pacific region, we have a unique opportunity to include in our culinary heritage the foods favoured by Pacific Islanders. The many different Island peoples who now live in New Zealand have created a demand for foods such as taro, cassava, mangoes, and pawpaws, to add to the long-time favourites — pineapples, coconuts, and bananas.

To add these ingredients to our cooking provides that touch of tropical colour that spells warm seas, white sands, and lush vegetation — the relaxed Pacific image. Discovering the versatility of these foods cooked in traditional ways or adapted to suit modern facilities, is exciting.

This is shown by the interest taken by different ethnic groups in feasts put on by Island peoples, including our own hangi.

Captions to preceding 4 pages.

Page 96/97: White Island — a steaming, active volcano off the Bay of Plenty coast. (photograph Robin Smith — Photobank).

Page 98/99: Pacific. An early morning visit to the Otara markets to make a choice from the extensive selection of produce and goods offered by the stallholders.

Facing page: The rocky heads and bay at Tutukaka, Northland. (photograph Peter Morath).

Polly's Bread

*Maori bread depends
on the preparation of a potato yeast
for its rising.*

Rewena
(potato water bug)

Original plant:

1 medium potato

1 cup water

1 teaspoon sugar

2 cups flour

Starter plant:

1 tablespoon original plant

½ cup warm, unsalted potato water

1 teaspoon sugar

Original plant: Peel the potato, and cut into 3 slices. Cook in the unsalted water until soft. Add the sugar, and mash well.

Cool to lukewarm. With a fork, mix in the flour to form a soft dough.

Cover, and leave in a warm place until next day to prove.

Starter Plant: Take a tablespoon of dough from the original plant and put in one litre glass jar. Add the warm, unsalted potato water. Cover lightly, and keep in a warm place.

Next day, add the sugar, then cover, and keep in a warm place. Continue adding potato water one day, and sugar the next, to keep the plant growing.

The plant is ready to use in 3 to 5 days.

Make up several of these jars of starter plant, and use them in rotation, so that the plant has time to grow between use.

Note: Do not use salted potato water, this will kill the plant.

Rewena Paraoa

5 cups flour

1 teaspoon salt

1 teaspoon sugar

Rewena (potato water bug))

Put flour, salt and sugar into a large mixing bowl. Make a well in the centre, and add enough Rewena to make a soft dough. This will be almost all the bug. If necessary, add lukewarm water to help form the dough.

Turn out on to a floured board, and knead well — about 10 minutes.

Take off about 1 tablespoon of dough to start a new plant. Grease a round oven dish or dutch oven about 20 centimetres across. Put the dough in, smooth side up. Stand in a warm place until doubled in bulk.

Bake at 200 degrees C for about 45 minutes until golden brown.
Makes 1 loaf.

Pawpaw Pie

250 grams sweet short pastry

2 cups peeled pawpaw flesh

½ cup brown sugar

2 tablespoons lemon juice

½ teaspoon ground ginger

¼ cup desiccated coconut

Line a 20 centimetre pie tin with the sweet short pastry, and bake blind at 190 degrees C for about 15 minutes. Remove baking blind material, and continue cooking for a further 10 minutes. It may be necessary to cover the edges to prevent over-browning.

Have the pawpaw peeled, seeds removed, and the flesh cut into pieces. Place this, the brown sugar, lemon juice and ginger in a saucepan, and simmer until the fruit is tender.

Turn the fruit mixture into the cooked pie shell, and sprinkle with coconut. Serve warm or cold, with or without cream.
Serves 4 to 6.

A Maori concert party performing.

Pawpaw Ice Cream

(photograph left)

2 cups pawpaw puree

¾ cup sweetened condensed milk

2 tablespoons lemon juice

1 cup cream

Peel the pawpaw, and remove the seeds. Process in food processor or blender, or pass through a sieve to get a puree. Add the sweetened condensed milk and the lemon juice. Mix well.

Beat the cream until soft peaks form. Fold into the puree.

Turn into a freezer container, cover, and freeze for about 1½ hours. Remove from freezer, and stir gently, so that freezing outside edges are stirred into the centre of the mixture. Cover, and return to the freezer until firm.
Makes 4 cups.

Mango Fluff

(photograph left)

2 mangoes

2 passionfruit

2 egg whites

Peel mangoes and remove the stones. Cut up roughly, then place in food processor or blender and process until smooth. Place in a bowl.

Scoop pulp from the passionfruit. Reserve a little for garnishing, and add the rest to the mango puree and stir through.

Beat egg whites until stiff. Fold them into the mango puree.

Spoon into serving glasses, and chill. Garnish with reserved passionfruit pulp.
Serves 4 to 6.

Tropical Fruit Salad

(photograph right)

3 bananas

3 tablespoons lemon juice

1 orange

¼ cup crystallised ginger

1 tablespoon grated chocolate

Peel the bananas, and cut diagonally into 2 centimetre pieces. Brush with lemon juice to prevent browning. Sprinkle any remaining lemon juice over the bananas.

Peel the rind and pith from the orange. Cut the orange horizontally into 1 centimetre thick slices.

Chop the ginger in half.

Just before serving, mix the bananas, orange slices and ginger together. Place in a serving bowl, and sprinkle with grated chocolate.
Serves 3 to 4.

Fresh Pineapple Ice Cream

The fresh pineapple for making this can be scraped from the shells. The coarse section of the pineapple can be minced or grated and used as part of this measurement as well.

1 egg

1 tablespoon flour

1 cup sugar

2 cups milk

1 cup cream

2 cups grated fresh pineapple

In a saucepan, mix together the egg, flour and sugar, and blend to a smooth paste with a little of the measured milk. Gradually add the rest of the milk. Heat gently, stirring all the time, and cooking until the custard thickens.

Pour into an ice cream tray, and freeze until the mixture is starting to go firm on the edges. Turn into a bowl, and beat lightly.

Whip the cream until thick, but not stiff. Fold in to the custard mixture. Carefully fold in the pineapple.

Return to freezing trays, and place a piece of waxed paper over the top. Freeze until firm.
Makes about 5 cups.

Glazed Pineapple Slices

6 to 8 slices 3 millimetres thick, fresh pineapple

½ cup sugar

½ cup water

2 tablespoons white vinegar

3 or 4 pieces crystallised ginger

Cut the pineapple, and reserve any syrup that forms during cutting. Put this syrup, together with the sugar, water and vinegar into a saucepan.

Finely chop or crush the ginger, and add to the mixture. Bring to the boil, and simmer for about 5 minutes. Add the pineapple slices, and continue simmering until they are clear and have absorbed most of the syrup.

Serve hot with pork, ham or chicken, or chill and serve cold with or without cream for dessert.
Serves 4.

Curried Pork and Pineapple

500 grams lean pork or pork pieces

1 onion

1 tablespoon butter

1 tablespoon curry powder

1 cup water

½ teaspoon salt

1 to 2 tablespoons lemon juice

1 cup fresh pineapple cubes

Fine white breadcrumbs

Butter

Cooked rice

Cut the meat into cubes, trimming off any excess fat. Chop the onion.

In a pan, melt the first measure of butter, and in it fry the onion lightly. Add the curry powder, and continue to fry. Add the pork, and fry until coloured all over, adding a small amount of extra butter if necessary. Carefully add the water and salt. Lower the heat, cover, and simmer gently for about 1 hour or until the meat is tender. Add the lemon juice.

While the meat is cooking, cut the pineapple into cubes, and roll them in fine breadcrumbs. Heat the unmeasured butter in a separate pan, and lightly fry the pineapple until golden all over.

Pile the cooked rice in a large bowl. Pour the curried pork over this, and place the fried pineapple pieces on the top.
Serves 4.

Bananas

The versatile banana is enjoyed by most people as a fresh fruit, but it also has a place in our baking, in cakes, puddings or as a vegetable.

Banana Casserole

500 grams kumara

3 bananas

8 gingernuts

¼ cup chopped seedless raisins

25 grams butter

¼ cup orange juice

¼ cup water

1 tablespoon brown sugar

Peel, then boil the kumera until they are just tender, then cut them into thick slices. Peel and cut the bananas into slices. Crush the gingernuts, and mix with the chopped raisins.

In a greased ovenware dish, arrange layers of kumara, bananas, and the crumb mixture, ending with the crumb mixture.

Chop the butter into small pieces, and scatter over the top.

Mix the orange juice, water and brown sugar together and pour over.

Place a cover on the dish, and put in a 200 degree C oven and cook for about 25 minutes. Remove the lid and allow to brown for a few minutes. Serve hot with ham, pork or chicken.
Serves 4 to 6.

Deep Fried Bananas

4 bananas

3 tablespoons oil

1 tablespoon lemon juice

½ teaspoon salt

¼ teaspoon paprika

Batter:

½ cup flour

½ teaspoon salt

¼ teaspoon pepper

2 teaspoons oil

½ cup water

Oil for deep frying

Peel the bananas, and cut in half lengthways.

Mix together the oil, lemon juice, salt and paprika. Pour over the bananas, and leave to marinate for 20 minutes.

Batter: Sift flour, salt and pepper into a mixing bowl. Mix in the oil and water. Beat well, and leave to stand for 30 minutes.

Heat the oil in a deep fryer or large saucepan. Drain the bananas, and dip them in the batter mixture. Fry until golden brown — about 5 minutes. Serve with chicken, pork or fish.
Serves 4.

South Sea Bananas

4 bananas

½ cup brown sugar

1 teaspoon cinnamon

25 grams butter

¼ cup orange juice

½ cup coconut

Peel the bananas, and slice in half lengthways.

Butter an ovenware dish thoroughly, and arrange the bananas in this.

Mix the sugar and cinnamon together. Sprinkle over the bananas. Cut the butter into small pieces, and scatter over this. Carefully pour in the orange juice and sprinkle the top with the coconut.

Place in a 180 degree C oven, and cook for about 20 minutes, or until the coconut is coloured and the fruit soft. Serve hot.
Serves 4.

Fish and Banana Curry

(photograph below)

2 bananas

½ cup pineapple juice

1 onion

1 clove garlic

1 green pepper

50 grams butter

1 teaspoon salt

2 teaspoons curry powder

250 grams diced white fish

Peel the bananas and cut into 1 centimetre thick slices. Place in a bowl, and pour the pineapple juice over them. Leave to stand while preparing the remaining ingredients.

Peel and chop the onion and garlic. Remove the seeds from the green pepper, and shred the flesh.

Heat the butter in a pan, and fry these vegetables until they are just tender. Sprinkle in the salt and curry powder, and stir well.

Have the fish cut into small cubes. Add this to the pan, stir again, and cook until the fish just starts to whiten. Carefully add the bananas and the pineapple juice. Stir well, cover, and simmer for about 15 minutes. Serve with rice.
Serves 2.

Baked Bananas

4 firm bananas

Melted butter

Salt

Cut off the ends of the bananas. Carefully remove one strip of peel, about 2 centimetres wide, from each banana. Brush the bananas with melted butter, and sprinkle lightly with salt.

Place in a baking dish and put in the oven at 190 degrees C. Cook for about 15 minutes, or until the peel has become dark and the banana is tender when pierced with a fork. Serve hot as a vegetable with pork, chicken or ham.
Serves 4.

Baked Banana Pudding

3 eggs

1 cup milk

¼ cup brown sugar

½ cup mashed bananas

½ cup desiccated coconut

½ teaspoon almond essence

Beat the eggs, and blend the milk and sugar into them. Stir well. Mix the mashed bananas, coconut and almond essence into the egg mixture, and pour into a greased 3 cup ovenware dish.

Stand the dish in a pan of hot water, and bake at 180 degrees C for about an hour.

Chill before serving.
Serves 4.

Banana Nut Cake

125 grams butter

1 cup sugar

2 eggs

¾ cup mashed banana

2 cups flour

½ teaspoon nutmeg

1 teaspoon baking soda

½ cup lightly toasted chopped cashew nuts

Cream the butter and sugar. Beat the eggs, and add to the creamed mixture, a little at a time, beating well after each addition.

Mash the bananas immediately before use, and fold them into the creamed mixture. Sift the flour, nutmeg and baking soda together, and stir in. Finally, add the chopped nuts. Pour into a buttered and floured 20 centimetre cake tin.

Bake at 180 degrees C for about 50 minutes.

When cold, either ice with a vanilla-flavoured icing, or dust the top with icing sugar.

Boiling mud, Rotorua.

Coconut

Fish in Coconut Cream

2 cups desiccated or freshly grated coconut
1 cup boiling water
1 onion
4 to 5 small fish steaks or fillets
Butter
1 tablespoon cornflour
2 tablespoons cold water
Salt and pepper
Lemon slices
Tomato slices

Place the desiccated or grated coconut in a bowl, and pour boiling water over it. Leave for about half an hour, then squeeze to extract as much coconut cream as possible. It may be necessary to pour a little more boiling water over the coconut to get sufficient liquid to use in this dish.

Peel the onion and slice it very thinly.

Trim the fish as necessary.

Generously butter a shallow ovenware dish, and place the sliced onion on this. Arrange the pieces of fish on top, then pour over sufficient of the coconut cream to almost cover the fish.

Cover, place in a 160 degree C oven, and cook for about half an hour or until the fish is set.

Lift the pieces of the fish on to a serving plate, and tip the liquid into a saucepan. Have blended the cornflour and water, seasoned lightly with salt and pepper. Stir this into the saucepan. Cook gently until the sauce just thickens. Pour over the fish, and garnish with slices of lemon and tomato.

Note: If a lot of liquid comes out of the fish, it may be necessary to increase the amount of cornflour.
Serves 4 to 6.

Tahitian Fish Salad

The fish for this must be absolutely fresh

500 grams fresh fish
Lemon juice
Coconut cream
1 onion
Salt and pepper to taste
Garnishes:
Sliced hard-boiled egg or sliced tomato or sliced cucumber.
Sprigs of parsley or mint

Skin and bone the fish, and cut into 2 centimetre pieces. Place in a shallow dish, and squeeze lemon juice all over the fish until it is almost covered. Set aside in a cool place for several hours. During this time, turn the fish occasionally in the juice.

Meantime, prepare the coconut cream by pouring 1½ cups of boiling water over one cup of desiccated coconut. Leave to steep for about half an hour, then strain the resultant cream through a muslin.

When the fish has become white, lift it out and place in a bowl together with the finely chopped onion. Season well with salt and pepper, and pour in coconut cream to almost cover. Garnish with whatever suitable garnish is available, and serve very cold.
Serves 4.

Coconut Milk

Freshly grated or desiccated coconut steeped in hot water, then squeezed out, produces coconut milk or cream of richness varying according to the amount of water used. Tinned coconut cream or milk can be used instead.

Eggplant in Coconut Milk

1 cup rich coconut milk
1 large or 2 small eggplants
1 onion
½ teaspoon salt
1 hot chilli pepper or pinch chilli powder

Prepare the coconut milk, using as little water as possible, so that it is rich in flavour. Peel the eggplant, and cut in thick slices. Arrange in a lightly greased, deep ovenware dish.

Peel and slice the onion, and scatter over the eggplant. Sprinkle salt over the top, and if chilli powder is being used, mix this with the salt. If a fresh chilli is being used, remove the seeds and finely shred the flesh. Scatter over the top. Pour in the coconut milk.

Cover, and bake at 180 degrees C for about 1 hour.
Serves 3 to 4.

Miki

The coconut milk in this recipe is the liquid drained from a fresh coconut, not the milk made by grating and steeping the flesh.

1 cup coconut milk drained from the coconut
¼ cup water
1 tablespoon finely chopped onion
1 teaspoon chopped chives or spring onion
¼ teaspoon salt
Shake pepper

Mix together the coconut milk and water. Add chopped onions, salt and pepper. Chill.

Serve as a pre-dinner drink in the coconut shell, with a sprinkle of chopped chives or spring onion.
Makes 1.

Coconut Ice Cream

½ cup desiccated coconut

¾ cup hot water

1 x 400 gram tin sweetened condensed milk

1 cup cream

½ cup shredded coconut

Put the desiccated coconut in a bowl, and pour the hot water over it. Leave to soak for 30 minutes, then pour through a muslin and squeeze out the liquid.

Measure three quarters of a cup of this, and blend with the condensed milk. Chill in a freezer tray until very cold, but not frozen.

Whip the cream until stiff, and fold into the chilled milk mixture. Pour into freezer tray and cover with waxed paper. Freeze until mushy. Beat until smooth with a fork or beater, and stir in the shredded coconut.

Return to freezer tray, and cover with waxed paper. Freeze until firm.
Serves 6 to 8.

Treasure Island Pie

½ cup sugar

½ cup flour

½ teaspoon salt

1¾ cups milk

3 eggs

25 grams butter

1 teaspoon vanilla

1 cup desiccated coconut

1 cooked 20 to 23 centimetre pie shell

¼ cup sugar

Mix the first measure of sugar, the flour and salt in a saucepan, and gradually blend in the milk, stirring to form a smooth paste. Cook this over gentle heat, stirring all the time, until the sauce thickens and starts to boil. Do not allow to boil.

Separate the eggs, and beat the yolks until mixed. Add half a cup of the hot sauce to the eggs, and mix well, then return this to the sauce in the pot, and cook for 2 minutes, stirring constantly. Add the butter and vanilla, and two thirds of the coconut to the cream sauce.

Allow to cool a little, then pour the mixture into the cooked pie shell.

Beat the egg whites until stiff, and beat in the second measure of sugar to form a meringue. Pile in peaks all over the cream sauce, and sprinkle with the remaining coconut.

Bake at 200 degrees C for 7 to 10 minutes to brown the meringue.
Serves 6.

Pacific Coconut Cake

Western Samoans have a reputation for making the most feathery sponge cakes.

Sponge:

1 cup flour

1 teaspoon baking powder

Pinch salt

4 eggs

¾ cup sugar

2 tablespoons hot water

¼ teaspoon vanilla essence

Coconut filling:

1 cup coconut cream

1 cup milk

4 tablespoons cornflour

1 egg

¾ cup sugar

1 tablespoon brandy or rum

Assembling:

2 tablespoons coconut cream

About ¾ cup desiccated coconut

Orange jube slices

Grease a deep 20 centimetre round cake tin, and line with paper.

Sift the flour, baking powder and salt on to a paper.

In a cake mixer, beat the eggs for about half a minute, until frothy. Add the sugar, and beat on high until the mixture is thick and will hold its shape. Add the water and essence down the side of the bowl. Using a large spoon, fold in the sifted dry ingredients, about half at a time. Do not overmix. Pour into a prepared tin. Bake at 190 degrees C for 35 to 40 minutes.

Allow to cool slightly in the tin, then turn out on to a wire rack to cool completely. Split into 3 layers.

Coconut filling: Put the coconut cream and half the measured amount of milk in a saucepan. Heat slowly.

Mix the rest of the milk with the cornflour to make a smooth paste.

Separate the egg. Beat the yolk and sugar together. Beat the egg white until stiff. Stir the cornflour paste into the egg yolk and sugar mixture. Stir some of the hot mixture into this. When evenly mixed, return to the hot milk in the saucepan, and stir over gentle heat untill it boils and thickens.

Remove from the heat, cool slightly, then fold in the brandy or rum and the stiffly beaten egg white.

Assembling: Spread the bottom layer quickly with one quarter of the coconut filling.

Place the second layer on top, and sprinkle it with half the coconut cream. Spread one quarter of filling on this.

Place the third layer of the cake on top, and sprinkle with remaining coconut cream. Spread the top and sides with coconut filling, and sprinkle generously with desiccated coconut. Decorate with orange jube slices.

Yam Fritters

¾ cup flour

¼ teaspoon salt

1 tablespoon melted butter

½ to ¾ cup lukewarm water

1 egg white

Fat or oil for frying

200 grams yams

Sift flour and salt into a bowl. Add melted butter and lukewarm water. Mix well with a wooden spoon.

Beat egg white until stiff, and fold into the batter.

Set aside for 10 minutes.

Peel and slice the yam into rounds about 3 millimetres thick. Heat the oil. Dip the yam slices into batter. Fry until golden brown. Drain on kitchen paper. Serve hot.
Serves 4.

Kumara Baked in Coconut Cream

400 grams kumara
2 onions
2 tablespoons flour
Salt
Pepper
1 cup water
1 cup coconut cream
Pinch cayenne pepper

Wash and peel the kumara and cut into slices about 1 centimetre thick. Slice the onion into rings.

Place the flour, salt and pepper in a paper bag. Add the prepared vegetables, close the top of the bag, and shake well to coat vegetables with flour.

Mix the water and coconut cream together. Arrange the floured kumara and onion slices in a shallow ovenproof dish. Pour over the water and coconut cream. Top with a light sprinkling of cayenne pepper.

Bake at 180 degrees C for 35 minutes, or until tender. Serve hot with roast chicken.
Serves 4.

Sweet Potato Poi

2 cups grated raw kumara
¼ cup grated raw coconut
1 teaspoon salt
Buttered foil

Mix the freshly grated kumara and coconut together, and season with salt.

Line a small ovenware dish with buttered foil, leaving sufficient overlap to cover the vegetables. Place the mixture in the buttered foil, and fold the foil over to completely cover the mixture.

Bake at 180 degrees C for about 1 hour. Remove from the oven, and serve as a starch with meats, either hot or cold.
Serves 2 to 3.

Taro

Taro Fritters

3 cups cooked mashed taro
1 cup flour
1 teaspoon baking powder
½ teaspoon salt
About ½ cup minced corned beef or ¼ cup chopped cooked bacon
Fat for frying

Mix the taro, flour, baking powder and salt together to get a smooth paste. Add the meat of your choice, and mix well. Shape into round cakes.

Heat a small quantity of fat in a pan, and fry cakes in this until golden brown. Turn once during the frying. Drain on paper.

Serve very hot.
Makes about 15 fritters.
Note: To cook the taro, bake for 1½ to 1¾ hours. (See page 109) Mash the cooked starch in much the way you would potato. Alternatively, the root can be boiled, drained and mashed.

Taro and Corned Beef Salad

(photograph left)

500 grams cooked taro
1 green pepper
1 small onion
2 stalks celery
1 cup cold cooked peas
½ cup salad dressing
250 gram tin corned beef
6 to 8 lettuce leaves
Freshly grated nutmeg

Dice cold cooked taro. Remove seeds from pepper and dice. Peel and dice onion. Slice celery.

Combine taro, pepper, onion, celery, peas and salad dressing. Cut corned beef into cubes and mix through salad lightly.

Line serving dish with lettuce leaves and arrange salad in them. Sprinkle with nutmeg.
Serves 6.

A salad combining the popular local and imported Pacific Island ingredients taro and tinned corned beef.

Mashed Taro

Taro can be used
in similar ways to potato.
It is more starchy
and denser than potato,
and is a greyish-white colour
when cooked.
It goes very well
with pork, chicken or fish.

500 grams taro

1 cup water

½ teaspoon salt

2 tablespoons butter

2 tablespoons milk

¼ teaspoon white pepper

Peel taro and cut into chunks. Place water and salt in a saucepan, and bring to the boil. Add taro, and boil gently for 15 to 20 minutes, or until the taro is tender when tested with a skewer. Drain well.

Mash with a potato masher. Add butter, milk and pepper, and keep mashing until the mixture is smooth.
Serves 4 to 6.

Fa'ausi

"The Pig without Legs"

This dish is considered a delicacy
in Western Samoa,
and is so complicated to make
that it is rated as important as pork.
The taro is normally wrapped
in palm leaves,
but our recipe uses foil instead.

1 taro, about 1 kilogram (select one with a reddish top)

Butter for greasing

1½ cups coconut cream

1½ cups water

1 teaspoon vanilla

¾ cup sugar

1 tablespoon cornflour

2 tablespoons water

Peel, then grate or mince the taro.

Grease a 30 by 50 centimetre sheet of foil with butter. Place grated taro on it in a cake 4 centimetres thick. Fold foil over.

Bake on an oven tray at 180 degrees C for about 40 minutes. When done, a toothpick poked into the taro will come out dry.

Unwrap, and leave taro to cool.

In a heavy-based saucepan, caramelise the sugar over very low heat.

Mix coconut cream and water together. Add to sugar. Return to heat. Stir over low heat without boiling until sugar is dissolved. Add vanilla. Thicken with cornflour and water mixed to a paste.

Cut cooled taro in 3 centimetre cubes. Place in a salad bowl. Pour sauce over, making sure all cubes are covered. Chill until serving time.
Serves 6 to 8.

Baked Taro

1 x 500 gram taro

Scrub the taro well. Dry.

Place in the oven at 190 degrees C and bake for 1½ to 1¾ hours, or until soft when tested with a skewer.

Split open and, if wished, add seasonings and butter before serving.
Serves 4 to 6.

Manioc

Manioc Parcels

1½ cups finely grated manioc (cassava)

1 small onion

Thick coconut cream

3 tablespoons tinned corned beef

Cut three 18 centimetre squares of foil or banana leaf.

Divide manioc into 3 even portions. Pat it out on to the squares to cover about 10 by 8 centimetres.

Slice onion, and place pieces of onion and corned beef, moistened with coconut cream, on to patties. Fold in half. Seal by tying or folding edges.

Bake at 200 degrees C about 1 hour, or until manioc is slightly browned.
Serves 3.

Manioc Crisps

Manioc (cassava)

Oil for frying

Peel and slice manioc very thinly. Dry well.

Deep fry in hot oil. Drain on absorbent paper.

Serve salted hot or cold.

Manioc Bread

600 grams manioc (cassava)

1 cup grated ripe coconut

25 grams butter

½ cup sugar

1 teaspoon baking powder

1 teaspoon allspice

1 teaspoon cinnamon

1 teaspoon vanilla essence

About ½ cup milk

Peel and finely grate manioc. Mix with grated coconut, and cut in butter. Mix in sugar, baking powder, allspice, cinnamon, vanilla essence and milk to combine.

Put into an ovenproof dish, leaving 2 to 3 centimetres at the top for the bread to rise. Bake at 180 degrees C for 1½ hours, or until golden brown.

Serve hot as a dessert, or cold as slices.
Serves 6 to 8.

Breadfruit Casserole

This is a very rich dish.
Ordinary milk can be substituted
for thin coconut cream.

1 breadfruit

1 onion

1 clove garlic

1 teaspoon salt

¼ teaspoon chilli powder

2 cups thin coconut milk

1 cup thick coconut cream

Peel, core and slice breadfruit into cubes about 5 centimetres thick. Measure 500 grams. Place in a casserole.

Dice the onion. Crush garlic with salt. Add onion, garlic, salt, chilli powder and coconut milk to the casserole. Cover.

Bake at 180 degrees C for 1½ to 1¾ hours, or until breadfruit is cooked. Stir in the thick coconut cream.

Cook for a further 5 minutes. Serve hot.
Serves 8.

LADIES A PLATE

Many a migrant woman to New Zealand has known the embarrassment of turning up at a function with an empty plate, to learn that this customary 'entry fee' to a gathering means a plate of food suitable to share.

Generations of New Zealand women have taken to small and large functions their favourite cake, sausage roll, pikelet, sandwich, stuffed egg, or biscuit. Often, a considerable reputation for a baking skill and recipe is gained, and that lady's plate is always in demand.

How much poorer our culinary heritage would be, if we didn't continue to foster this generous attitude to sharing, that our forbears instituted.

Captions to preceding 4 pages.

Page 110/111: Pony day at Duvauchelle, Banks Peninsula. (photograph Peter Morath).

Page 112/113: A long established and continuing New Zealand tradition, requiring each lady to bring a plate of food for the function, shows the quality of our cooking and the warmth of our hospitality.

Facing page: Daffodils blooming in spring at Geraldine, South Canterbury.

(photograph Bob Wells — Photobank).

Cakes

Sponge
(photograph left)

3 eggs

½ cup sugar

¾ cup flour

¾ teaspoon baking powder

pinch salt

2 tablespoons hot water

Decoration:

Jam

Whipped Cream

Icing sugar

Grease and line two 18 centimetre sponge tins.

Place eggs and sugar in a deep bowl, and beat until the mixture is thick and will hold its own shape. Sift flour, baking powder and salt together. Pour the hot water down the side of the bowl. Fold in sifted dry ingredients, about half at a time. Pour into the prepared tins.

Bake at 190 degrees C for 15 to 20 minutes, or until the sponge springs back when touched lightly.

Cool for a few minutes in the tins, then remove to a wire rack to complete cooling. When cold, spread jam on one layer. Pile whipped cream on top of the jam, and spread it out to the edges. Sift icing sugar on to the second layer of cake, and carefully position it on top of whipped cream.

Chocolate Souffle Roll
No party is complete without a chocolate log.

4 eggs

½ cup sugar

115 grams dark chocolate

¾ cup cream

2 tablespoons icing sugar

2 tablespoons brandy

Icing sugar

Separate the eggs. Beat the yolks until frothy. Add sugar gradually, and beat until thick and pale.

Break chocolate into small pieces, and melt in a bowl over simmering water. Add to the creamed yolks and sugar.

Beat egg whites until stiff. Carefully fold into chocolate mixture. Turn into a greased and floured 20 by 30 centimetre sponge roll tin, which has a sheet of greaseproof paper on the bottom. Bake at 190 degrees C for 15 minutes.

Remove sponge from the oven. Cover with a layer of damp kitchen paper. On top of this, place a dry tea towel. Place in refrigerator for 15 minutes, or until quite cold.

Whip the cream, and add the measured icing sugar and brandy.

Sprinkle the second measure of icing sugar on to a sheet of greaseproof paper. Turn cold cake on to the paper. Peel off greaseproof paper from the bottom of the cake.

Spread the cake with cream. Carefully roll up from the short side, using the paper to aid rolling.

Lamingtons
Popular with jelly or chocolate, plain or piped with cream.

225 grams butter

¾ cup sugar

3 eggs

1 teaspoon vanilla

2¾ cups flour

2 teaspoons baking powder

Pinch salt

½ to ¾ cup milk

Grease and line a 20 by 30 centimetre sponge roll tin.

Cream the butter and sugar until light and fluffy. Beat the eggs well, and add them gradually to the butter mixture. Mix in the vanilla.

Sift together the flour, baking powder and salt. Add the sifted dry ingredients alternately with the milk.

Turn into the prepared tin. Bake at 180 degrees C for about 50 minutes. Turn out on to a wire rack to cool.

Next day, cut into 36 pieces, 4 by 5 centimetres.

Coat pieces, one at a time, with chocolate icing or thickening jelly. Roll in coconut. Place on a wire rack to set. Fill with whipped cream if wished.

Makes 36.

Jelly:

1 x 106 gram packet raspberry jelly crystals

1 cup boiling water

¾ cup cold water

Place the jelly crystals and boiling water in a bowl, and stir until the crystals dissolve. Add the cold water, and mix well.

Chill in the refrigerator until the jelly thickens to the consistency of egg white. Use to coat Lamingtons.
Makes enough for about 40 Lamingtons.

Chocolate Icing:

2 cups sugar

2 tablespoons cocoa

½ cup milk

½ teaspoon vanilla

Put the sugar, cocoa and milk into a saucepan. Heat slowly, stirring all the time, until the sugar is dissolved. Bring rapidly to the boil, and boil 2 to 3 minutes, or until the icing forms a thread when it is dripped from the spoon.

Remove from the heat, and stir in the vanilla.

Use to coat Lamingtons.

If the icing gets too thick, add a little water, or return to the heat for a moment or two.
Makes enough to coat about 40 Lamingtons.

Meringues

A standby
stored in an airtight container,
a party piece is always at hand.

4 egg whites

1 cup sugar

¼ teaspoon vanilla essence

Have the egg whites at room temperature. Beat the egg whites lightly in a bowl. Add half the sugar, a little at a time, beating well after each addition. Add remaining sugar and the vanilla. Continue beating until meringue is glossy.

Cover a baking tray with damp greaseproof paper. Using two teaspoons, place the mixture in mounds on the paper. Alternatively, pipe shape preferred. Allow space for the meringues to expand.

Bake at 120 degrees C for 1½ to 2 hours, or until dry. Allow to cool.

Store in an airtight container.

To serve, join the meringues together with flavoured whipped cream.

Suggested flavourings for the cream: A teaspoon of vanilla essence and 1 tablespoon of icing sugar; or ¼ teaspoon of orange or lemon rind and 1 tablespoon of icing sugar; or 1 tablespoon of your favourite liqueur can be added.
Makes 40 small meringues.

Biscuits

Afghans

200 grams butter

½ cup lightly packed brown sugar

1½ cups flour

½ teaspoon baking powder

3 tablespoons cocoa

2 cups cornflakes

Icing:

2 cups icing sugar

4 teaspoons cocoa

Water to mix

Walnut pieces

Cream the butter and sugar until soft and fluffy. Sift the flour, baking powder and cocoa into the creamed mixture, and mix well. Add the cornflakes, and mix in thoroughly.

Using 2 teaspoons, put clumps of the mixture on to a greased oven tray. Bake at 180 degrees C for 15 to 20 minutes.

Ice when cold.

Icing: sift icing sugar and cocoa together, and add sufficient water to form a stiff icing. Top each Afghan with icing and a piece of walnut.
Makes 40.

Choc Malt Refrigerator Biscuits

75 grams butter

¾ cup sugar

1½ teaspoons malt

1 egg

2 cups flour

½ teaspoon baking soda

1 tablespoon cocoa

Cream butter and sugar. Add malt, and beat well. Beat in the egg.

Sift flour, baking soda and cocoa together. Add to creamed mixture. Mix thoroughly.

Roll into two 20 centimetre lengths. Wrap in waxed paper, and leave in refrigerator overnight.

Cut into slices about 1 centimetre thick. Bake at 180 degrees C for about 10 minutes.
Makes about 40.

Melting Moments

(photograph right)

200 grams butter

½ cup icing sugar

½ teaspoon vanilla essence

1 cup flour

1 cup cornflour

½ teaspoon salt

Filling:

1½ cups icing sugar

½ teaspoon vanilla essence

Water

Cream butter and icing sugar until very soft. Add vanilla essence. Sift flour, cornflour and salt into the creamed mixture, and work until a smooth stiff dough is formed.

Pull off pieces of the dough and roll into balls. Place on a greased oven tray, and press with a fork to flatten, or pipe with a large star nozzle.

Bake at 160 degrees C for about 20 minutes. Do not allow the biscuits to colour too much.

When cold, sandwich together with jam or filling.

Filling: Sift the icing sugar, and add the vanilla and sufficient water to form a stiff icing.
Makes 24.

Muesli Squares

75 grams butter

3 tablespoons sugar

1 egg

1 teaspoon vanilla essence

2½ cups muesli

1 cup coconut

Put butter and sugar in a saucepan. Stir over low heat until the butter has melted.

Beat the egg. Stir into the melted butter. Add vanilla essence.

Remove from the heat. Stir in the muesli and coconut. Mix well.

Press the mixture into a lightly greased 18 centimetre square tin. Refrigerate until firm. Cut into small squares. Refrigerate in an airtight container. Serve from refrigerator.
Makes 16.

Iced Refrigerator Biscuits

(photograph below)

175 grams butter

¾ cup brown sugar

2 cups flour

¼ teaspoon salt

Decoration:

150 grams dark cooking chocolate

1 teaspoon white vegetable fat

Finely chopped walnuts

Coconut

Cream butter and brown sugar together until light and fluffy. Sift the flour and salt, and gradually add to creamed mixture to form a firm dough.

Place dough on a lightly floured board, and form into two, 10 centimetre long rolls. Wrap separately in greaseproof paper, and allow to chill for at least 30 minutes until firm or overnight.

Cut rolls into ½ centimetre slices, and place on greased oven trays. Bake at 160 degrees C for 15 to 20 minutes or until pale golden brown.

Cool on a wire rack.

Decoration: Melt chocolate and vegetable fat gently in the top of a double boiler. Remove from heat.

Dip biscuits in chocolate to half-coat them diagonally. Sprinkle them with chopped nuts or coconut.

When chocolate is set, store in an airtight container.

Makes 30.

Orange Jumbles

Biscuit:

100 grams butter

½ cup sweetened condensed milk

1 x 250 gram packet wine biscuits

½ cup coconut

½ cup cornflakes

1 tablespoon orange rind

Icing:

1½ cups icing sugar

1 tablespoon butter

2 teaspoons orange rind

2 tablespoons orange juice

Biscuit: Place butter and sweetened condensed milk into a medium-sized saucepan. Heat over medium heat until butter melts.

Crush wine biscuits into small pieces with a rolling pin. Add, together with coconut, cornflakes and orange rind, to saucepan mixture. Stir until all ingredients are throughly mixed.

Press into a greased 20 by 30 centimetre sponge roll tin. Place in a refrigerator until cold and firm.

Icing: Sift icing sugar into a bowl; add butter and orange rind. Mix to a smooth paste with orange juice.

Spread over base, and allow to set. Cut with a sharp knife into 4 by 6 centimetre pieces.
Makes 25.

Buttered Goods

Devonshire Scones
(photograph right)

This attractive presentation of scones has been adapted from its native Devon to flourish, with homemade jam and thick, whipped, New Zealand cream.

2 cups flour
4 teaspoons baking powder
Pinch salt
75 grams butter
¼ cup sugar
About ¾ cup milk
Butter
Raspberry jam
Whipped cream

Sift flour, baking powder and salt into a bowl. Cut the butter into the dry ingredients, until the mixture is like fine breadcrumbs. Stir in the sugar. Mix in sufficient milk to form a soft dough.

Roll out to about 1.5 centimetre thickness. Cut into circles, using a scone cutter or a floured glass.

Bake at 210 degrees C for 12 to 15 minutes.

Remove from the oven, and wrap the scones in a clean cloth. When cold, butter, spread with jam, and top with whipped cream.
Makes about 12.

Lemon Tea Bread

2 cups flour
¼ teaspoon salt
3 teaspoons baking powder
¾ cup sugar
100 grams butter
1 egg
1 cup milk
1 teaspoon grated lemon rind
2 tablespoons lemon juice
2 tablespoons chopped candied peel

Sift the flour, salt and baking powder together, and mix in the sugar. Cut in the butter until the mixture resembles coarse breadcrumbs.

Beat the egg, and mix with the milk. Add the grated lemon rind and juice and candied peel to the dry ingredients. Make a well in the centre, and mix in the egg and milk mixture. Mix well.

Pour into 2 well-greased 18 centimetre loaf tins, or one 23 centimetre loaf tin. Bake at 190 degrees C for about 35 minutes for the small tins, and about 50 minutes for the larger tin.

Allow to cool completely before cutting.

Fruit Bran Muffins

1 cup flour
½ teaspoon salt
1 teaspoon baking powder
1½ cups bran
¼ cup sugar
½ cup sultanas
1 teaspoon baking soda
1 cup milk
1 tablespoon butter
1 egg
1 tablespoon golden syrup

Sift flour, salt and baking powder together. Stir in the bran, sugar and sultanas.

Dissolve the baking soda in the milk. Melt the butter. Beat the egg lightly. Combine milk, butter, egg and golden syrup.

Make a well in the dry ingredients, and pour in the liquids. Stir to combine ingredients.

Drop spoonfuls into well-greased, deep patty tins. Bake at 200 degrees C for 10 to 12 minutes.
Makes 12.

Savouries

Sausage Rolls

(photograph left)

*Large or small, sausage rolls
find acceptance at any function.*

400 grams flaky pastry
375 grams sausagemeat
½ teaspoon finely chopped sage
¼ teaspoon pepper
Flour
Beaten egg

On a lightly floured board, roll the pastry to an oblong about 45 by 16 centimetres.

Chill while preparing filling.

Blend the sausagemeat with the sage and pepper. On a floured board, roll the sausagemeat to a roll 45 centimetres long. Lay the sausagemeat on one long side of the pastry. Brush the other long side with beaten egg. Carefully roll up the pastry, sealing the edges well.

Brush the surface of the pastry with beaten egg. Cut into 4 to 5 centimetre lengths. Prick each roll with a fork.

Place the rolls on a baking tray. Bake at 220 degrees C for 20 minutes. Lower the temperature to 190 degrees C, and continue cooking for a further 10 minutes to cook the sausagemeat throughout. Serve the rolls hot or cold.
Makes 9 to 12 rolls.

Fish Rolls

1 cut loaf fresh, white or brown bread
Butter
250 grams smoked fish
1 onion
2 tablespoons butter
2 tablespoons flour
¾ cup milk
1 tablespoon chopped parsley
Salt and pepper

Cut the crusts from the bread, and cut into 2, to get slices approximately 8 by 5 centimetres. Butter the bread on one side.

Flake the fish and put aside.

Auckland's Rangitoto Island at dawn.

Finely chop the onion. Melt the butter in a saucepan, add the onion, and cook until clear. Add flour, and when it bubbles, stir in milk, parsley and seasonings. Cook until thick. Add the flaked fish, remove from heat, and cool.

Place a little of the mixture on the unbuttered side of the bread. Roll up, and place on a tray with the join underneath.

Bake at 200 degrees C for 10 to 15 minutes, or until crisp. Serve hot.
Makes 48.

Cheese Twists

1 cup flour
¼ teaspoon curry powder
Pinch mustard
¼ teaspoon salt
1 teaspoon baking powder
50 grams butter
¾ cup grated tasty cheese
1 egg
1 egg yolk
1 teaspoon water
Sea salt or parmesan cheese

Sift flour, curry powder, mustard, salt and baking powder together. Cut in the butter until mixture resembles fine breadcrumbs. Mix in the grated cheese. Lightly beat the egg, and add, mixing to a smooth dough.

Roll cheese pastry out on a lightly floured board, to a 24 centimetre square. Cut pastry into thin strips 12 centimetres long and 1 centimetre wide, using a knife or fluted pastry wheel. Lightly press two pieces together at one end, then, holding the other end of strips, twist the pastry. Place on a greased oven tray, and press ends lightly on to it.

Mix egg yolk with water, and lightly brush the cheese twists. Sprinkle with sea salt or parmesan cheese.

Bake at 190 degrees C for 10 to 15 minutes, or until pale golden.
Makes 24.

Eggs

Salmon Eggs
(photograph right)

6 hard-boiled eggs

½ cup mashed, tinned salmon including liquid

½ teaspoon salt

Generous shake pepper

1 to 2 tablespoons chopped parsley

Slice a thin strip off each hard-boiled egg on 2 sides, and halve the eggs lengthways.

Scoop out the yolks, and mash them, then mix in the salmon and seasonings, until a smooth paste is formed. Add the chopped parsley, and blend well. Pile into the whites.
Makes 12.

Mushroom Eggs
(photograph right)

6 hard-boiled eggs

6 mushrooms

1 tablespoon butter

Salt and pepper to taste

1 to 2 tablespoons top milk

Slice a thin strip of white off two sides of the eggs, then cut the eggs in half lengthways. Scoop the yolks into a bowl, and mash them.

Finely chop the mushrooms. Heat the butter, and fry the mushrooms in it, cooking until the mixture is completely soft.

Blend this and the seasonings into the mashed yolks, and add a little top milk as necessary to get a smooth filling. Pile this into the egg whites.
Makes 12.

Savoury Pink Eggs
(photograph right)

6 hard-boiled eggs

3 tablespoons tomato sauce

¼ cup finely grated cheese

Strips of gherkin

Take a thin slice of white off each end of the egg, then cut the eggs in half.

Put the white trimmings and the yolks through a food mill or sieve, and blend with the sauce and cheese until a smooth paste is formed.

Pipe this into the egg whites, and garnish each with two strips of gherkin.
Makes 12.

A reminder of colonial days — Voss farmhouse near Palmerston North.

Ham Baskets
(photograph right)

6 hard-boiled eggs

½ cup minced ham

½ teaspoon mustard

Freshly ground pepper

1 tablespoon juice from mustard pickles or sweet chutney

1 to 2 tablespoons mayonnaise

2 to 3 stuffed olives

Slice a thin piece of white from both ends of each egg, then halve the egg and scoop out the yolk.

Mash the yolk, and thoroughly blend in the ham, mustard, pepper, chutney and mayonnaise, adjusting the quantity of mayonnaise to get a smooth filling. Pile the filling high above the level of the egg white, and garnish with a slice of stuffed olive.
Makes 12.

Devilled Eggs
(photograph right)

6 hard-boiled eggs

¼ teaspoon salt

Freshly ground pepper

1 tablespoon onion juice

2 tablespoons mayonnaise

2 teaspoons mustard

½ teaspoon curry powder

From the round end of the egg, cut a thin slice of white, so the egg will stand flat. At the other end of the egg, cut off the top leaving a van dyke edge. This should be cut off far enough down to allow the yolk to be eased out of the white.

Mash the yolks with all the remaining ingredients, adding a little more mayonnaise if the mixture is not smooth enough to pipe.

Put the mixture into a forcing bag with a small star nozzle and fill the whites so the mixture flowers above them.
Makes 6.

Picturesque and pleasing, simple or stylish, the versatility of the stuffed egg ensures its place in entertaining of all types, all year round.

Asparagus Pinwheels
(photograph above)

Cooked fresh, or drained tinned asparagus

Salt and pepper

Fresh, thin sliced bread

Soft butter

Mash the asparagus, or puree it in a food processor. Season with salt and pepper.

Roll each slice of bread with a rolling pin to flatten. Butter one side of the bread, and remove the crusts. Spread the buttered side of the bread with a thin layer of the asparagus puree.

Roll the bread up firmly.

Wrap rolls in damp greaseproof paper, and place in the refrigerator until ready to serve.

Before serving, remove from refrigerator, and cut each roll into 1 centimetre thick slices.

Asparagus and Ham Rolls
(photograph left)

Soft butter

Prepared mustard

Fresh, thin sliced bread

Slices of ham

Cooked fresh, or drained, tinned asparagus

Salt and pepper

Butter the bread on one side, and spread with prepared mustard. Remove the crusts, making each piece of bread into a 10 centimetre square. Cut the ham slices to fit, and place on the buttered bread. Cut the asparagus spears into even-sized lengths to fit the bread.

Place 2 to 3 spears diagonally across each bread slice. Season with salt and pepper.

Roll the bread up from one corner to the corner diagonally opposite.

Cover the rolls with a damp cloth until ready to serve.

Asparagus Rolls
(photograph left)

Soft butter

Fresh, thin sliced bread

Cooked fresh, or drained tinned asparagus

Salt and pepper

Butter the bread on one side. Remove the crusts, making each piece of bread into a 10 centimetre square.

Cut the asparagus spears into even-sized lengths to fit the bread. Place 2 to 3 spears, depending on the size, diagonally across each buttered bread slice. Season with salt and pepper.

Roll the bread up from one corner to the corner diagonally opposite.

Cover the rolls with a damp cloth until ready to serve.

Sandwich Fillings
(photograph right)

Club Sandwiches

A. Minced ham and mustard.
   Cottage cheese, crushed pineapple.
B. Mashed tinned green peas.
   Peanut butter and crisp crumbled bacon.
C. Cheese and thin orange slices.
   Chopped celery and walnut.
D. Scrambled egg.
   Butter-fried sliced mushrooms.

Pinwheel Sandwiches

A. Bread spread with lemon butter, then with mashed tinned salmon mixed with cream cheese, fresh herbs and seasonings.
B. Mashed cooked dates with lemon juice spread on bread and topped with finely grated carrot.
C. Apricot jam topped with mashed banana.
D. Mashed avocado, lemon juice, seasonings and chilli sauce.

Single Filling Sandwiches

A. Mashed blue cheese and butter with sliced cucumber.
B. Minced cooked chicken with fresh peach or nectarine slices.
C. Finely chopped dried apricots and cashew nuts.
D. Curried hard boiled egg and desiccated coconut.
E. Mashed baked beans flavoured with chilli sauce. Sliced cheese and shredded lettuce.
F. Minced cooked lamb mixed with sweet chutney and freshly chopped mint.

The sandwich conjures up widely varying images for us all. The lunchbox style; the quick meal; the dagwood or the many shapely afternoon tea sandwiches with delectable fillings.

Tea Parties

Wattle Gateau
(photograph right)

Cake:

250 grams butter

1 cup sugar

4 eggs

2 to 3 drops almond essence

1 teaspoon grated orange rind

2 cups flour

3 teaspoons baking powder

1 cup ground almonds

Butter cream:

1½ cups water

1 cup sugar

6 egg yolks

300 grams butter

1 teaspoon grated orange rind

Decoration:

1 orange

70 grams flaked almonds

2 to 3 tablespoons orange marmalade jelly

2 to 3 tablespoons Grand Marnier

An old-fashioned garden setting at Harworth, New Plymouth.

Cake: Cream the butter and sugar until light and fluffy. Add the eggs one at a time, beating well after each addition. Add the almond essence and grated orange rind.

Sift together the flour and baking powder. Fold in the ground almonds, alternately with the sifted dry ingredients.

Turn into a well-greased 20 centimetre round cake tin. Bake at 170 degrees C for 55 to 60 minutes, or until a skewer inserted comes out clean. Leave to cool completely in the tin before turning out.

Butter Cream: Put the water and sugar in a small saucepan. Bring to the boil, stirring all the time, to dissolve the sugar. Boil steadily, without stirring, until a little of the syrup forms a thread when dropped from the tines of a fork.

Beat the egg yolks in a basin until creamy. Beat the syrup gradually into the yolks, and continue beating until mixture thickens. Allow to cool.

Add softened butter, a little at a time, beating continuously until thick, light and creamy. Beat in the orange rind.

Orange Garnish: Thinly peel slices of peel from an orange, scraping away any of the bitter white pith. Blanch in boiling water for 1 to 2 minutes, then refresh under cold water. Cut into very thin, even-sized shreds.

Almonds: Place the flaked almonds on an oven tray. Bake at 180 degrees C for 5 to 10 minutes, stirring once or twice throughout the cooking time, until an even brown is gained.

To Assemble: Slice the cake into three even layers.

Spread the bottom layer with 2 to 3 tablespoons of the butter cream.

Sandwich the second layer on top. Sprinkle with the Grand Marnier. Spread the orange marmalade jelly evenly to the edges, reserving some for garnish.

Sandwich with the top layer.

Completely cover the cake with the butter cream, reserving about ¼ cup for piping. Place the toasted almonds around the sides of the cake. Pipe a decorative edge around the cake, and a small inner circle. Fill the centre circle with remaining orange marmalade, then decorate with orange shreds.
Serves 12.

Mum's Coffee Cake

(photograph right)

6 eggs

¾ cup sugar

1 cup flour

2 teaspoons baking powder

¼ cup instant coffee powder

2 tablespoons hot water

Butter cream:

100 grams butter

1½ cups icing sugar

About 1 tablespoon instant coffee powder

3 tablespoons boiling water

2 tablespoons coffee liqueur

½ cup chopped walnuts

Icing:

1 cup icing sugar

4 teaspoons warm water

½ cup icing sugar

1 teaspoon instant coffee powder

2 teaspoons boiling water

Beat eggs and sugar until very thick. Test, by lifting the beater from the bowl, and drawing a figure 8 with mixture dropping from the beater. This should hold on top of mixture in the bowl until the 8 is completely formed.

Sift flour and baking powder together. Fold this into the egg mixture.

Dissolve coffee powder in the hot water. Fold into the mixture.

Turn into a greased and floured 22 centimetre cake tin. Bake at 190 degrees C for 40 to 50 minutes.

Leave sponge in the tin for 20 minutes before turning out on to a wire rack to cool.

Butter cream: Cream butter and sugar until light and fluffy.

Dissolve coffee powder in boiling water. Beat into butter and sugar, with coffee liqueur.

Split cake in half. Use about one quarter of butter cream to sandwich the cake together.

Divide the remaining butter cream in half. Spread side of cake with one half.

Roll the side of cake in finely chopped walnuts.

Icing: Sift the first measure of icing sugar. Add warm water, a little at a time, until the mixture is thick enough to coat the back of a spoon. Spread this icing evenly over the top of the cake.

Sift the second measure of icing sugar. Dissolve the instant coffee in boiling water.

Add coffee, a little at a time, until same consistency as previous icing.

Using a plain writing nozzle, pipe coffee icing in a spiral, starting from the centre of the cake.

Before icing has set, using the blunt edge of a knife blade, dipped in warm water, draw about 8 lines from the centre of the spiral to the edge of the icing.

Then, starting from the edge, draw the knife between intersections to the centre of the cake, creating a webbed effect. Using a star nozzle, decorate the edge of the cake with remaining butter icing.

Napoleon Cake

The contrast of pastry and sponge, fruit and cream, make this a delectable party cake.

A piece of sponge about 16 by 20 centimetres

About 500 grams puff pastry

1 cup raspberries

¾ cup cream

1¼ cups icing sugar

Pink colouring

Water

Trim the edges of the sponge neatly.

Roll out the pastry to 2.5 centimetre thickness, then cut two pieces, 2.5 centimetres longer and 2.5 centimetres wider than the piece of sponge.

Place pastry on an oven tray, and prick well with a fork. Bake at 230 degrees C for about 10 minutes, or until golden.

When cold, trim the pastry to fit the sponge exactly. Place the pieces of pastry on a flat surface ready for putting the cake together.

Whip the cream.

Mix the icing sugar with just sufficient water to make a smooth icing. Lift 3 or 4 spoonfuls into another basin. Colour with pink colouring.

Ice the top of one piece of pastry with the white icing, and while it is still moist, dribble some lines across it with the pink icing. Feather these backwards and forwards with a knife to make the pattern.

On the other piece of pastry, spread half of the raspberries, and cover this with a layer of cream. Neatly fit the sponge on to this, and press down gently. Coat the top of the sponge with the remaining cream, and spread the rest of the raspberries over it.

The iced pastry should be set by this time, and it can be easily picked up and placed in position on the sponge. Press gently, and keep in a cool place until wanted.

To serve, cut into slices with a sharp knife.

A symbol of special entertaining, a sign of craft skill, the ever popular brandy snap.

Small Fancy Cakes

Brandy Snaps

(photograph below)

*These scrumptious snaps
are very easy to make,
but require a little time.
They can be filled and eaten,
or used as containers for fruits
and creams
or to garnish special cakes or
desserts.*

75 grams butter

3 tablespoons golden syrup

¼ cup sugar

½ cup flour

1 teaspoon ground ginger

Whipped cream

Put the butter, syrup and sugar in a saucepan, and heat gently until the sugar has dissolved and the butter melted. Leave to cool slightly.

Sift the flour and ginger together, and stir into the melted butter mixture.

Place teaspoonfuls on greased baking trays, spacing well apart to allow room for spreading. A maximum of 4 per tray is recommended. Bake one tray at a time, at 180 degrees C, for 5 to 6 minutes, until golden brown.

Allow to cool briefly. Lift off with a spatula or broad-bladed knife, and roll around wooden spoon handles. When the snaps have hardened, gently slip them off the handles.

Store in an airtight container until ready to use.

When ready to serve, fill with whipped cream. Do this, using a small spoon or a piping bag fitted with a small nozzle, and filling the cream at each end of the snap.
Makes about 24.

Persian Balls

½ cup dates

1 cup dried figs

1 cup sticky raisins

¼ cup crystallised peel

¼ cup crystallised ginger

1 to 2 tablespoons lemon juice

About ¾ cup finely chopped walnuts

Put dates, figs, raisins, peel and ginger through the coarse blade of a mincer. Mix together well. Add lemon juice.

Roll into small balls, and coat in finely chopped walnuts.
Makes about 36

Whisky Balls

2 tablespoons cocoa

1 cup icing sugar

½ cup whisky

2 tablespoons golden syrup

2½ cups crushed wine biscuits

1 cup finely chopped walnuts

4 tablespoons melted butter

Icing sugar

Sift cocoa and sugar together. Mix whisky and golden syrup together. Add biscuit crumbs and chopped nuts. Add melted butter. Mix thoroughly.

Roll into small balls. Coat in icing sugar.
Makes about 45.

White Christmas

2 cups puffed rice breakfast cereal

¼ cup chopped cherries

¼ cup crystallised ginger

¼ cup currants

¼ cup sultanas

1½ cups coconut

1 cup icing sugar

1 cup powdered milk

¼ teaspoon vanilla

300 grams white vegetable fat

Place cereal, cherries, ginger, currants, sultanas, coconut, icing sugar, powdered milk and vanilla in a large mixing bowl.

Melt the vegetable fat over a gentle heat. It should be warm, not hot. Pour the fat on to ingredients in mixing bowl, and mix together well.

Press into a 20 by 30 centimetre sponge roll tin. Refrigerate until set. When set, cut into fingers 5 by 2 centimetres.
Makes 60.

Cream Horns
(photograph below)

250 grams puff pastry

1 egg

3 tablespoons raspberry jam

1 cup whipped cream

8 horn-shaped tins

Icing sugar

Roll the pastry thinly to a strip 60 centimetres long by 10 centimetres wide. Brush the surface all over with lightly beaten egg. Using a sharp knife, cut eight 1 centimetre wide strips from the pastry.

Starting at the tip of a cream horn tin, wind the pastry strips around it, overlapping 2 millimetres, and finishing neatly on the underside. The pastry should not overlap the rim of the tin.

Place the joined side down on a dampened oven tray. Bake at 220 degrees C for 10 to 12 minutes.

Allow to cool on the tins for a few minutes, then carefully twist each tin, and ease the pastry horn off. Allow to cool completely.

Fill the tip of each horn with a little jam. Spoon the cream into a forcing bag fitted with a large rose nozzle. Pipe a swirl of cream into each pastry horn, to meet the jam. Dust each one with a little icing sugar.
Makes 8.

Biscuits and Savouries

Shrimp Rolls

3 tablespoons butter

3 tablespoons flour

Salt

Freshly ground black pepper

1/4 teaspoon mustard

1 cup milk

200 grams shrimps

Butter

10 thin slices white bread

Melt the butter. Stir in the flour, and cook until foaming. Season with salt, freshly ground black pepper and mustard. Gradually add the milk, stirring constantly. Boil for 1 to 2 minutes, or until thick.

Wash and drain the shrimps, then stir into the sauce, and chill.

Butter the bread on one side. Remove the crusts. Spoon a little of the filling mixture along one edge of the buttered side of the bread, and roll it up.

Place with joined edge of bread down. Cover with a damp cloth until served.

Makes 10.

Honey Crunch Biscuits

100 grams butter

1/2 cup sugar

1 tablespoon honey

1 cup flour

1/2 teaspoon baking soda

1 cup cornflakes

Cream butter, sugar and honey together until pale and creamy. Add sifted flour and baking soda, then mix in cornflakes thoroughly. Roll into balls about three centimetres diameter.

Place on greased oven tray. Press lightly with a fork. Bake at 180 degrees C for 15 to 20 minutes, or until golden. Leave to cool on the tray.

Makes about 24.

Rows of roses near Levin.

Pineapple Sausage Pinwheels

Filling:

1 x 227 gram tin crushed pineapple

2 tablespoons finely chopped onion

2 tablespoons chopped parsley

1 egg

Salt

Freshly ground black pepper

350 grams sausagemeat

Scone dough:

1 1/2 cups flour

3 teaspoons baking powder

1/4 teaspoon salt

25 grams butter

1/2 to 3/4 cup milk

Filling: Drain pineapple. Place in a bowl with onion, parsley, egg, salt, pepper and sausagemeat. Mix together thoroughly.

Scone dough: Sift flour, baking powder and salt into a bowl. Cut in butter until the mixture resembles fine breadcrumbs. Add enough milk to give a soft dough.

Roll dough out on a lightly floured board into an 18 by 36 centimetre rectangle. Spread the dough with sausagemeat, filling to within one centimetre of edge. Brush edge with water. Roll up to form a long roll. Cut into 3 centimetre slices.

Place on a lightly floured oven tray. Bake at 190 degrees C for 20 to 25 minutes. Serve hot or cold.

Makes about 14.

Cheese and Almond Biscuits

1 cup flour

1/4 teaspoon salt

100 grams butter

1 tablespoon parmesan cheese

1/4 cup finely grated cheddar cheese

1/4 cup flaked almonds

1 egg

2 teaspoons water

2 tablespoons parmesan cheese

2 tablespoons flaked almonds

Sift flour and salt into a bowl. Cut in butter until the mixture resembles fine breadcrumbs. Add first measure of parmesan, the grated cheddar, and first measure of almonds. Mix well to combine.

Separate off 1 teaspoon of egg white, and reserve.

Beat remaining egg and water together. Stir into the cheese mixture to form a stiff dough.

Chill for about 20 minutes. Roll dough to about 0.5 centimetre thickness.

Using a plain 4.5 centimetre cutter, cut out the biscuits.

Place on a lightly floured oven tray. Brush each biscuit with reserved egg white. Sprinkle with a little parmesan and a few flaked almonds from second measures of these.

Bake at 180 degrees C for 20 minutes.

Makes about 30 biscuits.

FRESH BAKED

The need to be a competent baker arose in our early settling times, and included not only the yeast goods, but also the many quickly made scones, gems, muffins, and loaves, so popular for the men in the fields when 'smoko' was called.

This tradition has continued, especially in the country, but for many city dwellers, despite the nearby bakery and cake shop, pride is taken in being able to 'knock up a batch of scones' to welcome friends or serve for lunch.

The New Zealand women needed to bake, for provisioning and for the satisfaction they gained from achieving a high standard of skill.

Captions to preceding 4 pages.

Page 134/135: Crowds gather for the Royal A & P Show at Addington racecourse, Christchurch. (photograph Peter Morath).

Page 136/137: Freshly baked muffins, gems and shortbread displayed in the kitchen of Alberton, the Kerr-Taylor home of last century and now an Historic Places Trust Building.

Facing page: Harvesting grain at Culverden, North Canterbury. (photograph Peter Morath).

Buttered Goods

Oatcakes
(photograph left)

50 grams lard

1 cup hot water

3 cups medium oatmeal

½ teaspoon baking soda

½ teaspoon salt

Oatmeal for rolling out

Heat lard and water together in a small saucepan. Mix the oatmeal, baking soda and salt together in a bowl. Bring lard and water to the boil and stir into the oatmeal, using knife at first, and then bringing the mixture together with the hand.

Dust a board with oatmeal. Turn out the mixture, and before it cools, roll out to 3 to 4 millimetre thickness. Using a 7 centimetre round cutter cut out rounds.

Cook on a moderately hot ungreased griddle. Turn when sufficiently set to lift easily. Keep turning over until well crisped and lightly browned — about 30 to 40 minutes. Finish off by standing the oatcakes on edge on griddle. To use mixture left over after cutting out rounds, add a little more hot water and lard to mix again to a workable dough. Roll out as before.

Store in an airtight container. Serve buttered.
Makes about 28.

Pikelets
(photograph left)

1 cup flour

¼ teaspoon salt

1 teaspoon cream of tartar

½ teaspoon baking soda

1 tablespoon sugar

1 egg

1 tablespoon golden syrup

½ cup milk

2 to 3 tablespoons milk

Sift flour, salt, cream of tartar and baking soda into a bowl. Stir in sugar. Make a well in the centre of the dry ingredients, and add unbeaten egg and golden syrup. Using a knife, stir until ingredients are just combined. Carefully add first measure of milk. Stir in enough of the second measure of milk to form a batter that will drop easily from a spoon.

Very lightly grease a heavy frying pan or griddle, and heat over moderate heat. Drop tablespoonfuls of the mixture on to the greased surface. When bubbles form and break on the surfaces, turn the pikelets and cook on the other side. As pikelets are cooked, place them in a folded teatowel while cooking the remainder.
Makes about 24.

Welsh Cakes
(photograph left)

1½ cups flour

½ teaspoon baking powder

Pinch salt

25 grams lard

50 grams butter

6 tablespoons sugar

½ cup currants

½ teaspoon mixed spice

1 egg

2 tablespoons milk

Sift flour, baking powder and salt into a bowl. Cut in lard and butter until mixture resembles fine breadcrumbs. Add sugar, currants and mixed spice.

Beat egg, and add it with the milk to make a firm dough. Roll out dough on a lightly floured board to 1.5 centimetre thickness. Cut into rounds, using an 8 centimetre cutter.

Cook on a hot, greased griddle for about 5 minutes on each side, or until lightly browned.

Serve hot or cold.
Makes about 8.

Potato Scones

¾ cup mashed potato

1 tablespoon butter

About ½ cup flour

Salt to taste

It is best to have the potatoes still warm, but dry. Mix in the butter well. Work in the flour to make a soft, dry consistency. Add salt to taste.

Turn on to a lightly floured board, and knead lightly. Roll into a large thin circle of about 3 millimetre thickness. Cut into rounds, about 10 centimetres across, or divide circle into 8 segments.

Heat a girdle or heavy frying pan until fairly hot. Cook the scones for 2 to 3 minutes each side.

Cool in a clean teatowel, or eat hot with butter. These scones are best eaten fresh or reheated.
Makes 8 scones.

Oat Scones

1¼ cups flour

½ teaspoon baking soda

¾ teaspoon cream of tartar

1 teaspoon sugar

¼ teaspoon salt

½ cup oatmeal

25 grams lard or butter

About ½ cup sour milk or milk

Sift the flour into a bowl with the baking soda, cream of tartar, sugar and salt. Stir in the oatmeal. Cut in the lard or butter, until the mixture resembles fine breadcrumbs. Stir in the sour milk or milk, to make a soft, elastic dough.

Turn on to a lightly floured board, and knead lightly. Pat into a 1½ centimetre thick round. Cut into 4 with a floured knife.

Heat a girdle or heavy frying pan until fairly hot. Cook the scones for 5 to 7 minutes each side. Serve warm.
Serves 4.

Wholemeal Honey Scones

1 cup wholemeal flour

1 cup white flour

4 teaspoons baking powder

½ teaspoon salt

2 tablespoons butter

¼ cup honey

About ¼ cup milk

Sift wholemeal and white flour, baking powder and salt. Melt butter and honey together. Add milk, and mix with the dry ingredients to an easily handled dough.

Roll or press on a lightly floured board to 2 centimetre thickness. Cut in squares.

Bake on cold, ungreased oven tray at 220 degrees C for 10 minutes.
Makes 12 honey-flavoured scones.

Ginger Gems

(photograph page 136)
*Gems are a quick cooking item,
depending for their name
on the shape of the irons
in which they are cooked.
They have been retained
as part of our cooking heritage
from colonial days.*

½ cup golden syrup

100 grams butter

1 egg

½ cup sugar

2 cups flour

1 teaspoon baking powder

½ teaspoon salt

1 teaspoon cinnamon

1 teaspoon ground ginger

½ cup milk

1½ teaspoons baking soda

2 tablespoons hot water

Butter for irons

Preheat the gem irons in a 220 degree C oven.

Melt the golden syrup and butter, and allow to cool. Beat the egg and sugar until thick. Sift together the flour, baking powder, salt, cinnamon and ginger. Mix into the egg and sugar, alternately with the golden syrup and butter. Stir in the milk.

Dissolve the baking soda in the hot water, and stir in last.

Take the gem irons from the oven, and stand on a heat-proof surface. Place a small piece of butter in each iron. Spoon in the mixture to three-quarters fill each iron.

Bake at 220 degrees C for about 15 minutes, or until cooked.

Tip gems out on to a cloth, and wrap up. Repeat with remaining mixture.
Makes 24.

Banana Wholemeal Gems

1 cup flour

3 teaspoons baking powder

½ teaspoon salt

2 tablespoons sugar

1 cup wholemeal flour

1 egg

½ cup milk

3 tablespoons honey

25 grams butter

1 cup mashed banana

Butter for irons

Preheat the gem irons in a 220 degree C oven.

Sift the flour, baking powder and salt into a bowl. Stir in the sugar and wholemeal flour.

Beat the egg and milk together. Melt the honey and butter.

Add the mashed banana to the dry ingredients, then pour in the egg, milk, honey and butter all at once. Stir until blended, but do not stir too much.

Remove the preheated gem irons from the oven, and stand on a board. Put a small piece of butter in each iron. Spoon in the mixture to almost fill the irons.

Bake at 220 degrees C for about 15 minutes, or until they are well risen and golden brown.

Turn gems out of irons on to a cloth. Put more butter into irons before cooking the remaining batter.
Makes 20 to 24.

Butter Beer Muffins

*A useful way of using up
any left over beer.*

1 cup flour

¼ teaspoon salt

1½ teaspoons baking powder

3 tablespoons sugar

75 grams butter

1 egg

½ cup beer

Sift flour, salt and baking powder into a bowl. Add sugar. Melt butter, and cool. Beat egg lightly, and mix with the beer and cooled butter. Stir the liquid into the dry ingredients, until all is dampened.

Spoon into well-greased muffin tins to about two thirds full. Bake at 200 degrees C for about 15 minutes.

Can be served unbuttered if wished.
Makes 9.

Peanut Butter Muffins

2 cups flour

3 teaspoons baking powder

1 teaspoon salt

¼ cup sugar

½ cup peanut butter

½ cup chopped raisins

1 egg

1 cup milk

Sift the flour, baking powder and salt together, and stir in the sugar. Cut the peanut butter into the dry mixture, until it resembles coarse breadcrumbs. Stir in the chopped raisins.

Beat the egg well. Add the milk to the beaten egg, and stir into the other mixture, until the flour is just moistened.

Half-fill well-greased patty tins. Bake at 200 degrees C for about 15 minutes.
Makes 24.

Bran Muffins

(photograph page 137)

1 cup flour

½ teaspoon salt

1 teaspoon baking powder

1½ cups bran

¼ cup sugar

1 teaspoon baking soda

1 cup milk

1 egg

1 tablespoon melted butter

1 tablespoon golden syrup

Sift flour, salt and baking powder into a bowl. Stir in bran and sugar.

Dissolve the baking soda in the milk. Lightly beat the egg. Mix the milk, egg, butter and golden syrup together.

Make a well in the centre of the dry ingredients, and pour in the liquid. Stir until just mixed.

Three-quarters fill greased patty pans with the mixture. Bake at 200 degrees C for 10 to 12 minutes.
Makes 12.

Cakes

Orange Sultana Cake

2 cups flour

4 teaspoons baking powder

Pinch salt

100 grams butter

½ cup sugar

1 cup sultanas

3 tablespoons orange rind

2 eggs

2 tablespoons milk

Sift flour, baking powder and salt together. Cut in the butter until the mixture resembles fine breadcrumbs.

Mix together sugar, sultanas and orange rind. Add to flour mixture. Beat eggs and milk together, then add them, mixing to a soft dropping consistency.

Grease and line a 15 centimetre square cake tin. Spoon the mixture in. Bake at 180 degrees C for 45 minutes, or until cake springs back when lightly touched.

Lemon Date Cake

100 grams butter

½ cup sugar

½ cup brown sugar, firmly packed

2 eggs

2 cups flour

2 teaspoons baking soda

1 average-sized lemon

1 cup stoned dates

1 cup sour cream

Icing:

50 grams butter

2 tablespoons lemon juice

2 teaspoons vanilla

About 4 cups icing sugar

Finely grated lemon rind

Cream the butter and white and brown sugars together, until light and fluffy. Beat the eggs, and add to the creamed mixture, a little at a time, beating well.

Sift the flour and baking soda together.

Trim the ends from the lemon, then cut it into pieces, and remove any pips. Put it in a blender, food processor or mincer, and process until a fine, ground mass is formed. Add the dates, and process or mince well. Mix about half of the flour evenly through this lemon-date mixture.

Fold the remaining flour and the fruit mixture alternately into the creamed mixture. Carefully mix in the sour cream.

Spread the cake batter between 2 greased, paper lined and floured 20 centimetre sponge tins. Bake at 180 degrees C for about 35 minutes.

Allow to cool completely before filling.

Icing: Melt the butter, add the lemon juice and vanilla. Stir in sifted icing sugar until a thick, spreadable icing is formed.

Put a layer of this between the two cakes and decorate the top and sides with the remaining icing.

Scatter finely grated lemon rind over the top of the cake.

Marble Cake

175 grams butter

¾ cup sugar

3 eggs

2 cups flour

2 teaspoons baking powder

¼ teaspoon salt

¼ to ½ cup milk

½ teaspoon lemon essence

4 teaspoons cocoa

1 tablespoon water

½ teaspoon vanilla

Few drops red food colouring

½ teaspoon raspberry essence

Glace Icing:

¾ cup icing sugar

¼ teaspoon vanilla

1 to 2 tablespoons water

Prepare a 23 centimetre diameter guglhupf mould by creaming about 1 teaspoon each of butter and flour together to a paste. Using fingers, spread this over the inside of all the shaping in the mould.

Cream butter and sugar until light and fluffy. Add eggs one at a time, beating well after each addition. Sift together flour, baking powder and salt. Add sifted dry ingredients alternately with milk.

Divide the mixture into 3 equal parts.

Add lemon essence to one part, mixing well.

Mix cocoa, water and vanilla into the second part, to make it brown.

Colour the third part pink with red food colouring. Flavour it with raspberry essence.

Place spoonfuls into mould, alternating colours. Draw a knife through the mixture in a circular motion to merge the colours a little.

Bake at 180 degrees C for about 1 hour. Allow to stand in mould for 10 to 15 minutes before turning out on to a wire rack to cool.

When cold, sprinkle with icing sugar or ice with glace icing.

Glace Icing: Place icing sugar and vanilla in a small bowl. Add water gradually. Mix to a smooth, thin consistency, suitable for drizzling over cake.

Gingerbread

A plain cake which has been the mainstay of everyday cooking since early settlement times.

75 grams butter

½ cup brown sugar

¾ teaspoon baking soda

¾ cup milk

1½ cups flour

1½ teaspoons mixed spice

1½ teaspoons ground ginger

½ cup golden syrup

Cream butter and sugar until pale and fluffy. Dissolve baking soda in milk. Add to creamed mixture. Sift flour, spice and ginger together. Fold into the creamed mixture. Warm the golden syrup over low heat. Gently stir into the cake batter.

Pour into a greased 10 by 20 centimetre loaf tin. Bake at 160 to 180 degrees C for about 1 hour.

Leave gingerbread in the tin for 15 minutes, before turning out on to a wire rack to cool.

Wholemeal Spice Cake

75 grams butter

¼ cup honey

2 cups wholemeal flour

½ teaspoon salt

1 teaspoon mixed spice

½ teaspoon cinnamon

¼ cup sugar

¾ cup mixed dried fruit

¾ cup milk

1 teaspoon baking soda

1 tablespoon vinegar

Place the butter and honey in a saucepan, and warm together until melted. Cool.

In a large bowl, combine the wholemeal flour, salt, mixed spice, cinnamon, sugar and dried fruit. Make a well in the centre. Add the butter and honey mixture to form a thick batter.

Dissolve baking soda in milk. Add gradually to the mixture. Lastly, stir in the vinegar.

Quickly turn into a 20 centimetre square greased and paper-lined shallow tin. Bake at 180 degrees C for 35 to 45 mintues. Cool in the tin, about 15 minutes, before turning out on to a rack to finish cooling.

Bran Cake

100 grams butter

¼ cup brown sugar

1 egg

½ cup golden syrup

1½ cups flour

½ teaspoon baking powder

1 teaspoon baking soda

½ teaspoon salt

½ teaspoon ginger

1½ teaspoons cinnamon

½ teaspoon freshly grated nutmeg

1 cup bran

½ cup sour milk

Haymaking on a Wairarapa farm.

Cream the butter and sugar until pale and fluffy. Beat in the egg, and then the golden syrup.

Sift the flour, baking powder, baking soda, salt, ginger, cinnamon and nutmeg together. Stir in the bran. Add to the creamed mixture, alternately with the sour milk.

Turn into a greased 20 centimetre square cake tin. Bake at 180 degrees C for about an hour.

Note: If sour milk is not available, add about a teaspoon of lemon juice or vinegar to fresh milk, and leave 10 to 15 minutes.

Coconut Cake

125 grams butter

½ cup sugar

3 eggs

1 cup flour

1 teaspoon baking powder

½ teaspoon salt

1 to 2 tablespoons milk

1 teaspoon vanilla

3 tablespoons jam

½ cup sugar

1 teaspoon cornflour

1½ cups coconut

Cream butter and first measure of sugar until light and fluffy. Separate eggs. Beat the yolks into the creamed mixture.

Sift flour, baking powder and salt. Mix together the milk and vanilla.

Add the flour and liquid alternately to the creamed mixture.

Turn into a greased and lined 20 centimetre square cake tin. If available, a loose-bottom tin makes the cake easier to remove.

Spread warm jam over the cake mixture.

Beat egg whites until stiff. Gradually beat in the second measure of sugar. Mix cornflour and coconut together. Fold into the meringue mixture. Spread evenly over the batter in the tin.

Bake at 160 degrees C for 45 to 50 minutes, until lightly browned on top and the cake is coming away from the edges of the tin.

Stand in tin for 10 minutes, before lifting out with the aid of the paper lining or loose bottom. Do not turn the cake upside down. Cool on a wire rack.

Sultana Cake

2½ cups sultanas

Water

225 grams butter

3 eggs

1¼ cups sugar

2½ cups flour

1 teaspoon baking powder

1 teaspoon almond essence

Line a 22 centimetre square cake tin with 2 thicknesses of brown paper and 1 thickness of greased, grease-proof paper.

Place sultanas in a saucepan, along with sufficient water to cover. Boil 8 minutes. Drain. Cut butter into the hot sultanas.

Beat eggs and sugar until creamy. Add to sultanas and butter. Sift in the flour and baking powder. Add essence. Mix well, and turn into the prepared tin.

Bake at 160 degrees C for 1¾ hours. Cool in the tin.

Shortbread
(photograph page 136)
*One of the many variations
on the traditional
Scottish Shortbread which is now
as much a part of
New Zealand cooking
as in its original homeland.*

125 grams butter

½ cup icing sugar

1 cup flour

4 tablespoons cornflour

¼ teaspoon salt

Cream the butter and icing sugar until light and fluffy. Sift the flour, cornflour and salt together, and mix into the creamed mixture.

Knead well, and shape into 2 balls. Place each ball on a tray, and pat out to a circle about 1 centimetre thick. Pinch the edges, prick the surface with a fork, and mark each round into 8 pieces.

Bake at 170 degrees C for 15 to 20 minutes.
Makes 16 pieces.

Loaves

Date Tea Loaf

3 cups flour

6 teaspoons baking powder

½ teaspoon mixed spice

50 grams butter

1 cup dates

½ cup sugar

1 tablespoon golden syrup

½ cup water

1 egg

Sift flour, baking powder and mixed spice together. Cut in the butter until the mixture resembles fine breadcrumbs. Finely chop the dates, and stir into the mixture with the sugar.

Mix together golden syrup, water and egg. Pour into the cake mixture. Mix thoroughly.

Grease and line an 18 centimetre loaf tin. Spoon the mixture in. Bake in centre of oven at 180 degrees C for 1½ hours, or until the loaf is firm to touch.

Serve buttered.

Harvest Loaf

(photograph above)

1 large onion

50 grams butter

3 cups flour

2 tablespoons baking powder

½ teaspoon salt

Pinch cayenne pepper

About 1 cup milk

½ cup sour cream

½ cup grated tasty cheese

Chop the onion finely, and fry in the hot butter in a pan. Do not let it colour; just allow it to become transparent.

Into a bowl, sift the flour, baking powder, salt and cayenne. Stir the cooked onion and any remaining melted butter into the flour mixture. Add sufficient milk to form a soft, but manageable, dough. When this is mixed, lightly knead the dough a few times on a floured board.

Have greased ten an 18 centimetre round cake tin.

Cut the dough into 12 even-sized pieces. Roll each piece lightly into a ball, and place, almost touching, in the greased cake tin. Mix the sour cream and grated cheese together, and carefully spoon this over the top of the loaf.

Bake at 200 degrees C for about 30 minutes, or until the mixture is risen and golden. Take from the oven, and allow to rest in the tin for a few minutes before removing carefully.

When ready to serve, pull portions of the dough off the whole loaf.

Brunch Bread

1 cup wholemeal flour

2 cups white flour

5 teaspoons baking powder

¼ teaspoon salt

Pinch cayenne pepper

50 grams butter

1 cup milk

Cold water

Topping:

½ cup grated tasty cheese

2 teaspoons poppy seeds

1 tablespoon butter

Pinch cayenne pepper

Place the wholemeal flour in a bowl, then sift in the flour, baking powder and salt. Cut in the butter until the mixture is the consistency of fine breadcrumbs. Mix to a stiff dough with the milk and as much water as is required.

Turn on to a lightly floured board, and knead a few times to get a uniform dough. Shape into a round about 20 centimetres in diameter, but do not flatten too much. Place on an oven tray.

Topping: Mash the cheese, poppy seeds, butter and cayenne together well, and spread over the top of the bread.

Bake at 220 degrees C for about 12 minutes, then lower the temperature to 200 degrees C, and cook a further 10 to 12 minutes.

Serve warm or cold. If warm, tear off pieces rather than slicing them. Butter as for scones.
Serves 6 to 8.

Coffee Date Loaf

2 cups flour

4 teaspoons baking powder

1 teaspoon salt

½ cup sugar

¼ cup chopped walnuts

¾ cup chopped dates

2 teaspoons instant coffee

1 cup cold water

Pinch baking soda

1 egg

2 tablespoons melted butter

Sift the flour, baking powder and salt into a bowl, and add the sugar. Stir in the chopped nuts and dates.

Blend the coffee in the water. Add baking soda. Beat the egg well, and mix with the coffee. Stir in the melted butter.

Pour the liquid into the flour, and stir until the mixture is just dampened. Do not over-stir. Turn into a greased 10 by 20 centimetre loaf tin.

Bake at 190 degrees C for about 1 hour. Leave to cool on a rack.

Best kept a day before cutting.

Savoury Loaf

| 1 onion |
| 2 rashers bacon |
| 1 tablespoon butter |
| 2½ cups flour |
| 5 teaspoons baking powder |
| ½ teaspoon salt |
| 25 grams butter |
| ½ cup grated tasty cheese |
| 3 tablespoons chopped parsley |
| 1 egg |
| About 1 cup milk |

Peel and finely chop onion. Remove rind from bacon, and chop it finely.

Heat first measure of butter in a small saucepan. Add onion and bacon, and cook for 3 to 4 minutes or until onion is soft. Remove from heat, and set aside.

Sift flour, baking powder and salt into a bowl. Cut in second measure of butter until mixture resembles fine breadcrumbs. Add onion, bacon, cheese and parsley. Add lightly beaten egg and enough milk to give a soft dough. Turn mixture into a greased rib tin.

Bake at 190 degrees C for about 45 minutes.
Makes 1 loaf.

Parsley Loaf

(photograph above)

| 1 onion |
| 2 rashers bacon |
| 2 teaspoons butter |
| 2½ cups flour |
| 5 teaspoons baking powder |
| ½ teaspoon salt |
| 25 grams butter |
| ½ cup grated cheese |
| 3 tablespoons chopped parsley |
| 1 egg |
| About 1 cup milk |

Peel and finely chop onion. Remove rind from bacon, and chop finely.

Heat first measure of butter in a small saucepan. Add onion and bacon, and cook for 3 to 4 minutes, or until onion is soft. Remove, and set aside.

Sift flour, baking powder and salt into a bowl. Cut in second measure of butter, until mixture resembles fine breadcrumbs. Add onion, bacon, cheese and parsley. Add lightly beaten egg, and enough milk to give a soft dough.

Turn mixture into a greased rib mould. Bake at 190 degrees C for about 45 minutes.
Makes 1 loaf.

Fruit Tea Loaf

(photograph above)

| 2 cups flour |
| 2 teaspoons baking powder |
| ¼ teaspoon salt |
| 25 grams butter |
| 1 cup mixed dried fruit |
| 2 tablespoons sugar |
| 1 egg |
| About ½ cup milk |

Cherry Icing:

| 3 tablespoons icing sugar |
| 1 teaspoon water |
| 2 to 3 drops cherry essence |
| 2 to 3 drops red food colouring |
| 2 cherries |

Sift the flour, baking powder and salt into a bowl. Cut in the butter until the mixture resembles coarse breadcrumbs. Add the mixed dried fruit and sugar, and mix through.

Beat the egg until light and fluffy, and beat in the milk. Add to the dry ingredients, and mix to a soft dough.

Shape into a roll, and place on a greased oven tray. Bake at 190 degrees C for 20 to 30 minutes.

Spread with cherry icing, and sprinkle with chopped cherries.

Cherry Icing: Mix the icing sugar, water, cherry essence and colouring together to make a thin icing.

Chop the cherries into small pieces.

Yeast Baking

Savoury Tea Ring

½ cup milk
½ cup water
1 teaspoon salt
1 tablespoon sugar
50 grams butter
1 tablespoon dried yeast
3 to 3½ cups flour

Filling:

1 medium onion
25 grams butter
Shake pepper
Chopped parsley

Glaze:

1 egg yolk
2 tablespoons cold water

Scald the milk and water together, and pour over the salt, sugar and butter in a large bowl. Allow to cool to lukewarm. Sprinkle the yeast into the milk mixture. Leave to froth.

Add half the sifted flour, and beat well to form a smooth batter. Add the remaining sifted flour, until the dough is soft and able to be handled. Knead until smooth and elastic, then put into a greased bowl and brush the top of the dough with melted butter.

Cover, and set aside in a warm place to rise.

Filling: Chop the onion finely. Heat the butter in a pan, and fry the onion in it until it is tender, but not coloured. Stir in the pepper and parsley. Set aside to cool.

When the dough has doubled its bulk, knead again until it is elastic, then roll out to a rectangle 20 by 38 centimetres. Spread the onion filling over the dough, leaving a gap on the long edges of about 1 centimetre.

Roll up the dough, starting on the long side. Seal the edge. Turn the roll to form a circle, and seal the join. Place this on an oven tray, then cut with scissors at regular intervals of 2.5 centimetres. Lift and turn each section to lie cut side up. Mix the egg yolk and water, and brush over the ring.

Bake at 200 degrees C for about 25 minutes.

Cinnamon Buns

¼ cup lukewarm water
1 tablespoon dried yeast
50 grams butter
½ cup sour milk
1 egg
2½ to 3 cups flour
¼ cup sugar
1 teaspoon baking powder
¾ teaspoon salt
About 50 grams soft butter
2 tablespoons brown sugar
¼ teaspoon cinnamon
¼ teaspoon nutmeg
¼ cup finely chopped walnuts

Icing:

¾ cup icing sugar
Milk

Put the water into a large electric mixer bowl. Sprinkle the yeast over, and let stand until it is frothy.

Melt the first measure of butter. Add the sour milk, egg, and one cup of the flour with the butter, sugar, baking powder and salt to the yeast mixture. Beat 2 minutes at medium speed, scraping the sides of the bowl frequently. Stir in enough of the remaining flour to make the dough easy to handle, soft and slightly sticky.

Turn on to a floured board, and knead until springy and smooth. Use the remainder of the measured flour as necessary while kneading.

Roll the dough into a 27 by 22 centimetre rectangle. Spread with softened butter. Combine the brown sugar, cinnamon, nutmeg and chopped nuts, and sprinkle over the butter.

Loosen the rectangle from the board with a metal slice. Roll up from the long end. Cut into 9 equal parts with a piece of string. Place the slices sideways at equal intervals in a greased 20 centimetre cake tin.

Cover, leave in warm place, and let rise until double in bulk.

Bake at 200 degrees C for 25 to 30 minutes, or until cooked.

Cool in the tin for 5 minutes. Loosen the sides, and turn out. Invert on to a wire rack, and ice while still warm.

Icing: Put the icing sugar into a small bowl. Mix in enough milk to make a runny icing. Drizzle over the warm buns.
Makes 9.

No Knead Cheese Loaf

25 grams butter
1 tablespoon sugar
1½ teaspoons salt
Pinch cayenne pepper
1 cup water
1 tablespoon dried yeast
1 cup grated tasty cheese
1½ tablespoons poppy seeds
2½ cups flour
Melted butter

Put the butter, sugar, salt and cayenne pepper into a large bowl. Bring the water to the boil and pour over the butter mixture. Stir until the butter melts. Cool to lukewarm.

Add the yeast, and allow to stand until frothy.

Stir in the cheese, poppy seeds and 1½ cups of the flour, mixing until smooth. Beat with an electric mixer, food processor or a wooden spoon for 2 to 3 minutes, scraping the sides of the bowl frequently. Stir in the remaining flour to make a sticky dough.

Cover the bowl, and leave to rise in a warm place until double in bulk.

Stir down the batter by beating with a wooden spoon. Spread into a greased 18 by 10 centimetre loaf tin. Smooth the top, and sprinkle with poppy seeds. Cover, and let rise until double in bulk.

Bake at 200 degrees C for 10 minutes. Lower the heat to 190 degrees C for 30 to 35 minutes, or until the bread sounds hollow when tapped. Brush the top of the bread with melted butter. Leave in the tin for about 15 minutes before turning out.
Makes 1 loaf.

Grain harvesting at Methven, Canterbury.

Coffee Flavoured Coffee Cake

This coffee cake is coffee flavoured in contrast to the usual coffee cakes which are meant to be served fresh with coffee.

¼ cup sugar

¼ teaspoon salt

25 grams butter

½ cup milk

¼ cup water

1 egg

2 teaspoons dried yeast

3 to 4 cups flour

75 grams butter

¾ cup sugar

1½ tablespoons instant coffee powder

Put the sugar, salt and first measure of butter into a large mixing bowl.

Scald the milk and water. Remove from heat, and pour over the butter. Stir until most of the butter melts. Beat in the egg with a rotary beater.

Sprinkle the yeast over the lukewarm mixture, and leave in the bowl, covered, in a warm place until the yeast is frothy.

Beat in half of the sifted flour. Stir in enough of the remaining flour to make a soft dough, that is not sticky.

Turn on to a lightly floured board. Using some of the flour that remains, knead the dough until it is smooth and elastic.

Put into a greased bowl, and turn over. Cover, and leave in a warm place until double in bulk.

Punch down, then turn onto a floured board. Knead for only a few minutes.

Shape into a 30 centimetre roll, and cut into 26 even pieces. Roll the pieces with floured hands into small balls. Roll the balls in the melted butter, then in the combined sugar and coffee powder.

Grease a 20 centimetre ring tin. Place 17 of the balls around the outside edge of the tin, pressing to fit. Place the remaining 9 balls around the inside of the tin. Drizzle any remaining butter over the top.

Cover, and leave to rise in a warm place until double in size.

Bake at 200 degrees C for 30 to 35 minutes.

Cool for a few minutes in the tin. Loosen the sides, and turn out. Invert on to a serving plate.

To serve, break the pieces apart.

Canterbury Wheatfields.

Raisin Muffins

1 cup warm water

¼ cup sugar

1½ tablespoons dried yeast

1 egg

3 cups flour

1 teaspoon salt

4 tablespoons oil

1 cup raisins

Put the warm water and sugar in an electric mixer bowl, and sprinkle on the yeast. Leave for about 10 minutes, or until frothy. Beat the egg, and add.

Sift the flour and salt twice. Add half the flour and the oil to the yeast liquid. Beat with a dough hook, about 5 minutes, or until very smooth. Add remaining flour, and beat well for another 5 minutes until smooth and elastic.

Cover, and leave to rise in a warm place until double in bulk, about 30 minutes. Mix in the raisins.

Drop spoonfuls into greased patty tins to half fill. Leave to rise in a warm place, about 10 minutes, until almost double.

Bake at 200 degrees C for 15 minutes.

Makes 24.

Hot Cross Buns

(photograph right)

*The Hot Cross Bun
has a long history,
and has had many changes
and adaptations from its original
oval crib shape,
to the round one.
It is traditionally spiced,
and contains dried fruit.
It bears a cross either of dough,
or more simply, prepared icing.
The cross was believed
to ward off evil.
It is a sad reflection
that in recent times,
Hot Cross Buns have
been available for several weeks
before Easter,
whereas only a few years ago,
they were eaten only
at the Easter festival.*

1¼ cups milk

¼ cup sugar

1½ tablespoons dried yeast

4¼ cups flour

½ teaspoon salt

1 teaspoon cinnamon

½ teaspoon mixed spice

¼ teaspoon ground cloves

2 eggs

25 grams melted butter

1 cup sultanas

½ cup currants

¼ cup chopped peel

2 tablespoons chopped preserved ginger

Crosses:

½ cup flour

1 tablespoon melted butter

About 5 tablespoons water

Glaze:

1 tablespoon sugar

1 tablespoon milk

Heat milk to scalding point. Remove from heat, add sugar, and stir to dissolve. Cool to lukewarm. Sprinkle on yeast, and leave in a warm place for about 10 minutes, until frothy.

Into a bowl, sift together flour, salt, cinnamon, mixed spice and ground

cloves. Place half the flour mixture in another bowl. Make a well in the centre.

Beat eggs lightly. Pour yeast mixture, eggs and melted butter into the well. Beat with a wooden spoon. Add sultanas, currants, peel and ginger. Gradually mix in the rest of the flour to form a soft dough. Turn on to a floured board, and knead the dough until smooth.

Place in a greased bowl, turning mixture over to grease the top of the dough. Cover with a damp cloth. Put in a warm place to rise until double in bulk — about 1 hour.

Turn out on to a floured board, and knead lightly.

Divide into 24 even-sized pieces, and shape into balls. Place slightly apart on greased oven tray. Cover, and leave to rise again until doubled in size.

Dough for crosses: Sift flour, and stir in melted butter with enough water for dough to be piped. Using a fine nozzle, pipe crosses on each risen bun.

Bake buns at 220 degrees C for 25 to 30 minutes.

Glaze: Mix the milk and sugar together, and brush over buns about 5 minutes before baking is complete.
Makes 24.

The traditional baking for Easter, Simnel Cake (p170) and Hot Cross Buns.

Wholemeal Bread

¼ cup warm water

1½ tablespoons dried yeast

1 cup plain flour

1½ teaspoons salt

1 cup warm milk

1 tablespoon sugar

1½ cups wholemeal flour

Beaten egg

Place the warm water in a bowl. Sprinkle on the yeast, and leave in a warm place for 10 minutes or until frothy.

Sift the plain flour and salt into a large bowl. Make a well in the centre. Add the yeast liquid, milk and sugar. Beat well until smooth. Stir in the wholemeal flour.

Place in a greased bowl, cover with a cloth, and leave to rise in a warm place, until double in bulk, about 30 to 40 minutes.

Turn into a greased 6 cup loaf tin. Brush with beaten egg. Bake at 200 degrees C for 40 minutes.
Makes 1 loaf.

Basic Sweet Dough

50 grams butter
½ teaspoon salt
¼ cup sugar
1 cup milk
1½ tablespoons dried yeast
1 egg
About 3½ cups flour
Melted butter or oil

Put butter, salt and sugar into a large mixing bowl. Heat the milk until almost boiling. Pour the milk on to the ingredients in the mixing bowl. Stir until the butter melts and sugar dissolves. Leave until it cools to lukewarm. Sprinkle on the yeast, and leave in a warm place until frothy.

Lightly beat the egg, and add to the bowl. Gradually add 3 cups of sifted measured flour, beating until incorporated. Add more flour if necessary to make a smooth dough.

Lightly knead, then return to the bowl. Brush with a little melted butter or oil. Cover with plastic wrap. Leave in a warm place until doubled in bulk.

Punch dough down, and turn on to a lightly floured surface. Knead until smooth and elastic.

Use for making Cream Cheese Buns or Petit Pain au Chocolat.

Brioche

(photograph above)

*This is the traditional
French sweet yeast bun.*

½ cup milk
¼ cup water
125 grams butter
½ cup sugar
½ teaspoon salt
1 teaspoon sugar
1½ tablespoons dried yeast
About 3¼ cups flour
3 eggs
1 egg white
1 tablespoon sugar

Mix the milk and water together, and heat to scalding point. Set aside to cool until lukewarm.

Cream the butter until soft, and into it cream the first measure of sugar and salt, until a light fluffy mixture has formed.

Dissolve the second measure of sugar in the lukewarm liquid. Sprinkle the yeast on top, and leave until frothy — about 10 minutes.

Sift the flour into a bowl.

Pour the yeast liquid into another large mixing bowl. Add one cup of sifted flour to this, and work in the creamed butter mixture. Beat well. Add the well-beaten eggs, and continue to beat in the remaining flour until a batter is formed. At this stage, the batter must be well beaten until it is smooth. Cover, and set in a warm place until doubled in bulk.

Turn out on to a lightly floured board, and knead well. Divide the dough into 4 portions. Take one of these, and set aside. Cut each of the remaining 3 portions into 8 pieces. Shape each piece into a ball, and place in lightly greased brioche pans or patty tins.

Divide the remaining quarter of the dough into 24 small pieces, and shape each of these into a little ball. Poke a finger through the centre of the dough in each tin. Brush over the surface lightly with cold water, and place a small ball of dough on top of each hole.

Beat the egg white until just frothy, and mix in the sugar. Use this to lightly brush over the surface of the brioches. Cover, and set in a warm place to rise until double in size.

Bake at 190 degrees C for 15 minutes, or until they are golden and well risen.

Makes 24.

Petit Pain au Chocolat

(photograph above)

*French children
enjoy this as an afternoon treat.*

½ quantity sweet basic dough
About 24 small squares dark chocolate

Egg wash:

1 egg yolk
1 tablespoon water

To shape: Roll out dough to 5 millimetre thickness. Cut into rectangles 10 by 7.5 centimetres. In the centre of each piece of dough, place a row of 3 chocolate squares. Wrap the dough around it. Pinch the ends together lightly.

Place on a greased oven tray with join underneath, allowing room for rising. Cover, and leave until doubled in size.

Mix egg yolk with water. Brush the dough with this egg wash.

Bake at 200 degrees C for 12 minutes. Eat while still warm.

Makes about 8.

The evocative smell of freshly baked yeast goods in the tempting forms of buns and savarin (p163).

Butteries

(photograph above)

Butteries are a rich yeast dough, Scottish in origin, and following a similar process to the making of croissant dough.

1 teaspoon sugar

1 cup warm water

1 tablespoon dried yeast

About 2½ cups flour

½ teaspoon salt

2 teaspoons sugar

50 grams softened butter

Dissolve first measure of sugar in the warm water. Sprinkle the yeast on to the water. Leave in warm place for about 10 minutes, or until frothy.

Sift the flour and salt together, and add the second measure of sugar. Make a well in the centre of the dry ingredients. Pour in the frothy yeast liquid, and mix to a fairly soft dough. Turn dough on to a lightly floured surface. Knead until smooth and elastic.

Return dough to a lightly greased bowl, cover with plastic wrap, and leave in a warm place until doubled in bulk.

Punch dough down, turn on to a lightly floured surface, and knead again until smooth. Roll the dough into a rectangle, 20 by 45 centimetres.

Divide butter into 3, and dot one portion over the top two thirds of the dough. Fold bottom third into centre, and top third over. Press edges lightly. Wrap in clear plastic wrap, and place in refrigerator for 5 minutes.

Repeat this process twice with remaining butter, giving half a turn for each rolling.

Refrigerate for 15 minutes. Roll out to 1 centimetre thickness, and cut into rounds or ovals of about 6 to 8 centimetres. Place on a lightly floured oven tray. Cover, and leave to stand in a warm place until doubled in bulk.

Bake at 200 degrees C for about 25 minutes, or until golden. Remove to cooling tray, cool slightly, then eat while still warm, with marmalade.
Makes about 16.

Dinner Rolls

¼ cup warm water

1½ tablespoons dried yeast

50 grams butter

¼ cup sugar

1 cup warm milk

1 egg

3½ cups plain flour

1 teaspoon salt

Milk

Put the warm water in a mixer bowl. Sprinkle on the yeast, and leave in a warm place for 10 minutes or until frothy.

Melt the butter and beat the egg. Add butter, egg, sugar and warm milk to the yeast mixture.

Sift the flour and salt. Add half the flour to the liquid ingredients, and beat with a dough hook for 5 minutes. Gradually add enough of the remaining flour to make a soft dough.

Cover, and leave to rise in a warm place for 45 minutes, or until double in bulk.

Punch down. Shape into small rounds or ovals. Place slightly apart on a greased baking tray. Cover, and leave to rise in a warm place until double in bulk.

Brush with milk.
Bake at 200 degrees C for 15 to 20 minutes.
Makes 18.

Kibbled Wheat Bread

½ cup warm water

3 tablespoons dried yeast

4 cups plain flour

1 tablespoon salt

1¼ cups kibbled wheat

2½ cups warm water

1 tablespoon milk

Place the first measure of warm water in an electric mixer bowl. Sprinkle on the yeast, and leave in a warm place for 10 minutes or until frothy.

Sift the plain flour and salt into a bowl. Add the yeast liquid to the bowl.

Mix the kibbled wheat and warm water, and add. Beat with a dough hook for 5 minutes. The mixture will be soft.

Place the dough in 2 greased, 6 cup loaf tins. Cover, and leave to rise in a warm place for 30 minutes, or until doubled in bulk.

Brush with milk. Bake at 200 degrees C for 40 to 50 minutes.
Makes 2 loaves.

Cream Cheese Buns

(photograph above)

1 x 150 gram pot cream cheese

1 egg yolk

½ teaspoon grated lemon rind

½ quantity sweet basic dough

Egg wash:

1 egg yolk

1 tablespoon water

Beat cream cheese until soft. Beat in the egg yolk and lemon rind.

Roll out dough to 5 millimetre thickness. Cut out rounds with a 10 centimetre plain cutter.

On half of each round of dough, place a spoonful of cream cheese mixture. Fold the other half over, sealing the edges well. Place on a lightly greased oven tray. Mix the egg yolk with the water. Brush egg wash over buns.

Bake at 200 degrees C for 12 minutes.
Makes about 8.

HOME ENTERTAINING

Aready invitation for New Zealanders to offer, has always been, "Come home and have a meal." The genuine welcome offered to visitors has gained us a reputation for being a friendly people. Sharing our food, be it the family dinner or a planned function, brings out the best in us, as we see others enjoying our cooking and local specialties.

At festivals and functions, food takes a dominant place, and in New Zealand, such occasions have an air of informality that stems from the sincerity of the people who have so frequently grown or caught the food that is being offered.

For our Christmas, celebrated in mid-summer weather, there are evolving a number of special dishes that suit the climate.

Outdoor entertaining suits our lifestyle, while traditions from other lands still hold a place in our culinary heritage.

Captions to preceding 4 pages.

Page 152/153: The night lights of Auckland city and the harbour bridge. (photograph International Press Ltd).

Page 154/155: Fireworks Entertaining. Set off a sparkle for the young with food that competes strongly with regular fireworks for showiness and imagination on this thoroughly British festival, Guy Fawkes.

Facing page: Entertaining outdoors is a popular summer pastime. (photograph Laurie Thurston — Photobank).

Waitangi Day Menu

The following recipes make a suitable meal to serve on Waitangi Day, February 6.

Pickled Pork

1 hand pickled pork about 1.25 kilograms

1 bay leaf

6 peppercorns

1 sprig parsley

6 allspice berries

Place pork in a saucepan with cold water to cover well. Add the bay leaf, peppercorns, parsley and allspice. Cover, bring to the boil, and simmer for about 2¼ hours, or until tender when pierced with a fork.

Drain, press into a loaf tin, skin side up. Cover with foil and place a heavy weight on top. Leave to cool.

To serve, cut into slices, and accompany with fresh tomato and cucumber pickles.
Serves 6.

Fresh Tomato and Cucumber Pickles

3 tomatoes

¾ cup chopped cucumber

2 tablespoons vinegar

1 tablespoon sugar

¾ teaspoon salt

¼ teaspoon freshly ground black pepper

Skin the tomatoes, and chop finely. Drain the juice from them. Peel the cucumber, and chop finely. Measure and drain.

Combine the tomatoes, cucumber, vinegar, sugar, salt and pepper. Serve as a fresh pickle.
Serves 6.

Note: To drain vegetables, place on a plate or board, and set at a slight angle. As the liquid forms, it will drain off the vegetables.

Kumara Salad

500 grams kumara

2 oranges

3 thin slices onion

2 teaspoons chopped parsley

¼ cup oil

1 tablespoon wine vinegar

½ teaspoon salt

¼ teaspoon freshly ground black pepper

Peel the kumara, and cook in boiling salted water until tender. Drain well, slice, and place in a bowl.

Peel the oranges so all the white pith is removed, and slice them crossways. Break up the onion slices into rings.

Add the oranges and onions to the kumara.

Chop the parsley. Place with the oil, vinegar, salt and pepper in a screwtop jar. Shake well, pour over the salad ingredients, and toss lightly. Place in a salad bowl, and chill until serving time.
Serves 6.

Cauliflower Salad

1 cauliflower

2 cups frozen whole kernel corn

1 green pepper

1 tablespoon oil

2 tablespoons sour cream

2 tablespoons white vinegar

1 teaspoon sugar

1 teaspoon salt

¼ teaspoon freshly ground black pepper

Remove florets from the cauliflower. Cook in boiling salted water for 10 minutes, or until just tender. Drain well, cover with cold water, leave for 1 to 2 minutes, and drain again. Place in a bowl to cool.

Cook the frozen corn in boiling salted water for 3 minutes, and drain well. Add to the cauliflower.

Deseed and chop the green pepper. Add to the cauliflower and corn.

Combine oil, sour cream, vinegar, sugar, salt and pepper. Pour over the salad, and chill until serving time.
Serves 6.

Peach Trifle

1 x 20 centimetre round stale sponge

¼ cup raspberry jam

3 tablespoons sherry

8 cooked peach halves

1 tablespoon cornflour

2 cups milk

2 eggs

2 tablespoons sugar

½ teaspoon vanilla

About 1 cup whipped cream

Toasted almonds

Spread the sponge with the raspberry jam. Cut into 2 centimetre pieces, and place in the bottom of a serving dish. Sprinkle the sponge with the sherry. Arrange the peaches over the sponge.

Mix cornflour with 2 tablespoons of the milk to form a smooth paste. Add to remaining milk. Beat milk and cornflour, eggs, sugar and vanilla together.

Cook in the top of a double boiler over simmering water, stirring constantly, until the custard thickens sufficiently to coat the back of a spoon. Allow to cool slightly, then pour over the sponge.

Chill for several hours, or overnight.

Spread whipped cream over the custard before serving. Decorate with toasted almonds.
Serves 6.

Outdoor Entertaining Barbecuing

New Zealanders' pleasure in outdoor living invites entertaining by way of barbecuing.

Long Bay Kebabs

For each Kebab allow:

2 rashers bacon

2 x 3 centimetre cubes green pepper

2 cocktail sausages

2 small boiled onions

4 cubes pineapple

Cooking oil

Remove the rind from the bacon, and roll each rasher into a tight roll.

Thread all the ingredients alternately on to skewers, and brush with cooking oil. Cook over hot coals for about 20 minutes, turning occasionally.

Makes 1 kebab.

Spiced Barbecue Fish

6 fish steaks

100 grams butter

1 onion

1 clove garlic

1 teaspoon salt

Freshly ground black pepper

1 teaspoon ground coriander

¼ teaspoon cardamom

2 tablespoons lemon juice

225 gram pot plain yoghurt

Wash the fish and dry it well. Peel and finely chop the onion and garlic. Melt the butter.

Mix the butter, onion, garlic, salt, pepper, coriander, cardamom, lemon juice and yoghurt. Brush the steaks with this sauce.

Barbecue over medium-hot coals, turning frequently and basting occasionally with the remaining sauce. The fish will take 20 to 25 minutes to cook, depending on the thickness of the steaks, and is cooked when it is lightly browned on both sides, and flakes easily with a fork.

Serves 6.

Curry Bread

1 long vienna or french loaf

50 grams butter

1 teaspoon curry powder

Pinch garlic salt

Foil

Cut the bread at 2 centimetre intervals along the loaf, and through to within 2 centimetres of the base.

Soften the butter, and blend in the curry powder and garlic salt. Spread each cut with some of the butter.

Wrap the loaf in foil and place in a 200 degree C oven for about 10 to 15 minutes. Unwrap, and serve it hot, pulling off a slice as required.

Serves 6 to 8.

Barbecued Whole Fish

Foil

1 whole snapper or similar fish

Oil or butter

1 bay leaf

1 strip lemon peel

1 sprig thyme

Salt

Freshly ground black pepper

25 grams butter

Lemon juice

Lemon slices

Select a piece of foil large enough to completely wrap up the fish. If heavy duty foil is not available, use two sheets.

Oil or butter the central area of the foil, and place the cleaned and scaled fish on this. Split the body cavity slightly, and in this, place the bay leaf, lemon peel and thyme. Season with salt and pepper inside and out. Score the fish 3 or 4 times on both sides. Sprinkle with lemon juice. Dot with the measured butter, and wrap securely in the foil, sealing it all round.

Place over the barbecue grill, and cook for 10 to 15 minutes, depending on the size and thickness of the fish. Do not overcook. Unwrap the fish, and garnish the slits on one side with slices or wedges of lemon.

The number of servings will depend on the size of the fish.

Barbecued Chicken Halves

2 x 1 kilogram chickens

Marinade:

1 medium onion

1 cup sauterne

½ cup oil

2 tablespoons crushed capers

2 teaspoons salt

2 teaspoons ground ginger

Split the chickens in half through the back and breast bones.

Finely slice the onion. Mix with wine, oil, crushed capers, salt and ground ginger. Pour the mixture over the chicken halves, and refrigerate overnight.

Spoon the marinade over chicken halves before placing them on barbecue grill, bone side down. Grill over slow coals, brushing them with marinade.

Cook 20 minutes, turn skin side down, and grill about 30 minutes longer, brushing frequently with marinade. Test by inserting a skewer into thickest part of the drumstick. If juice runs clear, the chicken is cooked.

Serves 4.

Barbecued Bananas

6 medium bananas

Foil

¼ cup lemon juice

½ cup brown sugar

¾ teaspoon cinnamon

½ teaspoon nutmeg

Butter

Peel the bananas, and place each on a piece of foil large enough to surround it. Sprinkle each banana with lemon juice. Mix the brown sugar and spices together, and sprinkle over the bananas. Place a small dob of butter on each banana, then wrap up in the foil so that the banana is completely sealed. Place over hot coals, and cook for 10 to 15 minutes, turning occasionally.

Serves 6.

Meal for a Hot Summer Night

Spiced Iced Coffee
(photograph right)

½ cup instant coffee powder

½ teaspoon cinnamon

Pinch ground cloves

Pinch allspice

1 cup boiling water

2 cups cold water

Ice cubes

Sugar

Cream

In a large jug, mix together instant coffee powder, cinnamon, ground cloves and allspice. Pour in the boiling water, and stir until the coffee is dissolved. Stir in the cold water.

Chill until ready to serve.

Place 3 or 4 cubes of ice in each of 4 tall glasses, and pour the coffee over this. Serve with sugar and cream if wished.
Makes 4 glasses.

Yoghurt Fruit Mould
(photograph above)
Strawberries, raspberries, boysenberries or loganberries are all suitable for this recipe.

3 teaspoons gelatin

1 cup plain yoghurt

1 cup orange juice

3 tablespoons liquid honey

2 apricots

2 nectarines

1 cup berries

In a bowl, sprinkle gelatin over the yoghurt, and let it stand for five minutes. Heat the orange juice to boiling point, and add it and the honey to the yoghurt. Beat well with an egg beater, or whirl in the blender until thoroughly mixed.

Cover, and chill until the consistency of egg white — about 1 hour.

Wash the apricots and nectarines, remove the stones, and cut fruit into even-sized pieces. Wash and drain the berries.

Stir the fruits into the gelatin mixture, and pour into a 4 cup mould. Cover, and chill until set.

To serve: Dip mould into hot water briefly. Place the serving plate over the mould, and turn both upside down. Shake gently to loosen the jelly. Garnish with extra berries.
Serves 6.

Whitianga Fish
(photograph right)

4 x 500 gram whole fish

1 teaspoon salt

1 tomato

1 small onion

1 lemon

1½ cups white wine

1 cup water

2 tablespoons butter

2 tablespoons flour

Salt and pepper

6 spring onions

Clean and scale the fish. Rub inside and out with the salt. Thinly slice the tomato, onion and lemon, and divide evenly among the 4 fish as stuffing.

Place the wine and water in a wok or large frying pan, and bring to the boil. Poach the fish in this, turning once, until just tender — about 7 minutes on each side. It should not be overcooked.

While the fish are cooking, knead together the butter and flour. Cut the spring onions in thin diagonal slices.

When the fish are cooked, push to the side of the cooking vessel. Add spring onions, and cook for a minute, then crumble in the flour and butter mixture. Stir until thoroughly blended and the liquid boils and thickens. Add the salt and pepper to taste. Pour the sauce over the fish.
Serves 4.

Holiday Rice Salad
(photograph above)

4 cups water

2 teaspoons chicken stock powder

2 tablespoons chopped onion

1 cup raw long grain rice

1½ tablespoons soy sauce

1 lettuce

2 to 3 tomatoes

1 green pepper

4 radishes

100 grams button mushrooms

Salad dressing

In a large saucepan, bring the water and chicken stock to the boil. Add the onion and rice, and boil until the rice is tender — about 15 minutes. Drain well, add soy sauce, and toss until evenly distributed.

Turn into a salad bowl. Chill.

Wash the lettuce, drain well, and break into pieces. Slice the tomatoes, green pepper, radishes and the mushrooms, and toss through the lettuce. Arrange on top of the rice. Serve with salad dressing.
Serves 4.

Guy Fawkes Menu

Celebrating Guy Fawkes Day is part of our culture. The occasion can be turned into a culinary one as well.

New Potato and Watercress Salad

(photograph page 154)

12 to 16 small new potatoes

Boiling salted water

2 stalks celery

100 grams cucumber

3 spring onions

50 grams watercress

2 tablespoons chopped parsley

Dressing:

½ cup sour cream

2 tablespoons mayonnaise

1 teaspoon curry powder

½ teaspoon lemon juice

Salt

Freshly ground pepper

Wash and scrape potatoes. Cook in a saucepan of boiling salted water until tender. Drain, and leave to cool.

Slice celery and cucumber. Chop the spring onions. Wash and trim watercress.

Arrange potatoes, celery, cucumber, spring onions and watercress in a salad bowl. Pour dressing over before serving, sprinkled with chopped parsley.
Serves 6.

Dressing: Combine sour cream, mayonnaise, curry powder, lemon juice, salt and pepper in a bowl.

French Onion Soup

(photograph page 155)

4 onions

50 grams butter

1 teaspoon sugar

1 tablespoon flour

4 cups beef stock

¾ cup dry white wine

Parmesan toasties:

1 or 2 plain muffins

2 tablespoons butter

2 tablespoons grated parmesan cheese

Peel and slice onions thinly. Heat butter in a saucepan. Add onions, and cook until they are tender, but not brown. Add sugar, and cook for 1 minute. Add flour, and cook until frothy. Gradually add beef stock, stirring well after each addition.

Cover, and simmer for 20 minutes. Add white wine, and reheat.

Serve soup with hot parmesan toasties scattered on top.
Serves 4 to 5.

Parmesan toasties: Split muffins in half, then cut each half into 8 segments.

Heat butter in a frying pan. Fry segments until golden brown on all sides. Add cheese, and toss to coat.

Skyrocket Skewers

(photograph page 155)

3 spring onions

500 grams mince

250 grams sausagemeat

1 egg

1 teaspoon prepared mild mustard

1 tablespoon tomato sauce

1 teaspoon Worcestershire sauce

3 tablespoons chopped parsley

Salt

Freshly ground pepper

8 wooden meat skewers

Oil

About 3 carrots

Boiling salted water

Thin strips tasty cheese

Finely chop spring onions. Combine spring onions, mince, sausagemeat, egg, mustard, tomato sauce, Worcestershire sauce, parsley, salt and pepper in a bowl. Shape mixture on wooden skewers to resemble fire crackers. Brush with oil on all sides.

Place under hot griller, and grill for about 5 to 10 minutes on each side.

Meanwhile, prepare the carrot tops. Peel carrots, and cut 8 slices about 3 centimetres thick. Using a potato peeler, round off one end to give a pointed shape.

Cook the carrot tops in boiling salted water until just tender. Drain, and set aside, but keep warm.

Place strips of cheese on one side of each meat firecracker. Return to griller for 2 to 3 minutes, or until cheese just begins to melt.

Place 1 carrot top on each skewer, rounded side up, above meat, before serving. Serve hot.
Serves 8.

Note: It may be necessary to put foil over wooden skewers to prevent them scorching under the grill.

Chocolate Roman Candle

(photograph page 154)

Cakes:

4 eggs

¾ cup sugar

¾ cup flour

¼ cup cocoa

1 teaspoon baking powder

Pinch salt

2 tablespoons hot water

Meringues:

2 egg whites

½ cup castor sugar

Few drops red food colouring

Few drops blue food colouring

Few drops yellow food colouring

Sherry cream:

1 x 300ml bottle cream

¼ cup icing sugar

1 tablespoon sherry

Hundreds and thousands

Cakes: Line a 20 by 30 centimetre sponge roll tin, and an 18 centimetre round tin with greaseproof paper. Grease well.

Place eggs and sugar in a bowl, and beat until mixture is thick and will hold its shape. Pour the hot water down the side of the bowl.

Sift flour, cocoa, baking powder and salt together. Fold in sifted dry ingredients, until well combined.

Turn about two-thirds of the mixture into prepared sponge roll tin, and the remaining mixture into the prepared round tin.

Bake at 180 degrees C for 15 to 20 minutes, or until cakes are set.

Have ready a clean damp tea towel placed on a board for sponge roll. Immediately the sponge is cooked, turn it out onto the teatowel. Roll up the sponge, using the teatowel to shape the roll. Leave to cool.

Leave the round cake in the tin to cool for 5 minutes, then turn out on a wire rack to cool completely.

Meringues: Beat egg whites until stiff, but not dry. Add sugar, a tablespoon at a time, beating well after each addition. The mixture should be smooth and glossy.

Divide the meringue among three bowls. Add red colouring to one

Set for dinner.

bowl, blue to the second bowl, and yellow to the third bowl, mixing each to give even colouring. Pipe or spoon each mixture onto greased, paper-lined trays to form small meringues.

Bake at 120 degrees C for 1 to 1½ hours, or until dry.

When cool, remove from tray, and store in an airtight container until required.

Sherry Cream: Whip cream until soft peaks form. Sift icing sugar. Gently fold icing sugar and sherry into the cream.

To Assemble: Unroll sponge and spread about half the cream on it. Roll up firmly.

Trim sponge roll to about 15 centimetres in length. Out of the centre of the round cake, cut a circle the same diameter as filled sponge roll.

Place the round cake on a suitable serving plate. Position the sponge roll in the hole in the round cake, making sure it is secure.

Spread remaining cream over both cakes to completely cover. Arrange meringues on top and sides of sponge roll. Scatter hundreds and thousands over meringues and base of cake.

Serves 10 to 12.

Tom Thumbs

(photograph page 154)

½ cup cream cheese

3 cups icing sugar

75 grams dark cooking chocolate

1 teaspoon grated orange rind

¾ cup coconut

Few drops red food colouring

Licorice

Beat cream cheese until soft. Sift icing sugar.

Melt chocolate in a bowl over a saucepan of hot water. Remove from heat, and add to cream cheese. Mix well. Add orange rind and icing sugar gradually, mixing well after each addition.

Into a screw-topped jar, put the coconut and a few drops of red food colouring. Shake to get pink coconut.

Cut licorice into thin strips, four centimetres in length.

Shape the cream cheese mixture into cylinders 4 centimetres long. Toss in pink coconut. Place a licorice strip in one end of each cylinder to resemble a wick. Chill until required. **Makes about 32.**

Egg Wheels

(photograph page 155)

4 eggs

2 tablespoons sour cream

2 tablespoons finely chopped chives

2 tablespoons chopped parsley

1 teaspoon Worcestershire sauce

2 tablespoons chopped gherkins

¼ cup crumbled cooked bacon

Salt

Freshly ground pepper

4 cheese flavoured muffins

Hard-boil eggs, cool, and remove shells. Place eggs in a bowl, and mash with a fork. Add sour cream, chives, parsley, Worcestershire sauce, gherkins and bacon. Season to taste.

Split muffins in half, and place on a grill rack. Toast the outside for 3 to 4 minutes, until lightly browned.

Turn over, and spread egg mixture on the untoasted split side. Return to griller, and grill for 3 to 4 minutes, until set. Serve hot. **Serves 8.**

The golden, bell-like flowers of the native Kowhai.

Two Menus for Overseas Visitors

Menu 1

(Menu for warm weather)

The meat must be lamb, because so frequently visitors to our shores want to taste it. See Meat, Chapter 2, pages 60 to 66 for suggestions.

Smoked Trevalli Mousse

250 grams smoked trevalli

2 hard-boiled eggs

1 tablespoon butter

1 tablespoon flour

1 cup milk

1 tablespoon gelatin

¼ cup warm water

¼ cup mayonnaise

½ teaspoon lemon rind

1 tablespoon lemon juice

½ cup cream

Freshly ground black pepper

Skin and flake the fish. Chop the hard-boiled eggs.

Melt the butter, stir in flour, and cook until frothy. Gradually add the milk, stirring continuously. Leave to cool.

Dissolve the gelatin in warm water. Mix with the mayonnaise, lemon rind and lemon juice. Stir in the fish and hard-boiled eggs.

Lightly whip the cream, and fold into the mixture. Season with freshly ground black pepper. Turn into an oiled 3 cup fish mould. Leave to set. Unmould, and garnish to serve. **Serves 6.**

Fruit Savarin

(photograph page 150)

Savarin:

1½ teaspoons dried yeast

1 teaspoon sugar

¼ cup warm milk

1½ cups flour

Pinch salt

2 eggs

75 grams butter

1 teaspoon sugar

Orange Syrup:

1 cup sugar

¾ cup water

3 tablespoons cointreau

½ cup orange juice

Whipped cream

4 kiwifruit

1 orange

Savarin: Mix together dried yeast and first measure of sugar. Sprinkle on to warm milk and leave until frothy — about 15 minutes.

Sift flour and salt into a warm mixing bowl.

Lightly beat eggs. Melt butter. Pour yeast mixture into flour. Add eggs, butter, and second measure of sugar.

Beat well with the hand for 15 minutes, or until the dough becomes smooth and forms a ball. The dough should be of a soft consistency.

Grease a 20 centimetre ring tin, and turn dough into it. Leave in a warm place until mixture almost reaches the top of the tin. Bake at 200 degrees C for 25 minutes, or until golden. Prepare the syrup.

Orange Syrup: Boil sugar and water in a saucepan until the sugar dissolves and the syrup becomes clear — 3 to 4 minutes.

Allow to cool slightly, then add cointreau and orange juice.

Remove the Savarin from the oven, and cool a little. Do not unmould. Spoon the syrup over the Savarin. Leave to stand for several hours, or overnight if possible. Turn out on to a plate. Decorate with whipped cream. Garnish with slices of kiwifruit. If kiwifruit are unavailable, garnish with orange segments and orange rind.

Serves 6 to 8.

Menu 2
(Menu for cool weather)

A menu to show off our foods to overseas visitors.

Oyster and Scallop Entree

1 egg
1 tablespoon milk
1½ dozen oysters
1½ dozen scallops
1½ cups fine dry breadcrumbs
4 tablespoons butter
Tartare sauce
Lemon wedges

Beat the egg with the milk until combined.

Drain the oysters thoroughly. Dip the oysters and scallops into the egg mixture, then lift out, letting any excess egg run off. Toss in fine dry breadcrumbs to evenly coat.

Heat the butter in a frying pan. Fry oysters and scallops for about 2 minutes, turning once, until golden brown and just cooked. Drain on absorbent paper. Serve hot with tartare sauce and lemon wedges.
Serves 6.

Roast Vegetables

Potatoes
Pumpkin
Parsnips

Potatoes: Peel potatoes, and cut into even-sized portions.

Arrange around the meat in the roasting pan, and turn to coat in pan juices, about 1 hour before meat is cooked.

Pumpkin: Cut into individual portions, removing the inside seeds and peeling if wished.

Place in the roasting pan 40 to 50 minutes before meat is cooked.

Parsnips: Peel parsnips, trim ends and, if large, cut in half lengthways, then again crossways. Cook in boiling salted water for 10 minutes. Drain.

Place in roasting pan about 40 minutes before meat is cooked.

Note: During roasting, turn vegetables to allow for even cooking and colouring.

When all vegetables are cooked, transfer to a heated plate, draining off excess fat. Keep hot until serving time.

Minted Peas:

Water
1 teaspoon salt
1 to 2 sprigs fresh mint
500 grams frozen peas
1 teaspoon butter

Place in a saucepan, enough water to just cover the bottom. Add salt and mint, and bring to the boil. Add frozen peas, and bring back to the boil.

Simmer for 5 to 7 minutes, until tender. Drain well; remove mint. Serve at once, topped with butter.
Serves 6.

Roast Lamb

1 x 2 kilogram leg lamb
2 teaspoons salt
Freshly ground black pepper
Sprigs fresh rosemary
2 cups vegetable water or stock
3 tablespoons flour

Rub the leg of lamb all over with salt and pepper. Make small slits in the fat with a sharp knife. Place a small sprig of rosemary in each slit. Place leg of lamb in a roasting pan.

Roast at 190 degrees C, allowing 15 to 20 minutes per 500 grams, plus an extra 20 minutes. Baste frequently during the cooking time.

Transfer cooked meat to a heated serving plate, allowing excess fat and juices to run off. Keep hot until ready to carve.

Strain off most of the fat from the liquid remaining in the pan, leaving about 3 tablespoons. Be careful not to let any of the meat solids run from the pan.

Sprinkle the flour over the pan. Mix into the juices, and cook for about 1 minute on top of the stove, until frothy. Pour in the water or stock, a little at a time, mixing to a smooth paste. Bring to the boil, and boil for 3 to 4 minutes. Strain gravy into a heated jug. Keep hot until serving time.
Serves 6.

Fruit Salad Pavlova
(photograph right)
Seasonal New Zealand fruits to offer overseas guests include passionfruit pulp, sliced kiwifruit, feijoas and tamarillos.

4 egg whites
¼ teaspoon salt
1 cup castor sugar
4 teaspoons cornflour
2 teaspoons vinegar
½ teaspoon vanilla
1 cup cream
Selected seasonal fruit

Prepare a baking tray by lining with foil and greasing with melted butter.

Beat the egg whites and salt until soft peaks form when the beater is lifted from the mixture. Add the sugar, a little at a time, beating well after each addition. Continue to beat until the mixture is very stiff. Add cornflour, vinegar and vanilla. Beat thoroughly.

Pile mixture into a circle about 20 centimetres round, on the prepared baking tray.

Bake at 125 degrees C for 1½ hours. Turn oven off, and leave pavlova in the oven with door closed, until completely cold.

Remove carefully from the foil, and place pavlova on a serving plate. Just before serving, whip cream until stiff. Spread it over the pavlova. Prepare fruit and arrange on cream.
Serves 6.

Traditional Christmas Dinner

For traditionalists, some Christmas specialties to make.

Christmas Mincemeat

1 large apple

2 cups raisins

1 cup sultanas

1 cup grated suet

½ cup chopped peel

½ cup sugar

1 tablespoon golden syrup

1 lemon

2 cups currants

1 teaspoon mixed spice

1 teaspoon cinnamon

½ teaspoon grated nutmeg

¼ cup brandy

Peel and core the apple. Mince the raisins, sultanas, suet, apple and the peel. Add sugar, golden syrup, lemon juice, grated lemon rind, currants, the spices and the brandy. Mix thoroughly, and put into jars, and seal.

New Zealand's native Christmas tree — the Pohutukawa.

Store in refrigerator if weather is very hot. Allow to mature for at least a week before using.
Makes about 8 cups.

Traditional Christmas Pudding

2 cups flour

2 teaspoons baking powder

1 teaspoon mixed spice

¼ teaspoon salt

2 cups grated suet

2 cups fresh breadcrumbs

2 cups sticky raisins

1 cup currants

1 cup sultanas

1 cup drained chopped pineapple

½ cup chopped dates

½ cup chopped dried apricots

½ cup mixed peel

1 cup brown sugar

3 eggs

1 cup golden syrup

1 teaspoon grated orange rind

1 teaspoon grated lemon rind

2 tablespoons lemon juice

1 tablespoon orange juice

½ cup sherry

Sift flour, baking powder, spice and salt into a bowl. Stir in suet and breadcrumbs. Add all the fruit and the sugar.

Beat the eggs, syrup, rinds and juices together.

Make a well in the centre of the dry ingredients, and add syrup mixture and sherry. Mix well.

Divide the mixture between two 5 cup, greased pudding basins, or use one 10 cup basin. Cover with greased paper and a pudding cloth or foil, and tie securely. Place on a trivet in a saucepan of water which comes three-quarters of the way up the basin.

Boil for 6 hours.

Cover with dry paper and clean cloths or foil, before storing in a cool dry place.

Boil for 2 hours before serving.
Small: 6 to 8 servings.
Large: 12 to 16 servings.

Fried Christmas Pudding

Thick slices of cold Christmas pudding

Butter

Ice cream, cream or sauce

Cut Christmas pudding into thick, even-sized pieces. It is best if the pudding is completely cold and firm.

In a frying pan, heat a little butter, and quickly fry the pudding first on one side, then turn to fry the second side.

Serve while it is still hot, with ice cream, cream or sauce, according to your preference.

Christmas Dinner Outdoors

There are many New Zealand families who spend Christmas on holiday out of doors, and to the amazement of those who come from the Northern Hemisphere, they can celebrate a Christmas New Zealand style in the searing sun.

Takatu Pate

375 grams lean veal

125 grams bacon

1 small onion

1 clove garlic

3 drops tabasco sauce

¾ teaspoon salt

¼ teaspoon pepper

1 egg

2 tablespoons brandy

1 bay leaf

Wholemeal bread

Gherkins

Tomatoes

Finely mince the veal, bacon, peeled onion and garlic twice. Add the tabasco sauce, seasonings, egg and brandy, and mix well.

Secluded Medland's Beach on Great Barrier Island.

Pack the mixture into a lightly-greased 17 centimetre loaf tin. Place the bay leaf on top. Cover with foil, and stand the tin in a pan of water.

Bake at 160 degrees C for 1 to 1½ hours, or until the pate is firm to touch.

Remove from the oven, and set aside to cool. Turn out, and refrigerate until required. Cut into slices, and serve with wholemeal bread, gherkins and tomatoes.
Serves 6.

New Potato Salad
(photograph page 169)

| 1 kilogram very small new potatoes |
| 1 onion |
| 2 sticks celery |
| 2 tablespoons chopped parsley |
| 1 teaspoon chopped mint |
| ½ cup whipped cream |
| 2 tablespoons vinegar |
| 1 tablespoon prepared mustard |
| Salt and pepper |
| Paprika |

Cook the potatoes in boiling salted water for 15 to 20 minutes or until soft. Drain, and allow to cool before removing the skins. Finely chop the onion and cut the celery into 1 centimetre slices. Place the potatoes, onion, celery, parsley and mint in a bowl.

Mix the cream, vinegar, mustard, salt and pepper together, and mix through the potato mixture, taking care not to break up the potatoes. Sprinkle with paprika.
Serves 6.

Pea and Mushroom Salad
(photograph page 169)

| 1 small onion |
| 100 grams small mushrooms |
| 4 tablespoons lemon juice |
| 1 tablespoon oil |
| Freshly ground black pepper |
| Salt |
| 2 cups green peas |
| Sprig mint |

Peel and finely dice the onion. Wash and slice the mushrooms. Combine lemon juice, oil, freshly ground black pepper and salt together in a bowl. Put onion and sliced mushrooms in the lemon juice mixture to marinate.

Chill, and leave several hours.

Cook the green peas in boiling salted water with the sprig of mint until tender. Drain, remove mint. Chill.

Combine the peas with marinated onion and mushrooms, including the lemon juice marinade.
Serves 4 to 6.

Pohutukawa Fruit Salad
(photograph page 169)

| About 1½ cups fresh cherries |
| About 1½ cups strawberries |
| Thick slice watermelon |

Wash cherries and strawberries. Do not remove the stalks of either fruit.

Cut the melon in cubes, and remove pips. Do this over a bowl to catch the juice.

Combine fruits in a glass jar or bowl, and pour over the retained melon juice.
Serves 4 to 6.

Rice Salad
(photograph page 169)

| 1 cup raw long grain rice |
| 1 bay leaf |
| 1 green pepper |
| ½ cup crushed pineapple |
| 2 tablespoons chopped parsley |
| Freshly ground black pepper |

Wash the rice. Cook it in boiling, salted water with the bay leaf for about 10 minutes, or until just tender. Drain in a sieve, remove the bay leaf, and run the rice under cold water.

Wash, deseed and finely chop the green pepper. Do not drain pineapple. Toss chopped pepper, pineapple and parsley into the rice. Sprinkle generously with black pepper.
Serves 4 to 6.

Honey Baked Chicken
(photograph page 169)

| 1 large chicken |
| Sprig fresh parsley |
| Thyme |
| Celery tops |
| 1 bay leaf |
| ½ cup honey |
| 1 tablespoon lemon juice |
| 1 tablespoon butter |
| Salt |
| Freshly ground black pepper |
| 1 bay leaf |

Dry the chicken thoroughly inside and out. Tie the sprigs of fresh herbs and bay leaf together, and place inside the chicken.

Gently heat the honey, lemon juice, butter, salt and pepper together. Brush over the chicken.

Place in a roasting pan, and roast at 180 degrees C for about 1 hour, basting frequently with the honey mixture.

When the chicken is cooked, remove from the pan, and cool it. Remove the herbs. Serve cold, garnished with fresh herbs and bay leaf.
Serves 4 to 6.

Little Barrier Island, Hauraki Gulf.

Iced Christmas Pudding

*Our climate lends itself
to spending Christmas outdoors,
and barbecued food is in keeping
with this way of life.
The trend is to break away
from cold climate tradition.
This Christmas pudding
is ideal for an
unconventional Christmas dinner
at the beach.*

1½ cups mixed fruit
½ teaspoon mixed spice
2 tablespoons brandy
1 x 2 litre tub vanilla ice cream
2 egg yolks
¼ cup icing sugar
1½ tablespoons gelatin
¼ cup water

Place the mixed fruit and spice in a bowl, and sprinkle with the brandy.

Scoop out the centre of the ice cream, leaving a shell of ice cream in the tub. Return the tub to the freezer.

Place the scooped out ice cream in the bowl with the fruit. Beat the egg yolks and sugar together until thick and creamy, and add it to the ice cream mixture.

Soak the gelatin in the water for 5 minutes, then stand over hot water, and stir until dissolved. Add this to the ice cream mixture, and mix well.

Place in the icecream shell and freeze until firm.

To transport to the barbecue, remove from the freezer just before leaving, and wrap in 4 to 6 layers of newspaper. Place in chilly bin with ice pads.

To serve, run a knife around the outside of the ice cream, and turn on to a plate. Cut into wedges.
Serves 6 to 8.

Christmas Cake
(photograph right)

*A cake with a thoroughly
New Zealand air is offered
for our summer Christmas.
What could be nicer
than sprigs of pohutukawa flowers,
giving the festival colour
of our own native plant?
There's also a simple outline
in the style
of a Maori rafter pattern,
and the warmest greetings
for Christmas and the coming year
in Maori.*

1 round fruit cake
Cornflour
Apricot jam
700 grams almond paste
550 grams fondant
Cake board or plate
Piping bag
No. 2 piping nozzle
Royal icing
Fresh pohutukawa flowers and leaves

Royal Icing:

1 cup icing sugar
1 egg white
Red food colouring
Gravy browning

Trim the top of the cake, if very uneven. Turn the cake upside down and place on a smooth surface that is lightly dusted with cornflour.

Gently warm the apricot jam, and rub it through a sieve. Brush the top and sides of the cake with warm jam.

Knead the almond paste until smooth. Press pieces of paste into any gaps on the cake to make the surface very even. It usually requires a lot around the base of the cake to fill it into the board.

Shape the remaining almond paste into a ball. Roll out on a very smooth surface, lightly dusted with cornflour, so that it is large enough to cover the top and sides of the cake.

Carefully lift the paste onto the cake with a rolling pin. Beginning from the centre of the cake, smooth the paste over the top and ease it over the sides. Trim excess neatly from around the base.

Leave for 24 hours.

Knead the fondant until smooth, and roll out on a very smooth surface, lightly dusted with cornflour, so that it is large enough to cover the top and sides of the cake.

Lightly brush the almond paste with water. Place the fondant on to the cake as for the almond paste. Trim around the base. Smooth the cake with the heel of the hand and fingertips. Run a straight-sided glass or bottle around the sides of the cake to smooth it.

Place on a cake board or plate.

Fill a piping bag, fitted with No. 2 piping nozzle, with red royal icing. Mark guidelines on the cake with a ruler so that the printing is straight. Pipe the Maori greetings, by making thick letters, by piping in a zig-zag fashion.

Pipe a simple stylised design, using red and black royal icing.

Just before serving, decorate the base of the cake with fresh pohutukawa flowers and leaves.

Royal Icing: Sift the icing sugar into a bowl, and beat in the egg white until it becomes a smooth, pipeable consistency. This may require a little more egg white or icing sugar.

Colour some red and the rest black by using red colouring and gravy browning.

Christmas Punch
(photograph right)

1 x 750ml bottle rose wine
Similar volume boysenberry and apple juice
2 tablespoons lime cordial
4 cups sparkling mineral water
Ice
Lemon slices

Combine the rose wine, boysenberry and apple juice, and lime cordial. Chill well.

Just before serving, add the chilled sparkling mineral water. Serve over ice, and garnish with lemon slices.
Serves 6 to 8.

Christmas in summer, a time to bring together commonsense and tradition with a menu suited to outdoor living, but retaining aspects of our northern hemisphere heritage.

Simnel Cake

(photograph page 149)

*One item that has become
associated with Easter,
the Simnel Cake has, in fact,
only in recent times
been linked to that festival.
It used to be associated with
Mothering Sunday,
mid-Lent Sunday,
when young women in service
went home, taking with them
a cake.
The 11 paste balls
represent the apostles,
with Judas being left out.*

Almond Paste:

3 cups ground almonds

½ cup castor sugar

1 cup icing sugar

1 egg

1 egg white

25 grams melted butter

Cake:

225 grams butter

¼ cup sugar

4 eggs

2¼ cups flour

½ cup ground rice

1 teaspoon baking powder

¼ cup candied peel

¼ cup crystallised cherries

3 cups currants

Glaze:

1 egg yolk

1 tablespoon water

Line the bottom and sides of a 20 centimetre round cake tin with 3 layers of paper. Grease the inside layer.

Almond Paste: Mix the ground almonds and sugars together in a bowl.

Lightly beat egg and egg white, and mix with the melted butter. Add egg mixture to almonds, and mix thoroughly. Knead until smooth.

Roll out a portion of paste into a 23 centimetre log, 2½ centimetres in diameter. Cut log into 11 equal pieces. Roll each piece into a small ball. Set aside.

Using icing sugar to prevent the paste sticking to hands and bench, take half of the remaining paste, and knead lightly a few times, until smooth.

Draw the size of the tin on a piece of greaseproof paper. Sprinkle the paper with icing sugar. Place the paste on it, and roll out to fit the circle drawn. Repeat with the second piece of paste. Cover, and set aside.

Cake: Cream butter and sugar until light and fluffy. Add the eggs one at a time, beating well after each addition.

Sift flour, ground rice and baking powder together.

Chop peel and cherries, and mix with the currants.

Add the flour and fruit alternately to the creamed mixture, starting and finishing with the flour.

Put half the cake mixture in the tin. With the help of the paper, place one circle of almond paste on top of the mixture. Spoon the remaining cake mixture on top. Smooth off the top, and sprinkle with a little cold water to keep the cake level.

Bake at 180 degrees C for 30 minutes, then lower heat to 160 degrees C for a further 2 hours.

Remove from the oven, and place the second piece of almond paste on top. Press lightly. Brush with egg yolk and water mixed together. Arrange the 11 paste balls around the outside edge, and brush with the egg wash.

Return to the oven, and cook for a further 15 to 20 minutes, or until lightly browned and the glaze has set.

Note: Do not use commercial almond paste, unless it is a genuine one, made from ground almonds.

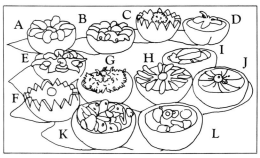

Starters
Grapefruit Starters

Many New Zealanders have prolific grapefruit trees in their gardens, and it is often difficult to know how to use all the fruit produced.

The sharp fresh flavour of grapefruit is an excellent starter to a meal, and many of us enjoy a simple grilled or mixed grapefruit hors d'oeuvre.

Here are some different ways of offering a meal starter that is essentially grapefruit. One or two of the ideas could be used to end a meal, if you prefer it that way.

A. Orange grapefruit
B. Grapefruit, grape and almond starter
C. Grapefruit with cream cheese
D. Minted grapefruit
E. Seafood grapefruit
F. Vandyked grapefruit
G. Rum grapefruit
H. Ginger grapefruit
I. Grapefruit and date starter
J. Grilled grapefruit
K. Grapefruit vinaigrette
L. Grapefruit Italian style

Prepare the grapefruit by cutting in half. With a serrated-edge knife, cut around each segment, so that it is freed from skin and pith, and may be easily removed with a spoon.

When removing the segments to mix with a filling, cut out flesh and membranes.

Chop flesh according to size of added ingredients.

Ideas

A. Segment an orange removing all rind and skin. Mix with the grapefruit segments, adding a little sugar and sherry to taste.

Rearrange the segments in the grapefruit.

B. Mix chopped grapes, almonds and mint leaves with the grapefruit segments.

Add a little French dressing, and decorate with grapes and almonds.

C. Mix cream cheese, grated walnut and honey to a paste. Pipe or spoon into the centre of a segmented grapefruit.

D. Decorate grapefruit with mint. For a fuller flavour, leave overnight to allow mint flavour to penetrate.

E. Mix shrimps and mayonnaise with the grapefruit segments. Garnish with shrimps and strips of tomato flesh.

F. Vandyke a grapefruit. Decorate with a cherry, and sprinkle with a little sugar.

G. Mix drained, crushed pineapple, coconut, brown sugar and rum with the grapefruit segments. Decorate with a walnut half.

This can be grilled, if wished, before garnishing with a walnut.

H. Decorate with slices of preserved ginger in syrup. Spoon a little of the ginger syrup over.

I. Mix chopped dates with the grapefruit. Decorate with whole dates and orange segments.

J. Sprinkle sherry and brown sugar over each prepared grapefruit. Grill until sugar melts and browns. Top with a cherry.

K. Mix the grapefruit segments with chopped ham, celery and green pepper. Add a little French dressing to taste. Garnish with tiny ham rolls and finely sliced green peppers and celery.

L. Mix chopped tomato and green olive with the grapefruit segments. Add a little Italian dressing. Garnish with olive slices and rolled anchovy fillets.

White Fish Terrine

(photograph below)

| 700 grams snapper or lemon fish fillets |
| 1 teaspoon salt |
| White pepper |
| 3 egg whites |
| 1 x 300ml bottle cream |
| Pinch cayenne pepper |
| 3 egg yolks |
| 1½ cups fresh white breadcrumbs |
| 3 tablespoons chopped parsley |
| 1 tablespoon chopped fresh tarragon |
| 1 tablespoon chopped chives |
| Salt |
| White pepper |
| 8 to 10 rashers bacon |

Select a terrine or loaf tin of about 6 cup capacity.

Set aside enough fish to make a layer of 1 centimetre thickness in selected dish.

Place remaining fish, the salt and white pepper in a food processor, and puree.

Take out about one third of the pureed fish, and place in a bowl.

With food processor motor running, add egg whites, one at a time, then one cup of cream, and lastly cayenne pepper. Set aside.

In the bowl with one third of reserved pureed fish, place egg yolks, remaining cream, breadcrumbs, parsley, tarragon and chives. Mix well to combine. Season with salt and pepper.

Remove rind from bacon rashers, and stretch them. Line the terrine or loaf tin with bacon rashers, leaving about 4 centimetres over at each end of rashers.

Spread half the creamy fish mixture on the base of the dish. Layer breadcrumb fish mixture, the reserved whole fillets, and the second half of creamy fish mixture.

Fold bacon rasher ends over the top of the fish mixture to cover.

Cover with a piece of greased foil. Place terrine in a pan of water. Bake at 150 degrees C for 1 to 1¼ hours. Chill to serve.
Serves 8 to 10.

Mushroom and Almond Pate

(photograph page 171)

½ cup blanched almonds

1 tablespoon oil

1 spring onion

300 grams mushrooms

50 grams butter

¼ teaspoon chopped thyme

Salt

Pepper

Coarsely chop the almonds. Spread them on an oven tray. Place in a 140 degree C oven for about 10 minutes, until evenly golden. Allow to cool.

Place almonds in food processor or blender, and process until smooth. With the blender still going, add oil until a paste is formed.

Chop spring onion and mushrooms finely. Heat butter in a frying pan. Cook mushrooms and spring onion for about 5 minutes, until moisture has evaporated. Add thyme, salt and pepper. Cool.

Beat in the almond paste until well combined. Turn into a bowl. Cover, and chill well.
Makes 1½ cups.

Terrine of Pork and Prunes

(photograph page 171)

300 grams belly pork

400 grams chicken livers

2 rashers bacon

1½ teaspoons salt

Freshly ground pepper

10 prunes

2 tablespoons brandy

1 onion

2 bay leaves

Remove bones from belly pork, and cut into 3 centimetre pieces. Place the pork pieces and half the chicken livers in a food processor or mincer. Process or mince until a coarse texture is reached. Place in a large bowl.

Process the second half of the chicken livers and the bacon finely. Place in the bowl. Season with salt and pepper.

Chop prunes finely. Add these and the brandy to the meat, and mix well to combine.

Cut onion into rings.

Turn meat into a 3½ cup dish. Arrange onion rings and bay leaves on the surface of meat. Cover with a lid or foil.

Stand the dish in a pan of water. Bake at 160 degrees C for 1 to 1¼ hours, until meat has shrunk away slightly from the sides of the dish.

Remove lid, place a piece of foil on top of meat. If foil was used to cover for baking, leave it in place. Weight down, and refrigerate several hours.
Serves 6 to 8.

Chicken Liver Pate

(photograph page 171)

400 grams chicken livers

2 rashers bacon

1 onion

1 cup milk

1 sprig parsley

6 black peppercorns

1 blade mace

25 grams butter

1 tablespoon flour

1 teaspoon salt

Bay leaves

Clarified butter

Mince chicken livers and bacon.

Slice the onion. Heat milk, onion, parsley, peppercorns and mace in a saucepan until small bubbles form. Cover, and allow to stand off the heat for 30 minutes.

In another saucepan, heat butter, and stir in the flour. Cook until bubbling.

Strain milk, and gradually add to the flour mixture. Cook, stirring, for 2 minutes. Add the hot milk sauce to the chicken livers. Season with salt.

Turn into a covered 4 cup oven-proof dish. Alternatively, turn into 6 to 8 small pots. Place bay leaves on top of meat.

Cover, and stand dish or pots in a pan of water. Cook in the oven at 180 degrees C for 50 to 60 minutes for a large dish, or 30 to 40 minutes for individual pots.

Remove bay leaves. Cover with clarified butter. Chill several hours before serving.
Serves 6 to 8.

Desserts

Hazelnut Gateau

(photograph right)

*Gateaux of this type
that call for rice paper,
can be made,
if the paper is not available,
by preparing the meringue on foil.*

Rice paper

Meringue:

6 egg whites

1½ cups castor sugar

Few drops vanilla essence

½ teaspoon vinegar

2 cups ground hazelnuts

Filling:

1 x 430 gram tin stoned cherries

Water

1 tablespoon sugar

3 tablespoons cornflour

1 tablespoon cherry brandy

Cream:

1½ x 300 ml bottles of cream

2 tablespoons icing sugar

Few drops vanilla essence

50 grams cooking chocolate

Prepare trays first: Grease 2 oven trays well, and dust with flour. Mark out three 20 centimetre circles and one 10 centimetre circle. Cut out 4 pieces of rice paper to fit the circles.

Meringue: Whisk the egg whites until stiff, then gradually beat in the castor sugar until very thick. Add the vanilla essence and vinegar. Using a large metal spoon, gradually fold in the ground hazelnuts.

Spread the mixture evenly over the 4 circles with a spatula. Bake at 190 degrees C for 35 minutes.

While still warm, trim the three 20 centimetre circles to even size, reserving the trimmings.

Remove all the circles from the trays, removing the paper while still warm, unless it is the edible rice paper. Allow to cool.

Cherry filling: Drain the cherries, reserving the juice. Make the amount of juice up to 1 cup with the water. Place the juice and sugar in a small saucepan, and bring to the boil.

Mix the cornflour to a paste with a little cold water, and stir into the hot liquid. Cook until thick and glossy. Stir in the cherries, reserving a few for decoration.

Allow the sauce to cool. Add the cherry brandy. The mixture should be quite thick.

Cream: Combine the cream, icing sugar and vanilla essence in a wide bowl. Whisk until thick. Do not over whisk.

Meringue crumble: Crush the off-cuts and the 10 centimetre meringue to crumbs, either in a food pro-cessor or with the aid of a rolling pin. Set aside.

To assemble: Place one of the circles of meringue on the plate the cake is to be served on. Pile the cherry filling on top, and spread it out evenly.

Place a second meringue on top. Spread this layer with 3 to 4 table-spoons of the whipped cream, and top with the third and last meringue.

Completely cover the whole gateau with the whipped cream, reserving about ¾ cup for piping. Press the crumbled mixture on to the side of the gateau, ensuring an even covering. Pipe a decorative border around the edge of the gateau.

Refrigerate the gateau until it is well chilled.

Chop the chocolate into rough pieces, and place on a saucer over warm water. Allow to melt, then cool slightly.

Make a piping bag with greaseproof paper, and using a very fine nozzle, pipe whirls of chocolate over the top of the cake. Decorate with reserved cherries.

Serves 10 to 12.

Caramel Choux

(photograph right)

½ cup water

50 grams butter

½ cup flour

Pinch salt

2 eggs

Whipped Cream:

1¼ cups cream

½ teaspoon vanilla

1 tablespoon icing sugar

Caramel Candy:

1 cup sugar

¼ cup water

1 teaspoon vinegar

Put water and butter in a saucepan, and bring to a full rolling boil. Add the flour, then remove the saucepan from the heat, and beat vigorously with a wooden spoon, until the mixture leaves the sides of the saucepan. Cool a little.

Add the unbeaten eggs, one at a time, and beat thoroughly after each addition. Beat until the paste is thick and satiny.

A food processor with metal blade in place, can be used for this second stage in making choux paste: place the dough from the saucepan in the bowl in 2 or 3 pieces. Add 1 egg, and beat until combined. Add the next egg down the feed tube while machine is running. Beat until the paste is glossy.

Pile or pipe on to a greased tray. Bake at 220 degrees C for 20 to 40 minutes, depending on size, before lowering temperature to 120 degrees C to dry out pastry. During the initial high temperature cooking, do not open the oven door. The time needed for drying out the pastry will depend on the size of the shells being made.

When shells are cooked, make a small opening underneath and, using a plain nozzle on the piping bag, fill the puffs with whipped cream. Arrange a layer of cream puffs on a serving plate.

Using tongs, dip the top of each puff in the caramel. Arrange on a serving dish.
Serves 10 to 12.

Whipped Cream: Whip the cream until stiff. Carefully fold in vanilla and sifted icing sugar.

Caramel Candy: Place sugar, water and vinegar in a saucepan. Stir to dissolve sugar. Boil, without stirring, until the candy begins to turn golden. Remove from heat.

Old Fashioned Puddings

What constitutes an old-fashioned recipe?

For the young, it's everything they cannot remember — and that can be only a few years ago. For older people, it's distant childhood memories of foods enjoyed in the family kitchen.

Blancmange

¼ cup cornflour

3 tablespoons sugar

2 cups milk

5 centimetre strip lemon rind

Mix cornflour and sugar to a smooth paste with a little of the milk.

Place the remaining milk and lemon rind in a saucepan, and heat to boiling point. Pour some of the heated milk into the cornflour mixture, then stir this back into the heated milk. Return to the heat, and cook while stirring, until the mixture thickens. Cook gently, with occasional stirring, for about 10 minutes longer.

Remove from the heat, remove rind, and pour into a wetted 2 cup mould. Leave to set. Unmould. Serve cold with fruit or jam.
Serves 4 to 5.

Apple Charlotte

1 kilogram cooking apples

2 tablespoons butter

1 tablespoon lemon juice

½ teaspoon lemon rind

3 tablespoons apricot jam

Sugar to taste

10 to 12 slices white sandwich bread

Butter

Sugar

Peel and slice the apples. Cook with first measure of butter and the lemon juice, rind and jam until a very thick puree is formed. Sweeten to taste.

Select a deep round cake tin about 16 centimetres in diameter.

Trim the crusts from the bread. Cut the bread into fingers about 3.5 centimetres wide, and long enough to cover the depth of the tin. Cut triangles of bread to cover the bottom of the tin.

Grease the tin well, and dust with sugar.

Heat the butter in a large frying pan, and when it bubbles, lightly fry the pieces of bread on one side only until golden. Lift out and drain.

Line the bottom of the tin with the bread, placing fried side down. Have the bread overlapping slightly to contain the apple. In a similar fashion, line the sides of the tin, reserving enough for the top.

Spoon the apple mixture into the lined tin, turn the edges of the bread on the sides over to fit the apple. Cover apple with remaining bread.

Bake at 190 degrees C for about 30 minutes, until the bread is crisp. Leave in the tin for about 10 minutes before unmoulding on to a plate. Serve warm with hot apricot sauce or cream.
Serves 6 to 8.

Spotted Dick

1 cup flour

¼ teaspoon salt

1 teaspoon baking powder

1½ cups fresh breadcrumbs

1 cup grated suet

1 cup sticky raisins

1 teaspoon grated lemon rind

½ cup sugar

¾ cup milk

Butter

Brown sugar

Sift flour, salt and baking powder into a bowl. Stir in breadcrumbs, suet, raisins, lemon rind and sugar. Mix to a soft dough with milk.

Spoon the mixture into a greased cylindrical tin with detachable ends, filling the tin only two thirds full. Fit ends into position. Boil for 2 hours.

Remove ends from the tin, and carefully remove the pudding on to a warm serving dish. Dot with small pieces of butter, and sprinkle with brown sugar. Cut into slices to serve.
Serves 6.

Treacle Tart

Treacle tart is an old fashioned dessert that has many variations, sometimes being made from golden syrup for those who prefer a less strong taste. The use of lemon and breadcrumbs with the treacle or syrup gives it the texture necessary.

300 grams short pastry

½ cup treacle

1 cup fresh breadcrumbs

1 teaspoon grated lemon rind

2 tablespoons lemon juice

2 tablespoons breadcrumbs

Roll out the pastry on a lightly floured board to 0.5 centimetre thickness. Use to line a 20 centimetre pie plate.

Mix together the treacle, first measure of breadcrumbs, lemon rind and juice. Spread over the pastry. Sprinkle the second measure of breadcrumbs on top. Bake at 220 degrees C for 15 to 20 minutes. Serve with cream or custard.
Serves 4 to 5.

Jam Roly-Poly

2 cups flour

2 teaspoons baking powder

½ teaspoon salt

1 cup grated suet

About ¾ cup water

1 cup stiff jam

½ cup plain cake crumbs

1 tablespoon lemon juice

Sift flour, baking powder and salt into a bowl. Stir in the suet, and mix until it is lightly coated with flour. Make a well in the centre, and add the water, using enough to mix to a soft dough.

Turn the dough on to a lightly floured board. Roll out to an oblong 26 by 20 centimetres.

Combine the jam, cake crumbs and lemon juice. Spread the jam mixture evenly over the dough to within 1 centimetre of the edges. Roll up as for a sponge roll, and press the edges together lightly.

Grease a piece of greaseproof paper large enough to enclose the roly-poly, and place it in it. Wrap the greaseproof paper around, then enclose the roly-poly in pudding cloth. Tie the ends securely, but allow room for expansion. Secure the middle of the cloth with a safety pin. Carefully lower the roly-poly into a pan of boiling water. Boil steadily for 1½ hours.

To serve, remove the cloth and paper, and cut into slices.
Serves 6.

Lemon Sago

3 cups water

½ cup sago

¼ cup sugar

¼ cup lemon juice

½ teaspoon grated lemon rind

3 tablespoons golden syrup

Put the water in a saucepan, and bring to the boil. Add sago. Boil gently, stirring frequently, until sago clears. Stir in the sugar, lemon juice, rind and golden syrup, mixing well.

Pour into a serving dish or individual dishes. Chill, and serve with cream if wished.
Serves 5 to 6.

Brown Bread and Apple Pudding

6 to 8 thin slices brown bread

Butter

¼ cup brown sugar

2 apples

2 cups milk

2 eggs

½ teaspoon cinnamon

¼ teaspoon ground cloves

Trim the crusts from the bread, and cut in half. Butter lightly, and sprinkle with the sugar. Peel, core and thinly slice the apples.

Layer the bread and apples in a greased 5 cup ovenproof dish, finishing with a layer of apples.

Place the milk, eggs, cinnamon and cloves in a mixing bowl. Beat lightly until thoroughly combined. Pour slowly into the dish so that the bread soaks up the milk.

Bake the pudding at 150 degrees C for 45 minutes, or until the custard is set and golden brown.
Serves 4 to 6.

The grand old homestead at Mt Peel station.

PUTTING DOWN FOR WINTER

More produce than can be used when it is at its seasonal flush is no problem in these days of freezers, but for generations in times past, turning it into something that would keep, became part of the homemaker's art. We still enjoy many preserves, despite the fact that most produce, commercially stored, is available almost without a gap, year long.

Jams, jellies, pickles, sauces, bottles of favourite fruit, plain or brandied, are the result of standing over a hot stove in summer heat. But the pride of the maker when the colourful collection can be tapped for later use, is without equal.

A surplus of any fruit or vegetable is soon converted into a tempting item to go with meats or toast or ice cream.

Preserving food allows us to enjoy more than just nourishment; it gives us tasty and distinctive items in their own right.

Captions to preceding 4 pages.

Page 176/177: Skiers at Porter Heights, Canterbury. (photograph Peter Morath).

Page 178/179: The abundant produce of summer and autumn, preserved variously, to enhance our menus and delight our palates the year long.

Facing page: A typical high country farm near the Remarkables, Central Otago. (photograph Eric Young).

Autumn reflections in Lake Wanaka, South Island.

Pickles

Bread and Butter Pickles

(photograph right)

*Bread and butter pickle
— what a strange term this is!
They are light cucumber pickles
that are crisp and fresh-tasting.
Very popular in America,
they can be served with
all manner of dishes,
from a hot hamburger
to a cold meat and salad.
They are a particularly useful
pickle to make when you have
masses of cucumbers in the garden.
As with any sort of pickle,
make sure the cucumbers
are not over-ripe,
or the seeds will be coarse and
hard.*

1.5 kilograms green cucumbers
500 grams medium onions
½ cup salt
About 8 cups cold water
3 cups vinegar
1¾ cups sugar
1 teaspoon celery seed
½ teaspoon curry powder
1½ teaspoons prepared mustard
1 cup water

Wash the cucumbers, score the skins with a fork, and slice thinly. Peel and slice the onions in rings.

In a glass or china bowl, arrange the vegetables in layers with the salt. Pour on the first measure of cold water. Stand in the refrigerator overnight.

Next day, drain the vegetables, and rinse thoroughly. Place in a saucepan with the vinegar, sugar, celery seed, curry, prepared mustard and second measure of water. Bring to the boil, and simmer 3 minutes.

Place in hot dry jars. Seal with plastic screw lids.

Makes 8 x 300 millilitre jars.

Pickled Onions

1.5 to 2 kilograms pickling onions
½ cup salt
Water to cover
For each jar allow:
2 peppercorns
1 clove
1 chilli
Cold vinegar

Peel onions, and put in a large china or glass bowl. Sprinkle with salt, and cover with cold water. Cover the bowl, and stand 24 hours.

Drain the onions, and place them in clean pickle jars. Stand upside down on thick newspaper to drain for a further 24 hours.

Into each jar, put the peppercorns, chilli and clove, and cover with cold vinegar.

Seal with a cork, and dip the end of the jar in paraffin wax, or use a non-metallic lid.

Keep 4 weeks before use.

Note: Cloves darken the onions, so they can be omitted if wished.

Pickled Cucumbers

1 kilogram cucumbers
5 cups water
½ cup pure salt
¼ cup sugar
1 tablespoon black peppercorns
8 whole cloves
6 bay leaves
2 centimetre piece root ginger
8 allspice berries
4 dried chillies
1 stick cinnamon
1 blade mace
2 teaspoons mustard seeds
1 tablespoon pure salt
2½ cups malt vinegar
2½ cups white vinegar
Fresh dill leaves

Choose young outdoor cucumbers, about 15 centimetres long. Wash and dry them, and then cut in quarters lengthways.

Boil the water and first measure of salt, and allow to cool. Put the cucumbers in a non-metallic bowl, and pour the brine over them. Stand in a cool place for 24 hours.

In an enamel or stainless steel saucepan, place the sugar, black peppercorns, whole cloves, bay leaves, root ginger, allspice berries, chillies, cinnamon stick, blade mace, mustard seeds, second measure of salt and malt and white vinegars. Bring slowly to the boil and simmer, for 3 minutes. Allow to cool and then strain.

Remove the cucumbers from the brine and rinse thoroughly in clear water. Drain well.

Allow to stand in a colander for about 2 hours to dry.

Pack the cucumbers upright in large jars, and fill up to within 1 centimetre of the top with the cool, spiced vinegar. Wash the dill leaves carefully, and place them on top of the cucumbers. Cover with a non-metallic lid. Store in a cool place. Ready to eat in 2 to 3 weeks.

Makes about 2 x 500 millilitre jars.

Pickled Courgettes

3½ cups white vinegar
1 cup sugar
4 teaspoons salt
1 teaspoon dill seeds
1 teaspoon mustard seeds
1 teaspoon tumeric
3 whole cloves
1 kilogram courgettes
6 small onions
2 green peppers

Place the vinegar, sugar, salt, dill and mustard seeds, tumeric and whole cloves in a deep saucepan. Bring to the boil. Cool.

Wash the courgettes, and cut into slices about 1 centimetre thick. Slice the onions, and separate out into rings. Deseed and slice the green peppers. Place the vegetables in a non-metallic bowl, and pour over the cooled vinegar. Stand for 1 hour.

Turn into a saucepan, and bring to the boil. Boil 3 minutes.

Pack into clean hot jars, and add the liquid to within 1 centimetre of the top. Cover with non-metallic lids. Ready to use in 2 weeks.

Makes 5 to 6 x 400 millilitre jars.

Mitre Peak in Milford Sound, Fiordland.

Beetroot and Raisin Relish

*Relishes of this type are good
for serving as an accompaniment
to all sorts of cold meats,
poultry and fish.
Hot meats, too,
can have the occasional
accompaniment of relish.
Beetroot and Raisin Relish
will make a sandwich filling
on its own,
or with thin slices of cheese,
and it can be used as
an added flavour for any
minced meat combinations,
such as patties or meat-loaves.*

1 kilogram beetroot

500 grams onions

2 cups raisins

1 tablespoon salt

6 whole cloves

6 allspice berries

6 whole peppercorns

1 small piece root ginger

1¾ cups sugar

1½ cups white vinegar

Wash the beetroot thoroughly. Trim root and stalk ends, leaving a little of the stalk on. Cook in boiling salted water for 30 minutes, or until tender, and skin will slip off. Drain, and leave to cool. Remove skins from beetroot, and cut into small cubes.

Peel and slice the onions. Place beetroot, onions, raisins and salt into a large saucepan or preserving pan. Tie the cloves, allspice berries, peppercorns and ginger in a piece of muslin. Add to the pan with sugar and vinegar.

Bring to the boil, and simmer until thickened to a jam-like consistency.

Remove spice bag. Pour into clean hot jars, and seal.

Makes about 3 x 100 millilitre jars.

Peppery Peach Chutney

1.5 kilograms peaches

1 lemon

2 cloves garlic

1 green pepper

1 cup seedless raisins

½ cup crystallised ginger

2 teaspoons salt

½ to 1 teaspoon cayenne pepper

2 cups brown sugar

3½ cups vinegar

Peel the peaches, and remove the stones, cutting the flesh coarsely. Place in a large saucepan.

Mince the lemon, discarding any pips, but using all the rind. Crush the garlic. Remove the seeds from the green pepper, and mince. Coarsely chop the raisins and ginger.

Add the prepared ingredients, salt, cayenne pepper, sugar and vinegar to the peaches. Bring to the boil, stirring frequently. Lower the heat, and simmer gently, still with frequent stirring, until the chutney is thick. This will take about 1¾ hours.

Pour into hot dry jars. Seal, and store for a few weeks before using. **Makes 2 kilograms.**

Capsicum Chutney

500 grams cooking apples

2 onions

3 large or 4 medium green peppers

3 tablespoons sugar

1 teaspoon salt

1 cup vinegar

Peel and core the apples, and peel the onion. Halve the peppers, and remove the seeds. Mince all these ingredients, making sure to catch the juice that is formed during mincing.

Put the minced ingredients, together with sugar, salt and vinegar into a saucepan, and bring to the boil. Once boiling, lower the heat, and continue to boil steadily, with frequent stirring, for about half an hour, or until the mixture has thickened to an almost jam-like consistency. Bottle in hot dry jars and seal.

Makes 1 kilogram.

Sweet and Sour Fruit Chutney

500 grams plums

500 grams peaches or apricots

1 x 454 gram tin crushed pineapple

1 cup cider or wine vinegar

2 cups brown sugar

Cut up the plums, discarding the stones. Peel and stone the peaches. If apricots are being used, these need no peeling. Put in a large saucepan with the tin of pineapple, including the juice, the vinegar and sugar.

Bring to the boil, stirring regularly. Lower the heat, and simmer with frequent stirring. Cook this way for about an hour.

At this stage, check the flavour to see that it has the sweet sourness preferred. If necessary, add a small amount more sugar, or a little more vinegar to adjust the flavour.

Continue boiling gently until the mixture is as thick as jam. This will take about another half hour.

Pour into hot dry jars, and seal.

Makes 2 kilograms.

Tamarillo Chutney

*Chutney is probably
one of the favourite uses
of this winter fruit
for preserving purposes.*

24 large tamarillos

4 onions

4 apples

½ cup crystallised ginger

1½ cups raisins

1 x 454 gram tin crushed pineapple

1 teaspoon cayenne pepper

2 teaspoons mixed spice

1 tablespoon salt

2 cups malt vinegar

1 kilogram brown sugar

Remove skins from tamarillos, by dropping into boiling water and leaving to stand for 2 to 3 minutes until skins burst. Rinse under cold water. Peel off skins. Peel the onions and apples. Chop onions finely. Core and chop apples. Slice tamarillos and preserved ginger. Add raisins.

Place these prepared ingredients in a large saucepan. Add pineapple, including juice, cayenne pepper, mixed spice, salt, vinegar and brown sugar.

Bring to boil, stirring to dissolve the sugar. Boil slowly for 1½ to 2 hours until thickened.

Pour into clean hot jars. Seal cold.

Makes 10 cups.

Spiced Kiwifruit

*Serve as a sweet pickle
with cold meats,
or an as ingredient in salads.*

1 cup white vinegar

2 cups sugar

1 tablespoon whole cloves

1 tablespoon whole allspice

1 x 5 centimetre length cinnamon stick

10 to 12 kiwifruit

Place the vinegar, sugar, cloves, allspice and cinnamon stick in a saucepan. Bring to the boil, stirring to dissolve the sugar. Boil for five minutes.

Peel kiwifruit, and cut into thick slices crossways. Strain the liquid, and discard spice. Add prepared kiwifruit, and simmer gently for 10 minutes.

Pack fruit into clean hot jars, and pour syrup over to cover fruit. Seal with a non-metallic lid.

Makes 1 x 1 litre jar.

Jam and Jelly

Strawberry and Rhubarb Jam

500 grams strawberries

500 grams rhubarb

1.5 kilograms sugar

1 teaspoon grated orange rind

Wash and hull the strawberries. Wash and chop the rhubarb to the size of the strawberries. Use young rhubarb, so it will not need skinning.

Put the fruit, sugar, and orange rind in a preserving pan, and simmer, stirring occasionally, until the sugar dissolves. Raise the heat, and cook briskly until a little will give a setting test when tried on a cold saucer. Cool a little before packing into hot dry jars. Seal with paraffin wax.

Makes 1 to 1.5 kilograms.

Cape Gooseberry and Apple Jam

3 green apples

Water

500 grams cape gooseberries

3 cups sugar

1 tablespoon lemon juice

Wash the apples thoroughly. Chop up roughly, and place in a saucepan with just enough water to cover. Bring to the boil, and simmer gently for about 30 minutes.

Strain through a jelly bag for several hours.

Place the apple liquid in a large pan with the crushed cape gooseberries, sugar and lemon juice. Stir until the sugar dissolves. Boil, stirring from time to time, until it gives the setting test. Pour into hot dry jars. Cover when cold.

Makes about 4 x 250 millilitre jars.

Gooseberry and Orange Jam

*Don't let
the gooseberry season go by
without storing a few for later
in the year, and this is a good way
to make a few survive
for later enjoyment.*

500 grams gooseberries

1 orange

75 grams raisins

250 grams sugar

Top and tail the gooseberries, and put into a saucepan.

Thinly pare the orange rind, and shred it finely. Remove the white pith from the orange, and discard. Roughly chop the pulp. Add rind and pulp to the saucepan.

Bring the fruit to the boil, and simmer until tender. Add the raisins and sugar. Bring to the boil, stirring to dissolve the sugar. Boil briskly until a setting test is given. Pour into hot dry jars, and seal.

Makes about 1¾ cups.

Old Fashioned Carrot Jam

500 grams carrots

1 cup water

500 grams sugar

½ cup lemon juice

1 teaspoon grated lemon rind

10 sliced blanched almonds

3 tablespoons brandy

Scrape the carrots, and cut into pieces. Put with the water, and boil until quite tender. Pass through a sieve or food mill.

Put the pulp, sugar and lemon juice in a saucepan, and bring to the boil. Stir regularly, and boil steadily for 5 minutes. Add the lemon rind and almonds. Boil 1 minute longer.

Remove from the heat, and add the brandy. Stir well. Pack into hot clean jars, and seal when cold.
Makes 2½ cups.

Melon and Passionfruit Jam

*There is one melon
that isn't for eating raw.
That is the cooking melon
or pie melon.
Pie melons make good jam.
It does take time to cook,
but has the advantage
of combining well with other fruits
such as citrus fruits,
tamarillos and passionfruit
to make distinctive jams.*

2 kilograms pie melon

8 cups sugar

24 passionfruit

½ cup lemon juice

Remove the rind and seeds from the melon. Grate the flesh finely, and place in a non-metallic bowl with half of the sugar. Leave to stand overnight.

Next day, pour the melon and sugar mixture into a large saucepan or preserving pan. Bring to the boil, and boil slowly until clear.

Add pulp from the passionfruit, remaining sugar and the lemon juice. Boil vigorously until the jam gives the setting test. Pour into clean hot jars, and seal.
Makes 7 x 300 millilitre jars.

Pawpaw and Orange Jam

1 kilogram pawpaws

½ cup sugar

Juice of 1 orange

2 cooking apples

1 cup water

Sugar

Peel the pawpaws, and remove the seeds. Chop coarsely, and sprinkle with the ½ cup sugar. Cover, and stand overnight. In the morning, grate the apple, and add with the orange juice and water. Boil until the fruit is tender.

Measure the pulp, and allow 1 cup of sugar for each cup of pulp. Bring this to the boil rapidly, and continue boiling until a setting test is reached. Pour into clean hot jars, and seal.
Makes about 1 kilogram.

Speckled Winter Preserve

2 lemons

2 sweet oranges

6¼ cups water

100 grams dried apricots

100 grams dried figs

100 grams stoned prunes

150 grams sticky raisins

Sugar

Squeeze the juice from the lemons and oranges. Place the skins, together with any seeds, in the cold water, and leave to soak overnight.

Bring to the boil, and boil until the skins are tender.

Strain all the liquid through a muslin-lined colander, discard the pith, and add the lemon and orange juices to the liquid. Measure the total liquid.

Chop the dried fruits roughly, add to the liquid, and bring to the boil. Continue boiling until the dried fruit is tender. Measure.

Add the sugar in the proportion of three-quarters of a cup of sugar to each cup of measured pulp.

Boil briskly until a setting test is given when a little is put on a saucer.

Take from the heat, and allow to cool for 10 minutes. Bottle in small, hot, dry jars. Seal when cold.
Makes about 1 kilogram.

Strawberry Jelly
(photograph above)

*Don't be surprised
if you find the whole berries
keep rising up to the top of the jar.
It is very difficult to keep them
evenly distributed,
and it doesn't seem to matter
once you open up the jar
and eat into it.
Use it as for any sweet jelly.
Its good colour
makes it ideal for glazing fruit
tarts.*

2 cooking apples

1 cup whole strawberries

2 cups chopped strawberries

3 cups water

2 tablespoons lemon juice

Sugar

Roughly chop the apples without peeling or coring. Hull, wash and drain strawberries.

Reserve 1 cup of whole, even-sized berries. Cut remainder in halves or quarters, depending on size. Measure.

Place apples, chopped strawberries and water in a saucepan. Bring to the boil, then boil for 20 minutes, or until tender. Pass the pulp through a muslin jelly bag. Leave it overnight if possible, until mixture stops dripping. Do not squeeze the bag.

Measure the juice into a saucepan. Add lemon juice, and bring to the boil. Add ¾ cup sugar for each cup of juice, then add the whole strawberries.

Bring to the boil, then boil rapidly until it passes the setting test. Leave the jelly to stand for 15 to 20 minutes, until it is beginning to set, then pour into hot dry jars and seal.
Makes about 1 x 300 millilitre jar.

Feijoa and Liqueur Jelly

(photograph above)

*A special jelly
for serving on hot scones or pikelets.
It is also suitable for serving
with meats such as lamb or game.*

1 kilogram feijoas

4 cups water

Sugar

¼ cup mandarin or orange
flavoured liqueur.

Wash feijoas, and cut them into quarters without removing the skins. Place them in a saucepan, and add the water.

Bring quickly to the boil. Boil for 45 minutes, or until very soft. Mash with a potato masher to break up all the fruit.

Pass through a jelly bag, leaving to strain overnight if possible. Do not squeeze the bag.

Next day, measure the juice, and add ¾ cup of sugar for every 1 cup of juice. Place juice, sugar and liqueur in a large saucepan.

Bring to the boil, and boil quickly until the jelly provides a setting test. Pour into hot dry jars. Seal when cold.
Makes 2 cups.

Matilda's Plum Conserve

1.5 kilograms plums

4 cups sugar

1½ teaspoons lemon rind

1½ teaspoons orange rind

2 tablespoons lemon juice

¼ cup orange juice

250 grams seedless raisins

½ cup chopped walnuts

Cut and stone the plums, and sprinkle with half the sugar. Let stand overnight.

In the morning, strain off the syrup into a large saucepan, and add to it the remaining sugar. Bring to the boil, stirring constantly. Boil for 5 minutes.

Add the plums, the rinds and juices. Cook for 30 minutes, stirring frequently. Add the raisins, and cook for about 25 minutes, or until jam gives a setting test. Add the walnuts. Bottle and seal.
Makes about 2 kilograms.

Three Fruit Marmalade

1 grapefruit

1 orange

1 lemon

10 cups water

Sugar

The total weight of the fruit should be 500 grams. Cut fruit finely, cover with the water, and soak overnight.

Boil 1 hour. Measure pulp, return to pan, and bring to the boil again. Add 1 cup of sugar for each cup of pulp. Boil again, until the marmalade gives a setting test. Pack into hot dry jars. Seal when cold.
Makes about 1.5 kilograms.

Apple Curd

2 large cooking apples

1 tablespoon water

2 lemons

1 cup sugar

2 eggs

50 grams butter

Peel and core the apples, and cut into small pieces. Put in a saucepan with the water, and cook gently until pulpy. Add the finely grated rind and juice of the lemons to the apple pulp, then stir in the sugar.

Beat the eggs, and mix into the apple. Cut the butter into pieces, and stir into the mixture while cooking it gently over low heat. Continue to stir and cook until the mixture thickens. Pour into small, hot, dry jars, and seal as for jam.

Kept in a cool place, this curd will store for about two weeks, or longer in the refrigerator. Use as tart filling, or as a spread instead of jam.
Makes about 2 cups.

Lemon Cheese

½ teaspoon grated lemon rind

¼ cup lemon juice

3 eggs

1 cup sugar

50 grams butter

Grate the rind of the lemon, and strain the juice. Put the rind, juice, lightly beaten eggs, sugar and butter in the top of a double boiler. Cook over steady heat, stirring regularly.

When the mixture is thick, turn into hot dry jars, and seal.
Makes 1½ cups.

Passionfruit Honey

50 grams butter

1 cup sugar

2 eggs

½ cup passionfruit pulp

1 tablespoon lemon juice

In the top of a double boiler, put the butter and sugar. Stand over hot water, and when the butter has melted, add the lightly beaten eggs, passionfruit pulp and lemon juice. Cook, with steady stirring, until the mixture thickens.

Turn into small hot, dry jars, and seal.
Makes about 2 cups.

Figs in Syrup

3 cups water

½ cup vinegar

2½ cups sugar

75 grams preserved ginger

2 kilograms fresh figs

Put the water, vinegar, sugar and preserved ginger into a heavy-based saucepan, and simmer for 30 minutes.

Wipe figs, and trim off the stems. Put figs into the syrup, and simmer very gently for 2 hours, stirring from time to time.

Pack into clean hot jars, and seal as for jam.
Makes 4 x 400 gram jars.

Brandied Fruit

1½ to 2 kilograms firm, ripe plums, peaches or apricots

½ cup water

½ cup sugar

¾ cup brandy

Cut in half, and stone the plums or apricots, and peel and halve the peaches.

Make the syrup by dissolving the sugar in the water, and boiling for 1 minute. Have a water bath ready for the jars.

Pack the fruit into the hot preserving jars, pressing the fruit gently under the shoulder of the jar to prevent floating. Pour over about ¼ cup of the boiling syrup, add ¼ cup of brandy, and then top up with syrup to 1 centimetre from the top.

Put the lids on, and the screw bands. Lower into the water bath. The water should come 2 centimetres above the lids. The jars should not touch each other.

Bring the water bath back to the boil. Boil for 20 minutes. Remove jars and cool. Check that the seals have domed down.

Keep several weeks before use.
Makes 3 x 500 millilitre jars.

Ginger in Sherry

*Most of us use
a little bit of root ginger,
then perhaps don't need it again
for a week or two,
so a large piece could deteriorate
during storage.
By preserving it in sherry,
it is always ready for use,
and of course, the sherry
will have taken on a ginger flavour,
making it quite a useful
ingredient when you want
to add sparkle to your next trifle.*

Root ginger

Sherry

Peel the root ginger, but keep it in large pieces. Place in a jar or bottle which has a screw-top lid. Cover the ginger with sherry.

Store either in the refrigerator or, for a shorter time, at room temperature.

When required for use, slice off the amount needed, and return the remainder to sherry.

Flavoured Vinegars

Those who are keen herb gardeners, or are interested in experimenting in the kitchen, will discover they can prepare their own flavoured vinegars, by using one of the white, wine or cider vinegars, and adding various herbs and other flavours.

This makes a fragrant vinegar to enhance salad dressings and other sauces.

Lemon Vinegar

*Use this in salads,
especially fish or cheese,
or on fruit mixtures.*

1 lemon

About 2 cups white vinegar

Using a potato peeler or sharp knife, finely peel the lemon. Place peel in a jar. Pour vinegar over.

Cover tightly, and leave for two weeks before using.

At the end of 2 weeks, strain, and discard lemon rind if wished.
Makes about 2 cups.

Garlic Vinegar

*Use where a light garlic flavour
is wanted on meats,
or in dressings or marinades.*

12 cloves garlic

¾ to 1 cup white vinegar

Peel the garlic, and leave it whole. Place it in a jar which has a close-fitting lid or a cork. Pour the vinegar over.

Leave to stand for 2 weeks before using. At the end of 2 weeks, strain and discard garlic cloves if wished.
Makes about 1 cup.

Tarragon Vinegar

*Use this in salad dressings
and hollandaise sauce.*

1 to 2 large sprays tarragon

About 2 cups white vinegar

Wash and dry tarragon well. Place in a large jar. Pour vinegar over.

Cover tightly, and leave to stand for 2 weeks before using. Leave tarragon in the jar as vinegar is used.
Makes about 2 cups

Herb and other flavourings, captured by infusion, in vinegar for later enjoyment.

Rosemary Vinegar

*Use this for cold lamb salads,
mint sauce or other vegetable
salads.
Use also to make mustard sauce
for corned beef.*

1 large spray rosemary

Vinegar

Wash and dry the rosemary. Place in a large jar. Pour the vinegar over it. Cover tightly, and leave to stand for 2 weeks before using.

Before using, strain the vinegar well and discard rosemary if wished.
Makes 2 cups.

Boysenberry Vinegar

*A refreshing drink can be made
from this concentrate
by adding 1 cup of iced water
to 2 tablespoons
of the berry vinegar.*

4 cups boysenberries

1 cup malt vinegar

Sugar

Combine the berries and the vinegar, and leave to stand for 24 hours.

Mash well, and strain. For each 2½ cups of juice, add 2 cups sugar. Boil for 20 minutes. Leave to cool.

Pour into clean bottles or jars, and cork. Store in a cupboard.
Makes 1¾ cups concentrate.

NEW ZEALANDERS
BY
ADOPTION

The fertile growing conditions that New Zealand offers have meant that plants brought here from abroad have adapted well. In fact, they have flourished to produce fruits of superior quality to the original.

Couple this with the skill of our scientists, and today we have kiwifruit originally from China; feijoas and tamarillos from South America; and from other lands, passionfruit, pepinos, persimmons, to name but a few of the fruits we now call our own.

While the summer sun warms this land, our produce fills the seasonal gaps in the Northern Hemisphere's supplies. New Zealand strawberries grace the tables of Americans at Thanksgiving, and our cherries add Christmas colour to festive tables in cold December.

Our adopted fruits are our success stories.

Captions to preceding 4 pages.

Page 188/189: Lush green farmland in the central North Island. (photograph Andris Apse — Photobank).

Page 190/191: Mellifluous Melons. Watermelon, piemelon, cantaloupe and honeydew; the sweet refreshing taste of summer. Melons are used mainly as a fresh fruit, except piemelon which is used in jam making.

Facing page: Fields of bright tulips at Hadstock bulb farm, near Christchurch. (photograph Grant Hunter).

Boysenberry Ice Cream

*This berry grows readily
in New Zealand,
and combines the qualities of size,
sweetness and tartness
in its large black-red form.*

250 grams fresh boysenberries

3 egg whites

Pinch salt

½ cup sugar

1 x 300ml bottle cream

Wash, drain then cut the boysenberries in half.

Whisk egg whites and salt until soft peaks form. Add the sugar and continue whisking until stiff. Whisk cream until thick, but not stiff, and fold it into the egg whites. Fold in the fruit.

Pour into an ice cream tray. Cover with foil or cling wrap. Freeze until firm. To serve, scoop into balls.
Serves 6 to 8

Gooseberries and Cream

500 grams gooseberries

½ cup sugar

½ cup water

2 tablespoons cornflour

2 tablespoons water

1 cup cream

Cinnamon

Tiny meringues

Wash gooseberries and top and tail them.

Place sugar and first measure of water in a saucepan, and bring to the boil, stirring to dissolve the sugar. Add gooseberries to the syrup, and simmer gently until just tender, keeping the fruit as whole as possible. Remove them on to a plate, using a draining spoon.

Mix the cornflour with the second measure of water. Measure half a cup of the syrup, and pour on to the cornflour mixture, stirring well. Bring to the boil, and cook, stirring, until the mixture thickens.

Allow to cool completely.

Whip the cream, and reserve one third of it. Fold the remaining cream into the thickened cornflour mixture.

Layer the cooked gooseberries and cornflour-cream mixture in individual dishes, ending with a layer of gooseberries. Garnish with the reserved cream and a sprinkling of cinnamon. Serve with tiny meringues.
Serves 4.

Tangelo Ice Cream

(photograph right)

*Recognise the ripeness of a tangelo
when the skin changes
from a rich orange-red
to a paler, blotchy yellow-orange.*

2 eggs

¾ cup icing sugar

1½ teaspoons finely grated tangelo rind

5 tablespoons tangelo juice

1 x 300ml bottle cream

Separate the eggs. Beat the yolks, icing sugar, tangelo rind and juice until the sugar is dissolved. Beat the egg whites until stiff. Whip the cream.

Fold the egg whites and cream into the tangelo mixture. Pour the mixture into freezer trays and cover with waxed paper. Freeze, without stirring, until firm.

To serve, spoon into individual glass dishes, and garnish with a curl of tangelo rind.
Serves 6.

Grapefruit Meringue Pie

*The New Zealand grapefruit
has a distinctive taste.
At the start of the season,
it is sharp and used
as a marmalade orange,
not too dissimilar to a Seville
Orange.
As the season goes on,
the fruit sweetens fully,
becoming suitable for eating as is.*

250 grams short pastry

¾ cup grapefruit juice

1 teaspoon grated grapefruit rind

25 grams butter

2 eggs

¼ cup golden syrup

¼ cup flour

½ cup cream

¼ cup sugar

Roll out the pastry, and line a 20 centimetre pie plate with it. Bake blind at 200 degrees C for 15 minutes. Remove the baking blind material, and continue cooking for a further 5 minutes to dry the surface of the pastry.

Place the juice, rind and butter in a saucepan, and heat until simmering.

While this is heating, separate the eggs and beat the yolks with the syrup and flour. Gradually combine this with the hot juice, and cook gently until smooth and thick. Allow the mixture to cool, then fold in lightly whipped cream.

Fill the pastry case with the mixture.

Beat the egg whites until stiff, then beat in the sugar, a tablespoon at a time. Pile the meringue over the filling, making sure the edges are covered. Return the pie to a 120 degree C oven for 30 minutes.
Serves 6.

Mandarin Imperial

5 tablespoons raw rice

1 cup milk

¼ cup sugar

25 grams butter

1 teaspoon vanilla

2 egg yolks

½ cup cream

½ cup tinned or fresh mandarin segments

¼ cup toasted whole, blanched almonds

Wash the rice. Cover it with cold water, and bring to the boil. Take from the heat, and set aside for 5 minutes, then drain.

Put the rice, milk, sugar and butter in a saucepan, and simmer gently until the rice is tender and the milk absorbed. Remove from the heat, and stir in the vanilla and egg yolks. Mix well, and set aside to cool.

When the rice mixture is cold, whip the cream until stiff, and fold into the rice.

Have the mandarin segments prepared — the tinned ones thoroughly drained, or the fresh ones peeled free of the white membranes — and fold these and the toasted almonds into the rice mixture. Turn into a glass serving dish or individual glass dishes. Chill until ready to serve.
Serves 3 to 4.

Strawberry Cheesecake

Base:

1½ cups vanilla wine biscuit crumbs

75 grams butter

1 teaspoon ground mixed spice

Filling:

1 tablespoon gelatin

¼ cup cold water

2 eggs

1 cup cream cheese

1½ tablespoons sugar

¼ cup milk

Pinch salt

¼ cup sugar

Topping:

200 grams strawberries

½ cup sugar

Pinch salt

3 tablespoons cornflour

2 tablespoons hot water

2 to 4 tablespooons lemon juice

5 to 6 extra strawberries

Base: Melt the butter, and mix with the biscuit crumbs and spice. Press into a 20 centimetre loose-bottomed cake tin that has been greased. Press up the sides for about 3 centimetres.

Filling: Mix the gelatin with the water. Allow to stand for about 3 minutes.

Separate the eggs. Beat the cream cheese with the first measure of sugar until smooth. Beat in the egg yolks one at a time, then the milk and salt.

Cook over low heat for about 5 minutes, stirring all the time, until heated through and thickened. Stir in the swollen gelatin until dissolved. Allow the mixture to cool until thick, but not set. Beat for 2 to 3 minutes until smooth and creamy.

Beat the egg whites until soft peaks form. Gradually add the second measure of sugar, beating well after each addition. Fold egg whites into the chilled mixture. Mix well. Spoon into the crumb crust and spread evenly.

Chill for about 2 hours, or until set.

Topping: Wash, hull and mash the first measure of strawberries. Mix the sugar, salt and cornflour in a saucepan. Add the mashed strawberries, water and 2 tablespoons of the lemon juice. Add more lemon juice if a sharper flavour is required.

Stir constantly over medium heat until the mixture thickens and boils. Boil 1 minute, stirring constantly. Put through a sieve, then cool for 5 to 10 minutes.

Pour over the cheesecake. Arrange the extra strawberries on top. Refrigerate until ready to serve.
Serves 6 to 8.

Strawberry Sour

2 cups strawberries

2 tablespoons sugar

3 eggs

¾ cup sugar

2 cups milk

3 tablespoons gelatin

¼ cup water

2 cups sour cream

Prepare a 5 cup souffle dish by tying a double-thickness band of greaseproof paper around the outside of the dish to stand 8 centimetres above the top of the dish.

Reserve a few strawberries for garnish. Hull the remaining strawberries, and chop roughly. Place in a bowl. Sprinkle the first measure of sugar over, and set aside.

Separate the eggs. Beat the yolks with the second measure of sugar until thick and creamy.

Heat the milk in a saucepan, and add to the egg yolk mixture. Return to the saucepan, and cook over a low heat until the mixture coats the back of the spoon. Set aside to cool.

Soak the gelatin in the water for 5 minutes, then stand over hot water, and stir until dissolved. Add to the cooled custard, and place in the refrigerator until the mixture starts to set.

Beat the egg whites until peaks form when the beater is removed from the bowl.

When the refrigerated mixture has thickened, fold in the strawberries, sour cream and egg whites. Pour the mixture into the prepared souffle dish, and place in the refrigerator until set. Before serving, garnish with the reserved strawberries.
Serves 6 to 8.

Pepino Salad

(photograph right)

This sweet, fragrant fruit, a more recent adoptee from South America, makes a fresh start to a meal.

1 pepino

2 tablespoons lemon juice

2 tablespoons brown sugar

2 pieces crystallised ginger

2 slices lemon

Cut the pepino in half lengthways. Sprinkle the lemon juice over each half. Sprinkle the brown sugar on the surface, and chill. Garnish with ginger and a lemon slice.
Serves 2.

Melon Salad

1 lettuce

2 to 3 slices water melon

1 large cucumber

2 to 3 spring onions

1 tablespoon chopped parsley

Dressing:

2 tablespoons white vinegar

Salt and pepper to taste

4 tablespoons salad oil

Wash and dry the lettuce. Tear the leaves into bite-sized pieces. Remove the rind and seeds from melon, and cut into 2 centimetre cubes.

Peel the cucumber, and cut into similar sized cubes. Chop the spring onions and parsley.

Combine the lettuce, melon and cucumber cubes and the chopped herbs.

Dressing: Mix all the ingredients together, and shake well. Just before serving, pour the dressing over the salad to coat all the ingredients. Turn into salad bowl, and serve immediately.
Serves 6.

Melon with Ham Starter

1 small cantaloupe melon

8 slices ham

4 lettuce leaves

Ground ginger

Freshly ground black pepper

Sprigs of parsley to garnish

Cut the melon into 8 wedges, and remove the seeds. Make several crossways cuts right through the flesh at 2 centimetre intervals, and ease the flesh from the rind, but leave it in position on rind. This makes for easier handling.

Trim and roll the ham slices.

Arrange the lettuce leaves on individual plates. Place two wedges of prepared melon and two rolls of ham on top of the lettuce. Sprinkle with the ground ginger and freshly ground black pepper. Garnish with sprigs of parsley.
Serves 4.

Fresh Plum Fritters

10-12 large, fresh, firm plums

1¼ cups flour

2 teaspoons baking powder

¼ teaspoon salt

1 tablespoon sugar

About 1 cup milk

1 egg

Oil for frying

Icing sugar

Wash, halve and stone the fruit.

Sift the flour, baking powder, salt and sugar into a bowl. Beat the egg and milk well, and stir into the dry ingredients to form a coating batter.

Dip each plum half into the batter, and fry in deep hot oil, allowing 3 to 5 minutes for frying each side. Drain well on paper. Serve hot, dusted with icing sugar.
Makes 20 to 24.

Fig Conserve

Figs for making this must be firm and in good condition.
No split or broken figs are suitable.
This can be served alone,
over ice cream, or topped
with sour cream.

2 kilograms figs

3 cups water

¼ cup vinegar

2½ cups sugar

125 grams preserved ginger

Wipe the figs and trim the stems.

In a large saucepan, put the water, sugar, vinegar and sliced preserved ginger, and simmer for 15 minutes. Place the figs in the syrup, and cook gently for 2½ to 3 hours, until the syrup is thick and honey-like in consistency. Stir occasionally during the cooking time to prevent catching.

Bottle in small preserving jars, and seal with a plastic screw top. Store several weeks to mature before using.
Makes about 2 kilograms.

Guava Honey

This small red or yellow fruit
which grows abundantly
in many gardens,
is mainly used in jelly making.
Juices, syrups and pulps
are other ways
to enjoy its dominant
and slightly piney flavour.

Guavas

3 egg yolks

1 cup sugar

½ teaspoon grated lemon rind

25 grams butter

Wash the guavas well, and place in a steamer. Cook over hot water until just tender, then press through a sieve, discarding the seeds. Measure this pulp to get 1 cup.

Beat the egg yolks and sugar together thoroughly. Add the lemon rind and guava pulp, and cook over hot water, stirring, until the mixture thickens. Add the butter, and blend in. Turn into small jars, cover, and keep in the refrigerator.

Use for cake fillings, pie fillings or as a spread.
Makes 500 grams.

Casseroled Quinces

This ancient fruit
is not suitable for eating raw,
but given long, slow cooking,
it is fragrant and delicious.
It can be combined with meat
mixtures,
and used also in jams,
preserves and desserts.

¼ cup honey

1 cup hot water

4 quinces

¼ cup sliced crystallised ginger

¼ cup sherry

Dissolve the honey in the hot water.

Peel and core the quinces, and cut into thick slices. Place these into an ovenware dish which has a close-fitting lid. Pour honey and water over the quinces. Scatter sliced ginger on top, and dribble sherry all over. Cover with a close-fitting lid.

Place in a 120 to 140 degree C oven, and cook for about 3 hours. Serve the quinces warm or cold with thick cream.
Serves 4.

Thick Cream: Into a shallow basin, pour 1 cup of cream and 1 cup of milk. Set in a dish of water, cover, and place in the oven along with the quinces. After about 3 hours, the thick cream will have risen to the top of the liquid.

Remove by carefully spooning it off into a container. The milk left over can be used in desserts or baking such as scones.

If wished, the same process can be carried out by heating the dish of water very gently on top of the stove.

Avocado Dip

2 ripe avocados

1 tablespoon very finely chopped onion

1 tablespoon finely chopped green pepper

½ teaspoon salt

¼ teaspoon crushed garlic

Peel the avocados, and remove the seeds. Retain the seeds. Mash the flesh to a smooth paste, and blend into the very finely chopped onion, pepper and garlic, as well as the salt. This mixture should be smooth.

Press the seeds into the mixture, cover, and chill in the refrigerator. The seeds will prevent darkening.

When ready to serve, remove seeds, and pile into a dish. Accompany with corn chips or raw vegetables.
Makes 1½ cups

Kiwifruit

This fruit, previously known as the Chinese Gooseberry, thus explaining its land of origin, has undoubtedly become New Zealand's most famous adopted fruit.

Kiwifruit and Ginger Dessert

6 kiwifruit

4 pieces preserved stem ginger

2 tablespoons ginger syrup

2 tablespoons rum

Whipped cream

Peel the kiwifruit, and cut into thick slices. Place in a shallow dish. Cut the stem ginger into thin slices. Scatter through the kiwifruit. Mix the ginger syrup and rum, and pour over the fruit.

Cover, and chill for several hours.

When ready to serve, spoon into small glass dishes, allowing a little syrup for each. Serve with whipped cream.
Serves 4.

Kiwifruit Rumpot

(photograph right)

This is a modified rumpot
to be used soon after making.
The fruit will lose colour on storing.

1 cup water

1 cup sugar

1 cup white rum

5 to 6 kiwifruit

250 grams strawberries

3 slices lemon

Heat the water and sugar until the sugar dissolves. Simmer for two minutes. Allow syrup to cool. When cold, mix in the white rum.

Peel the kiwifruit, and cut into thick slices. Wash and hull the strawberries. Cut the lemon slices in half.

Arrange the fruit in a jar, placing a layer of kiwifruit, then the strawberries, and finishing with a layer of kiwifruit. Carefully push the lemon slices down the outside of the fruit.

Pour the sugar and rum syrup over the fruit. Leave overnight.

Serve as a dessert alone or over ice cream.

More fruit can be added to the syrup, and left to absorb it. The syrup can also be used as a flavouring.
Serves 5 to 6.

Kiwifruit Supper Snack

4 thin slices bread

Butter

2 kiwifruit

100 grams cheese

½ rasher bacon

Using a griller, lightly toast the bread on both sides. Lightly butter one side of the toast.

Peel and slice the kiwifruit. Place 4 kiwifruit slices on each piece of toast.

Cut the cheese into thin slices, and place on top of fruit to cover completely. Cut the bacon into small pieces and sprinkle evenly over the cheese. Grill until the bacon is cooked and the cheese melts. Serve immediately.
Makes 4 snacks.

Te Puke Chops

4 pork chops

Salt

Freshly ground black pepper

3 to 4 kiwifruit

¼ cup orange juice

½ teaspoon cornflour

Trim the excess fat from the chops, and season with salt and pepper.

Peel kiwifruit, then slice them thickly.

Heat the frying pan. Add the chops, and fry until cooked, turning once. Remove the chops from the frying pan, and place in a warm serving dish.

Pour off the fat, and add the kiwifruit to the pan. Combine the orange juice and cornflour, and pour over the kiwifruit. Once the sauce bubbles, pour over the chops. Serve immediately.
Serves 4.

Kiwi Kebab

500 grams lean lamb

1 tablespoon oil

1 tablespoon lemon juice

Salt and pepper

6 kiwifruit

2 tablespoons oil

1 tablespoon brown sugar

Cut the lamb free of fat, and into large cubes.

Put the first measure of oil, the lemon juice, salt and pepper into a bowl, and mix in the lamb. Leave to marinate for about 1 hour.

Peel the kiwifruit, and cut in half crossways.

Mix the second measure of oil and brown sugar.

Thread pieces of kiwifruit and marinated meat alternately along a skewer. Brush over the fruit with the oil-sugar mixture. Place under a hot grill, and cook, turning the skewers, until the meat and fruit are browned lightly.

Serves 3.

Kiwifruit and Mandarin Compote

400 grams mandarins

½ cup sugar

¾ cup water

5 centimetre piece cinnamon stick

3 allspice berries

4 kiwifruit

Wash and dry one of the mandarins. Finely grate the peel to give a quarter teaspoon. Peel all the mandarins. Divide into segments, and remove the white pith. Prick several holes in each segment and set aside.

Place the mandarin rind, sugar, water, cinnamon and allspice in a saucepan. Boil together for five minutes. Remove from the heat, add the mandarins, cover, and allow to stand for a further five minutes. Remove the cinnamon and allspice, and allow mandarin mixture to cool to lukewarm.

Peel the kiwifruit, and slice in half crossways. Cut each half into 8 segments lengthways, and add to the mandarins. Chill before serving, or alternatively reheat and serve warm.

Serves 4 to 6.

Babaco

This large yellow fruit is another recent South American adoptee.

Green Ginger Wine Slush

250 grams unpeeled babaco

2 tablespoons icing sugar

3 tablespoons green ginger wine

4 ice cubes

Decoration:

Mint leaves

Orange slices

1 cherry

Cube the babaco, and freeze until firm. Place the babaco, icing sugar, green ginger wine and ice cubes in a food processor, and process until slushy.

Serve in a tall glass, garnished with mint leaves, orange slices, and a cherry.

Serves 1.

Rum Slush

250 grams unpeeled babaco

2 tablespoons icing sugar

3 tablespoons white rum

4 ice cubes

Decoration:

Lemon slices

Mint leaves

1 cherry

Cube the babaco, and freeze until firm.

Place the babaco, icing sugar, rum and ice cubes in a food processor, and process until slushy.

Serve in a tall glass. Garnish with a lemon slice, 2 or 3 mint leaves, and a cherry.

Serves 1.

Passionfruit

A popular fruiting vine that provides an aromatic, seedy pulp that is so well-liked for icings and topping.

Passionfruit is an essential ingredient in New Zealand fruit salads.

Meremere Fruit Salad
(photograph above)

| 1 cantaloupe melon |
| 2 tablespoons Grand Marnier |
| 125 grams seedless grapes |
| 3 passionfruit |

Cut the melon in half, and remove the seeds. Using a melon-baller, make balls from the flesh. Place in a bowl, and sprinkle with Grand Marnier.

Cut the passionfruit in half, and scoop out the flesh. Wash the grapes.

Just before serving, mix the fruits together, and place in a serving bowl. **Serves 3 to 4.**

Iced Surprise

| About 240 grams trifle sponge |
| 1/4 cup apricot jam |
| 1/2 cup passionfruit pulp |
| 1 tablespoon sherry |
| 1/2 litre vanilla ice cream |
| 1/2 cup cream |
| Extra passionfruit pulp |

Line a 21 by 9 centimetre ice box or loaf tin with waxed paper or plastic film.

Split the sponge horizontally to make three layers, 21 by 9 centimetres. Spread with jam.

Put a layer of sponge in the base of the tin. Mix the sherry and passionfruit pulp together. Soak sponge layer with one third of the pulp mixture. Divide ice cream into two. Place a layer of ice cream on top of the sponge. Smooth the surface.

Repeat layers of sponge, pulp and ice cream, finishing with the sponge. Cover with waxed paper or film. Freeze overnight, or turn freezer up to coldest setting and freeze for 2 to 3 hours.

Turn out by dipping quickly into hot water. Remove film or paper. Whip the cream. Spread a little over the top and sides of the cake. Pipe edges with remaining cream. Decorate top with extra passionfruit pulp.
Serves 6 to 8.

Cold Passion Fruit Souffle

3 eggs

1 cup sugar

½ cup seedless passionfruit pulp

1 tablespoon gelatin

¼ cup cold water

1 cup cream

Separate the eggs and put the yolks, sugar and passionfruit pulp in a saucepan. Whisk with a wire whisk or fork while cooking gently until the mixture thickens, then set aside to cool.

Set the gelatin in cold water to swell, and stand over hot water to melt. Stir this into the cooling egg mixture. Whip the cream, and fold into the cool egg mixture. Beat the egg whites until stiff, and fold into previous mixture.

Pour into individual glass dishes and leave to set. Garnish if wished. **Serves 6.**

Fruit Salad Bowl

1 cantaloupe melon

2 oranges

4 passionfruit

3 bananas

1 bunch grapes

2 to 3 tablespoons cointreau

2 tablespoons castor sugar

2 to 3 sprigs mint

Cut the top off the melon in a van-dyke pattern, using a small, sharp-pointed knife. Remove the seeds. Scoop out the flesh with a melon-ball cutter. Chill the melon shell.

Remove the peel and pith from the oranges, and cut into segments.

Remove pulp from the passionfruit. Peel bananas, and cut diagonally into 2 centimetre slices. Wash the grapes, and remove the stalks.

Toss all the fruits gently together. Sprinkle the cointreau over, and leave in the refrigerator to chill.

Sprinkle fruit with castor sugar just before serving. Spoon into chilled melon shell. Garnish with mint sprigs.
Serves 8.

Persimmons

Persimmons are known as the fruit that must be almost over-ripe to be ready to eat. Some newer varieties do not have the astringency, and can be eaten before they reach the very soft stage.

Baked Persimmon Pudding with Persimmon Sauce

75 grams butter

½ cup sugar

¾ cup persimmon pulp

½ teaspoon lemon juice

1½ cups flour

½ teaspoon baking soda

½ teaspoon baking powder

Pinch salt

1½ teaspoons ginger

½ cup raisins

Persimmon Sauce:

100 grams butter

¼ cup lemon juice

1 teaspoon lemon rind

2 egg yolks

½ cup sugar

1 cup ripe persimmon pulp

Cream the butter and sugar. Mash the persimmon pulp and lemon juice, or blend in the blender until smooth. Add to the creamed mixture, and beat well. It may curdle.

Sift together the flour, baking soda, baking powder, salt and ginger, and add with the raisins to the creamed mixture. Mix well.

Turn into a greased and lined 20 centimetre loaf tin. Bake at 160 degrees C for about 40 minutes. Leave in the tin for 10 minutes before turning out. Serve warm with the Persimmon Sauce.
Serves 5 to 6.

Persimmon Sauce: Place in a basin over boiling water, the butter, lemon juice and rind.

Beat the egg yolks and sugar together, and stir in. Add the ripe persimmon pulp. Leave in pieces. Stir continuously until the sauce thickens. Serve hot.
Serves 6.

New Zealand's export success — Kiwifruit.

Persimmon Bran Muffins

½ cup persimmon pulp

¾ teaspoon lemon juice

½ teaspoon baking soda

1¼ cups flour

2 teaspoons baking powder

½ cup sugar

½ teaspoon salt

½ teaspoon nutmeg

½ teaspoon cinnamon

¼ teaspoon ground cloves

¾ cup bran

½ cup sultanas

1 egg

½ cup milk

¼ cup melted butter

1 teaspoon grated lemon rind

Mash the persimmon pulp with a fork, or blend in the blender until smooth. Add the lemon juice and soda, and set aside.

Into a mixing bowl, sift the flour, baking powder, sugar, salt and spices. Add the bran and sultanas, and mix until sultanas are separated and coated with flour.

In another bowl, beat the egg lightly, and stir in the milk and melted butter. Add the egg mixture, lemon rind and persimmon pulp, all at once, to the dry ingredients. Mix to thoroughly moisten flour, but do not overmix.

Place in greased muffin tins, filling them three-quarters full. Bake at 200 degrees C for about 20 minutes.
Makes 12.

Tamarillos

The tamarillo which, in times past was called the tree tomato, crosses the flavour barrier between sweet and savoury. Its origins are in South America.

In New Zealand, its adopted home, it grows in areas that are mild and almost frost-free.

The red form is the commonest, but gold and yellow varieties are becoming popular.

Spiced Tamarillos

9 tamarillos

¾ cup white vinegar

1 cup sugar

6 whole cloves

1 x 5 centimetre length cinnamon stick

1 teaspoon grated lemon rind

Drop the tamarillos in boiling water. Remove from the heat and leave for 2 minutes, then drain and remove skins. Cut in half.

Place vinegar, sugar, cloves, cinnamon and lemon rind in a saucepan. Bring to the boil, stirring to dissolve the sugar. Add the halved tamarillos, and simmer for 10 minutes. Pack them into hot, clean screw-top jars. Pour the hot vinegar mixture over to fill the jars. Cover with plastic screw tops. Serve with cold meats.

Makes 2 x 300 millilitre jars.

Pork Chops with Tamarillo Sauce

(photograph above)

6 pork chops

Salt and pepper

Tamarillo Sauce:

6 tamarillos

Boiling water

1 onion

1 green pepper

2 tablespoons oil

3 tablespoons water

3 tablespoons brown sugar

Trim any excess fat from the pork chops, and season them with salt and pepper. Place in a cold frying pan with no added oil. Heat slowly, and when hot, cook the pork chops over a medium heat for 30 minutes or until done.

While the pork chops are cooking, prepare the sauce.

Tamarillo Sauce: Drop the tamarillos into boiling water and leave to stand for 1 to 2 minutes. Drain, cool, and peel off skins. Cut into thin slices.

Peel and chop the onion finely. Deseed and finely chop the green pepper.

Heat the oil in a saucepan. Add the onion and green pepper, and fry quickly for 2 minutes. Add the water, brown sugar and sliced tamarillos.

Bring to the boil, stirring all the time, and simmer gently for 10 minutes. Season to taste with salt and pepper. Serve with the pork chops.

Serves 6.

Tamarillo Pie

500 grams tamarillos

250 grams cooking apples

50 grams sticky raisins

½ cup brown sugar

Flaky pastry

Skin the tamarillos by plunging in boiling water for a few minutes.

Peel off the loosened skin. Chop into slices. Peel and slice the apples.

Put both fruits and the raisins into a saucepan, add the sugar, and cook over low heat until the fruit starts to soften. Turn into pie dish, and cool. Roll out pastry and cover pie top. Decorate.

Bake at 200 degrees C for about 15 minutes or until pastry is golden. Serve hot or cold.

Serves 6.

Feijoas

This fruit is known in some parts of the world as the Pineapple Guava.

Feijoa Cookies

½ cup feijoa pieces

1¼ cups flour

½ teaspoon baking powder

½ teaspoon baking soda

50 grams butter

½ cup sugar

1 egg

¼ cup chopped walnuts

½ teaspoon lemon rind

Peel the feijoas, cut into small pieces, then measure.

Sift flour, baking powder and baking soda. Cream the butter until soft, then beat in sugar until the mixture is fluffy. Add the egg and feijoa pulp, and beat well. Stir in the dry ingredients. Add chopped walnuts and lemon rind. Mix thoroughly.

On to a lightly greased oven tray, drop the mixture in teaspoonfuls, allowing space for spreading. Bake at 180 degrees C for 15 to 18 minutes.
Makes about 30.

Feijoa Coconut Roll

1¾ cups flour

3 teaspoons baking powder

¼ teaspoon salt

50 grams butter

¼ cup coconut

½ to ¾ cup milk

1½ cups sliced feijoas

½ teaspoon grated orange rind

2 tablespoons orange juice

¼ cup sugar

Melted butter

Coconut

Sift the flour, baking powder and salt into a bowl, and cut the butter into it until it is like fine breadcrumbs. Add the coconut. Cut in sufficient milk to make a stiff dough that can be rolled out. Roll out to 0.5 centimetre thickness, and rectangular in shape, about 20 by 30 centimetres.

Mix the peeled and sliced feijoas with the orange rind and juice and the sugar. Spread over the dough, leaving a border all around, then roll up like a sponge roll, starting on the long side. Place join down in a baking dish, and brush with melted butter.

Bake at 200 degrees C for about 20 minutes, then brush with more melted butter and sprinkle with coconut. Continue baking for 5 to 10 minutes until golden and crisp. Serve hot.
Serves 6.

Feijoa and Orange Fluff
(photograph below)

3 to 4 feijoas

Water

½ teaspoon grated orange rind

3 to 4 tablespoons orange juice

¼ cup sugar

1½ tablespoons quick cooking tapioca

1 egg white

Peel the feijoas, and slice roughly. Put in a pan with the water. Cover, and bring to the boil. Simmer for a few minutes until pulpy. Stir in the orange rind and juice. Sweeten to taste with the sugar.

Stir in the tapioca, and bring to the boil. Cook, stirring, for 1 to 2 minutes or until it clears. Allow to cool.

Whisk the egg white until stiff. Fold into the cool mixture. Pile into serving glasses, and chill.
Serves 3 to 4.

Feijoa Crumble

About 1 kilogram feijoas

About ½ cup water

Sugar to taste

Lemon juice to taste

2 tablespoons brown sugar

5 tablespoons flour

3 tablespoons melted butter

Peel and halve the feijoas, and cook in a little water with sugar and lemon juice. Turn into a 4 cup ovenware dish, and leave to go cold. The dish should have about 3 centimetres of space at the top.

Mix sugar and flour in a small bowl, and using a fork, work in the melted butter until the mixture is crumbly. Sprinkle this over the cold feijoas. Bake at 180 degrees C for 30 minutes.
Serves 4 to 6.

TUI FLOWER

Recently retired from her nineteen years as director of the N.Z. Newspapers Test Kitchen, Tui is well known for her lifetime interest in food — an interest which she pursued from Home Science School, to teaching, to Home Economist with Unilever, to journalism. A bursary to study in France extended her overseas experience and food knowledge.

Married to a former Auckland Star editor, Tui enjoys retirement that allows her to pursue her interests in homemaking and crafts.

In 1983 she was awarded the Queen's Service Medal for public service.

ROBYN MARTIN

An Aucklander, married, Robyn started her association with the Test Kitchen after leaving school. She then trained in Home Science at Otago University and was awarded the exchange study grant from the School of Home Science to Kansas State University U.S.A. where she took a masters degree. Returning to N.Z. Newspapers she worked in the Test Kitchen and later as a consumer reporter.

Robyn next took up the post of product manager with Auckland Milk Corporation and after five years returned to N.Z. Newspapers to the position she now holds as Head of the Food Section. She is keenly aware of the needs of the consumer.

JUDITH LONG

The principal food photographer for the Food Section of N.Z. Newspapers Judith combines enthusiasm and artistic talent to produce food pictures for the organisation. After training in a photographic studio she joined the company some thirteen years ago starting in the promotion department. She moved to the Food Section six years ago.

Judith is married and takes a keen interest in the restoration of old and historic buildings.

Contributing photographers — Food: Tong Wong, Michael Willison, Rees Osborne, Vickie Wardell.

Contributing photographers — Pictorial: Peter Morath, Eric Taylor, Eric Young, Judith Long, Roger Fowler, Anne McSweeney, Roy Sinclair, Grant Hunter, Richard Silcock, Bill Kleeman, Alistair Drew, Roger Gold, International Press, Laurie Thurston (Photobank), Robin Smith (Photobank), Pamela Karwowski (Photobank), Philip Paterson (Photobank), Andris Apse (Photobank), Michael De Hamel (Photobank), Bob Wells (Photobank), Martin Sewell (Photobank), Gregory Riethmaier (Photobank), Alan Gillard.

Index